Acknowledgements

- To our parents, Arvids & Emiliya Keikulis, who followed their Savior with fervent prayers and obedience.

- Dr. Tom Snipes, Professor of Appalachian University in the 70's, encouraged us to write the story. He used friends to type the first copy.

- Our brother John translated Papa's journal.

- Each sibling and Mari shared their memories.

- Marie Foshee urged us to move forward and made the copies.

- Brian Brown, going over corrections, adding photos and designing the cover.

- Thanks for many encouragements from many friends.

To God be the glory!

D1472635

Table of Contents

Prologue

Come Full Circle

At the corner of Fairmount Avenue and Marshall Street in Philadelphia, PA., lived a Latvian family, having emigrated from war-torn Europe on July 18, 1949. Their father, Arvids Keikulis, was the associate pastor of a Slavic church located next door to the parsonage. The family – which consisted of Arvids, his wife Cilite, and their five children – occupied the parsonage's second-floor apartment, with a large front room serving as their bedroom. The small sitting room contained a couch, table, and chairs. Next to the sitting room was a small kitchen. The only items that would fit into this small space were an icebox, a two-burner kerosene stove, a narrow table for food preparation, and a sink. Down the hallway was the bathroom. Even though the living quarters were a tight fit for a family of seven, the occupants were grateful for the privacy it provided – after years of living in cramped labor camps during World War II.

Brother Demetrus, as the people lovingly called Pastor Paul Demetrus; his wife, Ruth; and their two little daughters lived on the first floor of the parsonage. During World War II, Paul and Ruth had prepared to enter Russia as missionaries when the conflict ended. However, when the Iron Curtain came down with a forceful thud, excluding all western influence – especially that of Christianity – the couple turned their efforts to minister to Slavic immigrants entering America. They assisted the new arrivals in finding employment, setting them up in furnished apartments and registering their children in schools. The couple developed a talent for getting Philadelphians to donate clothing, furniture, and other useful household items to help establish foreigners in their new homeland.

Paul and Ruth Demetrus labored tirelessly, selflessly giving of themselves to the "least of these." Their vision and love became evident to all. Even the immigration officials of New York harbor called Paul regularly, seeking his help to place new arrivals when sponsors did not show up or had changed their minds. Paul and Ruth never failed to offer assistance to those in need.

* * * * * * * * * * * * *

Anna Keikulis Has a New Homeland

In early 1950 the promise of spring was in the air. An occasional bird could be heard from the vacant lot next door to the church building. I hurried my three sisters to get dressed for church. Papa and Mama had already gone several hours before, leaving me in charge. As usual, Judite, 13, and Modra, 9, were carefully checking their appearance in the long mirror hanging on the back of the bedroom door. Mama had altered some donated clothing to fit them perfectly. The clothes were washed, ironed, and looking like new purchases.

"Just because we are poor doesn't mean we have to look poor or act poor," Papa always reminded us.

Ilze, 6, had enough spunk for all of us and did not appreciate anyone, especially her older siblings, giving her orders. Her response to my urging was, "You are not my boss!"

No wonder this little one survived the hardships of the war, I thought with a smile.

"Ready!" she finally announced. Swinging the door open so hard it nearly fell off its hinges, she ran ahead, jumping on the banister, riding it all the way down, and skipped out the front door into the street. Giggling, we hurried to catch up with her.

I squinted in the bright sunlight, breathing in the fresh air. What a wonderful day! This spring would bring several new beginnings in my life. In just a few weeks I would cross a huge milestone that was called "Sweet Sixteen" in America. Certainly it must be an important event to have such a wonderful name, I thought. Also, I would be finishing my special English classes and starting high school. Indeed, this promised to be an eventful year.

Modra and Ilze attended the elementary school across the street, and they loved it. They had never seen such beautiful textbooks with vibrant pictures, plenty of pencils and paper, and crayons in many colors. School was a pleasurable experience for both of them.

Judite and I attended school a couple of city blocks past Independence Hall. The entire school building was devoted to immigrant teens studying not only the English language, but also being immersed in American history and culture. Philadelphia, with its rich heritage, provided dozens of opportunities to visit sites where history had been made. More than once we visited Independence Hall, each trip followed by a class discussion of the declaration document itself, its meaning, and the personal cost to those who signed it.

Pointing out the crack in the Liberty Bell, our teacher, Mrs. Brasso, asked, "Why display a bell that not only is broken but also never rang in celebration of our independence?"

After some discussion, she quietly remarked, "That is what makes America uniquely different. It accepts the broken, the weary, giving all an opportunity to make a contribution."

Mrs. Brasso loved America and transferred her passion to her students. Wherever our field trips took us – to City Hall to observe William Penn's statue atop its pinnacle, to Betsy Ross's 18th-century home, or to the Benjamin Franklin Museum in Philadelphia's historic district – she pointed out the contributions that made our country unique. In class we were exposed to patriotic songs, as well as folk tunes. The first time we heard the Battle Hymn of the Republic, I could hardly contain my emotions.

The words of the old hymn clearly speak the gospel, as evidenced in lines from its verses and chorus:

> *Mine eyes have seen the glory of the coming of the Lord...*
> *I can read His righteous sentence by the dim and flaring lamps...*
> *Let the Hero, born of woman, crush the serpent with His heel...*
> *Oh, be swift, my soul, to answer Him! Be jubilant, my feet...*

He is wisdom to the mighty; He is honor to the brave...
In the beauty of the lilies Christ was born across the sea,
With a glory in His bosom that transfigures you and me;
As he died to make men holy, let us live to make men free;
While God is marching on!

Glory! Glory! Hallelujah! Glory! Glory! Hallelujah!
Glory! Glory! Hallelujah! Our God is marching on.
(Julia Ward Howe)

What a wonderful country is this America, I thought, where the gospel is sung openly and all glory given to God for His truth and sovereignty! We were inspired and grateful for our new homeland.

On one occasion Mrs. Brasso asked us to bring a vegetable for the next day's lesson. We were not told what to bring; it had to be the student's choice. Her contribution was a beef bone, a large pot, and a hot plate. The pot was filled with water, and all the vegetables were scrubbed and sliced. All morning the savory aroma of the brewing soup filled the classroom. Finally it was ready, and we thoroughly appreciated the product of our contributions.

"This is America," our teacher said, pointing to the pot. "This is what makes her great. Each citizen contributes for the good of all."

For the remainder of the afternoon we discussed the contributions of each ethnic group, all the citizens at large, and even ourselves. We were challenged to be contributors in our new homeland.

My thoughts returned to the present as we entered the front hall of the church building on this day of worship. Truly this United States of America is a magnificent country. I can be sure no one will break down the front door of this building to arrest Papa for preaching the gospel or threaten Mama for allowing her children to be instructed in the Christian faith. There are no threats of a firing squad for meeting together for family Bible reading and prayer.

As we ascended the flight of steps to the second-floor sanctuary, the murmur of the kneeling congregation filled the air. This was the custom of these grateful people. They had suffered much during the war. Now they were preparing their hearts for the preaching of God's Word. Scanning the kneeling worshipers, I was comforted by their obvious devotion and love for their Lord and Savior. They were living examples of free citizens living in a free country where people worship without fear or intimidation.

My pleasant thoughts were abruptly interrupted by the sight of the "fun crowd" seated on the back row with their eyes piously closed, pretending to be in prayer. If their parents only knew what kind of party their teens had attended the night before, they would be shocked. Furthermore, when I had refused to participate in their newfound freedom in this new land, they renamed me "Gordaja" (the proud one). The label stung because I felt I didn't deserve criticism just because as the associate pastor's daughter I needed to be an example of godly behavior.

My sisters and I found our usual seats in the second row. While I participated in worship that morning, my thoughts centered on my wounded heart. However, at the close of Papa's preaching, I dutifully went all the way up to the left of the platform and knelt. This, too, was the custom of the Slavic people, to kneel and consider what had been preached from God's Word and apply it. Sighing deeply and unable to pray, I lifted the eyes of my heart toward heaven and whispered, "Lord, you know my heart."

Suddenly, it seemed as if the celestial curtains of His glory parted and the Father was looking deeply into the crevices of my heart saying, "I do." I felt totally exposed before Him, His all-seeing eyes penetrating my being, yet without condemnation. I knew very well what the Father spoke through His prophet Jeremiah about the condition of the heart, that is both deceitful and sick (Jeremiah 16:9) and much in need of divine intervention. Also, through the prophet Isaiah, God had warned that our righteousness, or efforts to be good, is like covering ourselves with a filthy garment (Isaiah 64:6). His righteousness – through Jesus Christ's sacrifice – is the only adequate covering.

The Father had a wonderful plan for my life. I was but a small lump of clay in His hand. In trying to be good and in all my efforts to be an example of goodness, I did not succeed. It was only as I submitted to Him that He would place me on the potter's wheel and mold me into something worthwhile for Him.

I rose from my knees filled with hope and joy and a new freedom in my heart. No longer did I feel the need to impress but simply to allow the Father's hand to shape my life.

At that moment my eyes fell on my dear papa and mama. They were talking to a group gathered by the side door. Their faces are aglow with the contentment and peace of being vessels in the hands of their loving Lord, I thought, and useful ones at that!

Trying to be good had become a heavy burden to me – actually too much to bear. Under this self-imposed load, my heart had begun to judge others severely. Now, with my sight on the Potter's wheel, I understood that the trials, persecutions, and watching their children suffer in Nazi prison camps had formed my parents into faithful servants of the Lord.

They had come full circle in their walk of faith.

Our Peace Guardian

Do not be anxious about anything, but in everything,
by prayer and petition, with thanksgiving, present your
requests to God. And the peace of God, which transcends
all understanding, will guard your hearts and your minds
in Christ Jesus.

Philippians 4:6-7

On the following pages is the true story of the Keikulis family – their trials, persecutions, and discouragement.

It is also the story of faith and hope – perseverance, worship, witnessing, and triumph – told from the pages of their father's journal, their mother's words, and their own memories.

It is the story of a family's unique, courageous journey...

Chapter 1

God's Recruitment Campaign

Latvia is a small country nestled between Estonia and Lithuania, just across the Baltic Sea from Sweden. The Letts, an ancient people, were among Europe's earliest settlers. Latvians and Lithuanians are their descendants. In the far north, Latvia has a large gulf, the Gulf of Riga, which is a warm water seaport that does not freeze over in winter. For this reason, Latvia's history is filled with occupations and wars by would-be world powers needing a place for their conquering battle-ships to harbor.

Most northern European seaports have the problem of icing over during freezing winters, so Latvians had to live as serfs under the barons and royalties of Norway, Sweden, and Poland, but most often under Germany and Russia. Life under Sweden was called the "Golden Years" because children were permitted to attend school.

While their culture and language bear some influence of these ties, Latvians take pride in their own nationality and identity. The land is a wealth of natural resources, and landscapes are outlined with scenic forests of tall pines and masses of birch trees. The people love music and singing and have penned hundreds of folksongs, called "dainas," that tell about their country and their lives. These songs kept their souls alive during the difficult times.

Karlis Keikulis, a Latvian by birth, was a dreamer with various talents. He mixed pharmaceuticals at night and sold them. When offered money to work for a pharmacy, he was too proud to accept it because of his lack of formal education. His wife, Anna, came from proper, well-to-do ancestry.

Arvids Keikulis was born to Karlis and Anna on Feb. 10, 1901, the middle child in a family of four sons and a daughter. A brother and a sister had died in infancy. Karlis called Arvids "Veed," meaning "middle." Whenever the father needed his son, he said something like, "Veed, come and show me where it is." Usually Arvids was able to find the misplaced object.

Although they were church members, the Karlis Keikulis family found themselves in services only once a year, as tradition required. At home Karlis criticized the church and doubted the experience of God. When Arvids was a small boy, his dad said, "When you die, you are dead and there is nothing else. It is over!"

No one dared to blatantly disagree, but Arvids did not accept his father's opinions. "I cannot believe that. It just cannot be that after you are buried it is all ended", he reasoned. He could not be persuaded otherwise.

"This boy will be a minister," Karlis said sarcastically. "He is smarter than I am, and I cannot convince him to think as I do."

On occasions when Karlis was angry or bragging, he took God's name in vain and cursed. This upset Arvids, and he would cry, "Papa, please do not talk like that about God." Then Karlis would back off and change the subject.

An incident in church would have a lasting impact on young Arvids' life. When he was 12, a friend invited him to hear a missionary from India. Arvids traveled to hear her twice, and something stirred within him. Before, he had found it difficult to sit through a church service, but now he felt a love that he did not comprehend. The missionary's personal testimony about Christ made a profound impression on him. He never caught her name, but he and the other boys wanted to be near her so they assisted in taking her suitcases to her destination outside the city.

After hearing the missionary speak, Arvids still did not feel motivated in ceremonial church services, but the message of love he had heard from her inspiring testimony remained in his heart.

As he grew older, he became aware of tragedy in his family. His father was living in adultery, and the gossip was prevalent. Prior to this, Arvids had done well in school and achieved three grades ahead of his age. In his teens he became aware of his father's lifestyle, and he became disheartened and could no longer concentrate on his studies.

Whenever one of the children misbehaved, Karlis would send Arvids outside to get a ripe birch branch for the discipline. Once when scolded by his dad, the bitterness and hurt inside the boy erupted, and he uttered a sharp retort.

"How dare you talk back to your father?" Karlis seethed. "Do you know better than me?"

"Are you a father to us?" Arvids replied.

From that moment, Karlis said little to his son and never disciplined him again, but Arvids' feelings of hurt and rejection continued.

Arvids' education was interrupted when World War I came to Latvia's borders. The combat zone was actually on the family's property, half belonging to Russia and the other half to Germany. The Russian army issued the order, "Do not leave a rooster crowing or a dog barking. Destroy the crops."

This devastation caused a famine and economic crisis. The Keikulis family's livelihood was gone; most of their savings and personal belongings were lost as a result of the war. With his last thousand lats, Karlis purchased a house in Riga, the capital. (The lat was Latvia's currency, eventually replaced by the euro.)

The war situation was critical. After Arvids' brother had already left for the front, Karlis, who was older than draft age, and Arvids, not yet 15, were both called to come with their horses to bring supplies to the war zone. They were then conscripted into the Russian army. During the night, Karlis and Arvids brought supplies to throw into the bunkers. The bitter winter made the job difficult for both them and the horses due to freezing temperatures. Building a fire was prohibited, since any type of light would have attracted unwanted attention.

As youths that lacked experience, Arvids and the other boys were cocky and headstrong. They hated the war and its intervention and took careless risks. They had to ride horses through long winter nights – sometimes lasting 16 hours – to bring supplies to the warfront. On one occasion the freezing and thawing of the ground had caused deep ruts, and Arvids' horse stumbled into one, breaking a wheel on the buggy. There was no way to repair the wheel; and because he was late in delivering barbed wire to its destination, he was arrested by the Red Army. The ensign taking him to jail was a Cossack. (Cossacks were predominantly East Slavic people who became known as members of democratic, semi-military communities, mostly located in Ukraine and southern Russia.)

Arvids realized he needed to get out of this situation. He was familiar with the land and the terrain, having been born and raised there. They came to a place where a plank bridge over a swamp area was part of a route for transporting needed war supplies. Arvids knew the swamp like the back of his hand, so he took the risk of jumping off the bridge and began running, zigzagging into the swamp and across the quick-sand. The Cossack shot at him but missed, not able to run into the swamp for fear of stepping into quicksand.

Arvids made his escape.

Karlis had a beautiful horse, though old, and he had the job of driving a coach for an officer. Arvids immediately went to his father's regiment and explained the circumstance. The officer came in and heard the story. He asked for the name of Arvids' officer, which in Russian was Dolgi, meaning "the long one."

"It is a good thing he took so long in deciding to shoot you," the officer said, with humor. "I would have taken care of it immediately. Do not worry; we will take care of this."

Arvids was then able to join his father's regiment and to continue serving there.

Throughout 1915 Karlis and Arvids took supplies to the army engineers who were building roads and bridges. The following year was even more severe. It seemed that winters were longest and coldest in times of war, producing brutal blizzards. It became increasingly more difficult to take supplies through deep snow with the horses. Working through long nights, when they finally returned to their bunker, they practically fainted as they went to sleep. When Arvids developed a serious ear infection, he decided his only hope for survival was to run home. He had carefully figured out how to get by the gate, but when the sentry saw the youth's condition – so near collapsing – he said, "Go on!"

However, before reaching the final checkpoint, a stern Russian refused passage, and Arvids was forced to take a long detour to get around the post. The temperature was far below zero as Arvids trudged through 20 miles of snow. He could feel his strength ebbing out of him, and his body yearned to stop. He knew that going to sleep in the freezing snow would be a fatal mistake. As he momentarily sank down, he felt calm. He desperately wanted to give in to the temptation to float into a restful sleep, but something inside warned that he would surely die if he did not press on.

Forcing himself to stand, he resumed the journey and made it home, where he collapsed. When he awoke, he had pneumonia and could not move.

When the battlefront had passed over the area near their home, Arvids went walking among the dead and wounded bodies lying on the ground in an effort to find his brother, whom the family had not seen nor heard from since his departure for the warfront. For three days Arvids stepped over bodies, lifting caps to see if he recognized one as his brother. The stench was terrible, but he became accustomed to it and continued to search. He paused momentarily when he found a Bible on one of the bodies.

This had been a gruesome task, permanently imprinting the scenes of war in his mind. As dusk approached, he felt weary, so he dropped down into a bunker and fell asleep.

When he awoke, he realized that he had slept next to a dead soldier.

* * * * * * * * * * * *

In 1918, after two-and-a-half years, Germany won the war and occupied Latvia. The Germans had used up their food supplies, so the first thing they wanted to do was build fences and claim food supplies for their armies. Riga was surrounded by an electrical barbed-wire fence to prevent people from leaving the city in search of bread. It became a familiar sight to see people dropping dead in the middle of a street.

During this period Arvids had two unusual experiences.

He knew he needed to go home but felt weak and hungry, since he had not eaten during the three days he had searched for his brother. The only sight was death all around. It was springtime – and a long distance to any town or farmhouse. He wondered what he could find to eat. He had walked a mile from the front, still thinking about his hunger.

As he wandered down a seldom traveled country road, sparse green grass was beginning to come through the ground. Looking down, he noticed a large piece of pressed meat that seemed to be a sausage or bologna, perhaps weighing two pounds. In his hands it felt cold and moist as if it had recently been removed from an icebox. He was so delighted that he ate it all.

He wondered how he had come upon it.

Later, after he arrived back home and was living with his family in Riga, he had a dream. In the dream he heard a voice say, "Go out to the road that is seldom traveled on. There you will find gold."

In the dream he saw ruts in the road made by wagon wheels. The ruts had grown up with long, wild grass and weeds. He saw a clump of grass with large roots clinging to it. He awakened and immediately walked to the road he had seen in his dream. Because of the war, the road was left unfinished and grass had grown over it. Grazing animals had eaten the grass almost down to the roots.

Walking down the road, he came to the clump of grass he had seen in his dream. As he stopped, he saw a bare glimmer of metal. He stooped down to pick it up and uncovered a five-ruble gold piece. At this point he did not consider how he was able to find the gold piece or how the entire episode could have happened – just like the food he had found earlier on the road.

When Arvids arrived back home, a woman was talking to his mother.

"See, neighbor, if only we had money!" he overheard her say. "A Jewish man is secretly selling wheat, but only for gold."

After hearing this, Arvids went and bought a sack of flour, which fed his family through the devastating famine.

* * * * * * * * * * *

The long hours in the nights during the first war and the tragedy in his family had crushed Arvids' spirit. By the time he was 18, he had become backward and shy, having no feeling of self-worth or confidence that he could accomplish anything. He knew he needed to work in order to exist and had heard that a railroad company needed foresters to supply their lumberyard. Mustering up his courage, he finally went and applied for a job.

The government director to whom he spoke pointed to a crew that was loading lumber and said, "Go and supervise that group."

Arvids thought that perhaps the director took pity on his small frame and pale countenance and figured that he could not handle heavy work. Timidly, Arvids walked over and joined the crew, trying to fit into the scheme of things. As he pulled with the other workers on the rope tying down the load of lumber, he joined in the shout, "One, two…"

"I told you to supervise!" the director yelled out.

Thus Arvids was forced to start giving orders and to immediately learn the requirements of the job. Later that day the boss gave him additional good advice. It was hard work – but satisfying. Now that Arvids could do something and get results, he felt like he was growing into manhood.

After two years as a forester, Arvids joined the army and was placed in officer's candidacy school. He realized how weak-headed he had been and that the experience in forestry and the army was teaching him the self-respect and discipline he had sorely lacked.

Yet God had other plans for him.

After four years of hard training, Arvids was disappointed to be passed over for promotion. He felt slighted and did not sign up for the next term. Later he learned what had happened.

While still in the army, he had once walked into a crowded restaurant. When no table was available, he asked the waiter if he could share a table with two gentlemen who were already seated, and he was granted permission to sit there. The men were Russians, who engaged in conversation over the meal.

Not realizing they were Russian soldiers in plain clothes, Arvids did not know he was being observed and suspected of giving them military information. Though he was never charged or questioned about it, the incident was recorded in his files that he was suspected of befriending

Communists. This had prevented his promotion.

Still, army life had provided the discipline he needed to mold his weak character into manliness.

Following his release from the military, Arvids spent three months in a sanatorium. Like many of his family members, he had contracted tuberculosis and was admitted for treatment. The place was depressing because everyone was sick, and they had little hope for improvement. With the disease spreading and no cure available, treatment consisted only of rest and observation by medical personnel. Nevertheless, patients were checked daily to see if they had gained weight or developed any signs of progress. There were no restrictions to force patients to remain institutionalized.

Discouraged, Arvids decided to leave the sanatorium, choosing instead to live among healthy people. He hoped that leaving would lift his morale and at least take his mind off his condition. He did not want to return to his family, since that situation depressed him.

He went to another city, Dobele, to get away from it all. Dobele was approximately 40 miles southwest of Riga. There he found an office job working for a wealthy landowner and railroad builder.

After settling into an upstairs apartment, Arvids looked out the window at the steeple of the Lutheran church and began speaking to God in his thoughts. He was aware that tuberculosis was incurable, but he had an irrepressible desire to live.

"God, couldn't you give me just 25 years to have a family and enjoy them?" he asked.

The immorality of his father had caused him to be shy and backward around women, so he typically avoided contact with them.

Below his apartment was a bakery and candy shop owned by his boss. One day he decided to buy some confections and started down to the shop. As he approached the door, he was surprised to hear a small voice in his mind saying, "The woman inside is to be your wife."

Upon entering the store, this shy young man saw an attractive, dark-haired girl whose smile made him comfortable, so he asked for the finest candy in their showcase. After paying for the candy, Arvids picked up a piece and held it out to the girl's mouth.

When surprising someone with a treat, Latvians were known to say a familiar ditty, "Open your mouth and close your eyes." As Arvids said the words, the pretty girl behind the counter leaned over obliging, opening her mouth and closing her eyes – at which time Arvids quickly popped the candy into his own mouth. She blushed, and they both laughed.

It turned out that Emilija Cecilija (Eh-me-li-yuh Tse-tsee-li-yuh) Paulina Kasparovics was the boss's niece. Everyone called her Cilite.

The two got along so well that Arvids asked Cilite if he could meet her after work to take a walk together. She accepted the invitation.

On their first "date," they met an old woman as they crossed a bridge. She stopped and addressed them in a kind voice. "You know, children, you ought to be married," she said. "You really belong to each other."

The shy young man and his new friend blushed – but laughed comfortably.

* * * * * * * * * * *

Cilite Kasparovics' family had moved to Moscow, Russia, during World War I. There was an epidemic of scarlet fever in Latvia, and the Russian army took a large population of children to Russia to keep them from contracting the disease. Also, there was the problem of severe famine. Hoping to find work, Cilite's father thought it best for the family to move to Moscow.

Ansis Kasparovics went out daily looking for food and work; however, favorable conditions were not to be found. People were arrested for carrying food and accused of carrying contraband for illegally selling the items. It was bitter cold as Cilite's father walked around in search of something – anything – and it nearly cost him his life. Strict curfews were enforced and punishable by death.

Czar Alexander Romanoff had lost the confidence of the masses. The socialistic idealism of Karl Marx and Friedrich Engels was spreading among the intelligentsia. Its promises of equality and bread for everyone fed the hopes and minds of the population. However, dissatisfaction soon erupted among the majority of the people, and the movement to overthrow the czar took to the streets. Eventually the royal family was captured and murdered.

The declining economy and widespread famine that overtook Russia spread into Latvia – to the same extent or worse. Hundreds of children were starving to death.

In 1917, two revolutions swept through Russia, ending centuries of imperial rule and setting in motion political and social changes that would lead to the formation of the Soviet Union. In March, growing civil unrest, coupled with chronic food shortages, erupted into open revolt, forcing the abdication of Nicholas II (1868-1918), the last Russian czar. Just months later, the newly installed provisional government was itself overthrown by the more radical Bolsheviks, led by Vladimir Lenin (1870-1924) [history.com].

Vladimir Lenin became the hero of the Bolshevik Revolution and the premier of the Communist Party.

Soon after the revolution, when Cilite was 13 years old, she was sent to a comfortable "dacha," a Russian country home serving as a boarding school. There was no explanation as to why she was chosen or if she would ever return to her home again. The dacha employed numerous capable teachers and staff to run the school. As a new Communist country, there was no fee or charge for the students. Along with the regular school curriculum, Cilite received instruction in Russian arts, dances, music, and songs. She realized she was attending school and living with children of the new elite, the Communist leaders. She was eating well while countless others were starving. She liked learning Russian literature and arts but wondered how her family was faring and if she would see them again.

A year later, with no known reason, Cilite was put on a train headed back to Moscow. She was unsure whether someone would meet her at the station. Upon arrival, she searched the mass of faces but found no one who looked familiar. She then started walking to where she hoped to find her family's apartment. She trudged for several hours trying to remember the way and not knowing if her family still lived there. Finally, as she approached the familiar street, her heart began to beat wildly. In the distance she saw a young girl. Could it be her sister Rolite? The two girls stared. Coming closer, they screamed and ran toward each other. For a few minutes, the sisters rejoiced in a happy reunion; then Cilite recognized that her family was in poor health while she had been doing well.

She never understood why she had been privileged above others, but Russian became her education language.

The Kasparovics family returned to Latvia for Cilite to finish her senior year in Liepaja, a large city on the Baltic Sea. The family home faced a scenic park separating their street from the beach. When she was 18, Cilite went through confirmation classes and a ceremony in church. They had lived through many hardships, and her father had turned to alcohol as an escape. The strong drink affected his behavior, often resulting in cruelty to his family. Cilite and her sisters saw their mother quietly endure the episodes, and it brought them much sorrow. Cilite prayed, asking God to allow her to have a "real" family.

The experience of Russian culture revealed Cilite's talent in singing and music. Upon returning to Latvia, she began training in opera and agreed to have a publicity photo made. She was soon performing in the background chorus of the Opera House in Riga and eventually chosen to rehearse as the understudy to the leading lady. When the opera star became ill, Cilite was asked to step into the role. Her singing performance was so well received that the newspaper published her photo with the caption, "A starlet is born."

As she proceeded with her newfound stage life, she found herself immersed in activities that brought discomfort to her soul and left her unfulfilled. The vanity of a performer's life behind the scenes had choked her spirit. To take time to sort things out, she left the opera and went to Dobele, where her uncle lived and had become involved in various businesses.

That was when she met Arvids Keikulis, and her priorities began to change.

Arvids' and Cilite's fondness for each other was growing. With their sorrows behind, it was as if they had captured a joy of living. They knew that marriage was forthcoming. However, most of Cilite's relatives disapproved of her marrying a man whose destiny appeared to be an early death from tuberculosis. To the couple, however, their love was so fulfilling that the presence of tuberculosis was not important. Their strong relationship made the disease seem remote, and they forgot about it. Cilite inspired boldness in Arvids, and in her he saw a side of life that he had not experienced. It awakened in him the desire for laughter and contentment. The zest for living that Cilite possessed filled a void in his own life. He had not known how to laugh, but with her beside him they shared much happiness. Her trained, melodic voice brought music into his life.

Cilite's pleasure in discovering a relationship with Arvids, who was vastly different from her father, made her lose interest in returning to the opera. She felt as if she had been set free.

While Arvids was away visiting his parents, Cilite's aunt tried to convince her of the hopelessness of marrying a man with a terminal disease and into a family that had lost most of their possessions during the war.

"He is poor, sick, and dying," her aunt argued. "Cilite, you can have anyone you want. Why settle for a failure? If you marry a sick man, love will fly out the window, and poverty will walk in the door."

Unwittingly, Cilite broke the engagement and went sobbing to her mother in Liepaja. Paulina Kasparovics spoke words of wisdom to her distressed daughter.

"Darling," she said, "if God was so unmerciful not to give love to the poor, there would be no God. It is better to have a few good years with a man who loves you than to have a lifetime of misery."

Paulina alone encouraged Cilite that love was strong enough to endure such a test, and Cilite made up her mind to follow her heart.

With new resolve and gladness in her heart, Cilite packed her small suitcase and took the train for Riga to meet Arvids' family. Wearing her best suit of pink and gray in the style of the day, with a matching drooping hat, she arrived at the house and met Arvids' mother, Anna. As Cilite explained the situation, Anna Keikulis became excited and suggested the girl hide in Arvids' room to surprise him. He was expected to walk in any minute. He had been depressed, thinking about Cilite's relatives' disapproval of the marriage.

Arvids arrived and went straight to his room. Once inside, he turned around and caught Cilite's eyes looking at him from behind a partition. Startled, his face turned ashen. Cilite jumped out, threw her arms around him and told him she had come to marry him – and that was that.

The wedding date was set for Oct. 28, 1927, and the ceremony would take place at a lavish estate owned by Cilite's uncle.

For the ceremony Cilite wore an elegant gown in the latest style. Her dress of organza had a coordinating loose coat with a wide sash around the hips. She wore a matching hat that came down over her forehead. She felt – and looked – stunning. Arvids was handsome in his formal tuxedo. An orchestra was hired to play music during the festivities. Preparations and cooking were done four days in advance, and the maids roasted 12 geese that were specially selected for the event. It was an elaborate affair, with guests remaining for three days of feasting and celebrating at the grand manor.

* * * * * * * * *

After spending the early months of their marriage in Dobele, the couple returned to Riga and settled into a second-floor apartment above the store where Arvids worked.

Every day Arvids rose before daybreak to meet the delivery carts. Often he made cocoa and brought it upstairs to Cilite. Then they would talk until they heard another delivery cart downstairs.

One morning as he was preparing to go down, Cilite called out, "Instead of cocoa could you bring me an onion, dear?"

"An onion for breakfast?" Arvids asked, not sure he had heard correctly.

"Yes, a nice fresh, juicy onion," Cilite answered. "You know, we have some in the pantry."

Puzzled, Arvids took her the onion. This continued for several weeks, and the new bride smelled like onions. They soon learned that this was a sure sign that an addition to the family was on the way. Expectant women were encouraged to eat a lot so the baby would be large and healthy.

In time, Arvids and Cilite were blessed with their firstborn, a son, Janis, who was delivered by a midwife in October 1929 and weighed a whopping 13 pounds.

In 1931 Arvids landed a job as store manager in the small rural community of Pampali. He managed a general store stocked with everything a farmer or country resident would need. There were two such stores serving the community, the other a cooperative approximately six miles away. The village had a creamery, bakery, doctor, and flour mill. Farmers brought their crops and dairy products to town for processing. Then they bought food, as well as farming and living supplies, at the country stores.

The rural location was better for Arvids because he had difficulty breathing in the cities due to lingering tuberculosis. By now, the illness was common in the area. Cilite's sister, Rolite, was afflicted; and the disease had claimed the lives of Arvids' three brothers and a sister.

* * * * * * * * * * *

World War I left Latvia in ruin, and the recovery had been slow. The happiness of Arvids' and Cilite's relationship restored a sense of normalcy for them, except for the problem of his illness. Although there was no cure for tuberculosis, they had each other and their new baby – albeit no hope for the future. If it were not for the seriousness of the illness, they could have been content in their circumstances. They had many friends and good status in the community, but the disease was destroying the life they were endeavoring to build. There was no apparent way out. Arvids perspired heavily during the nights, requiring a change of pajamas and bedding. He became too weak to lift his arms and in his nervous tension became a heavy smoker.

Cilite's days were filled with tears as she watched her husband grow weaker. At times the burden seemed too heavy to bear, so she went to visit her mother in Liepaja for comfort and consolation.

Once again, Paulina Kasparovics offered valuable advice, this time for brokenness. She invited her daughter to a gospel meeting where a newly converted man was scheduled to preach. Arvids Kumins (Koo-minsh) had responded to God's call, having left his career as a construction engineer to preach the good news that had changed his life. Brother Kumins had received an engineering degree in Philadelphia, Pa., and was converted at Highway Tabernacle in that American city. The Lord had so changed his life and direction that he felt led to abandon his engineering career to spread the good news of the gospel. Upon his return to Latvia, the local newspapers ridiculed him.

At first it was difficult for Cilite to think about this meeting; she did not want any part of it. Religions outside the state church were looked upon as dangerous sects. However, Paulina persuaded her that attending this service would not be improper.

Cilite had previously attended a service with her mother where they had heard a Latvian-born missionary from America named James Arthur Gravinc (Gray-vinsh). It was through him that Paulina and other residents first heard the gospel. When Brother Gravinc returned to America, the seed was sown and revival had spread in Latvia.

When Cilite's sister, Rolite, was dying of tuberculosis, her mother – although a God-fearing woman – did not know how to comfort her daughter. She decided to call Brother Gravinc. He came and prayed with Rolite, explaining his message from the Bible that eternal life begins the moment one accepts Christ. Through his testimony Cilite's mother and sister were saved. Just before dying, Rolite told those around her that she had met Jesus, that He was taking her to greener meadows, and that she had perfect peace. Her loved ones were confident that she died in victory.

When Paulina followed the Lord in water baptism, Cilite attended the service. She did not understand the commitment her mother was making and was perplexed.

"Daughter, you need peace in your troubled heart," Paulina said. "Come to Christ. Only He can give you the peace you need."

Both bilingual and musically inclined, Cilite began to help Mr. Gravinc translate Russian hymns into Latvian. Her heart was stirred at the message of the hymns, but concern for her husband was uppermost in her mind.

Now, in the meeting, for the first time the young mother heard preaching with such power and conviction that her resistance vanished. The hunger in her soul caused her to respond when she heard of a living Christ who died and was resurrected that all mankind might be changed and given new life. Never before had she heard such enthralling words, and her heart was touched. At the conclusion of the service, Brother Kumins asked those who wanted to respond to Christ's call and receive Him into their hearts as personal Savior and Lord to come to the front. As people went forward, Cilite felt resistance and struggle return to her soul.

"Dear daughter, this is the only way," said her soft-spoken mother as she took her hand. "You, too, must respond to Christ's call."

With that, Cilite found herself in front of the congregation, and she opened her heart to receive Jesus Christ. The burden that had pressed so heavily was released.

She returned home with new hope and meaning in her life.

When she arrived back in Pampali, Arvids became intensely aware that his wife was completely changed. For the first time there was a Bible in their home. Arvids surmised that what had happened could not be bad. Curiously, their lives seemed to become more stable. He noticed that Cilite would read the Bible for hours and then pray. Singing of hymns replaced sadness with joy. He was moved to see Cilite praying quietly and yet so naturally to God, calling Him "Father." He never asked what was going on and dared not interrupt because he knew something holy was taking place. Before retiring for the night, Cilite knelt by the bed, praying silently. Arvids pretended to be asleep, but he was curious and wondered what his wife could find to talk to God about and what she found interesting to read for so long.

One evening after Cilite had fallen asleep, Arvids tiptoed into the kitchen and opened the Bible on the table. His eyes fell on John 3:3, which says, "Truly, truly, I say to you, except a man be born again he cannot see the kingdom of God." As he read these powerful words, he felt as if a strong voice had spoken directly to him. He promptly slammed the book shut, but the truth had pierced his heart like a bolt.

On the advice of Brother Kumins, who had said, "Without a word, go home and win your husband," Cilite had not tried to share her newfound faith in words, but through love. Arvids was aware that she was genuinely committed, and he could not help but respond with respect. For the first time in their relationship, he knew that Cilite knew something he did not. Thankfully, he understood enough to realize that it was a positive change, although he could not comprehend it himself. Each night after Cilite fell asleep, he went into the kitchen where she had left her Bible and continued to read. Its truth spoke to his hungry heart.

Secretly, he read the Bible through in several weeks.

When Christmas arrived, Arvids and Cilite traveled to her parents' home in Liepaja to join the festivities. They found themselves among worldly people, celebrating the holiday without mention of the Christ they were supposedly honoring. Cilite's heart longed for something more, and she slipped away to seek fellowship at Brother Kumins' house. Arvids had known this preacher before his conversion. They had worked together at the railroad company, and Arvids knew where the man lived. Inconspicuously, he decided to leave the party to follow Cilite. Just as suspected, he found her at the preacher's house.

The Kumins family received Arvids graciously. Soon the wives went into another room, and the visitor found himself facing Brother Kumins alone. After a cordial discussion, their conversation turned to spiritual matters in which Arvids only listened, since he could not converse on the topic. Brother Kumins spoke in a natural, flowing way and with such conviction that there was nothing with which Arvids Keikulis could argue or disagree.

Brother Kumins had recently returned from a trip to America. There he was deeply affected by the spiritual awakening and had ministered across the United States as revival fires spread. He brought back with him the spirit of revival and renewal. There was no doubt that when this man spoke he was anointed from on high.

Arvids Keikulis had always been certain of his own philosophy of life and never wavered from it. Now he knew he had met a man with whom he could not argue and be truthful at the same time. What he did not realize was that his soul was under conviction of the Holy Spirit, and his heart heard every word; yet intellectually he was hesitant to embrace the truth. Brother Kumins quoted to Arvids the words of Jesus from John 14:6: "Jesus said to him, I am the way, the truth and the life. No man comes to the Father except through Me."

"Where do you get all of this from?" Arvids finally asked.

Brother Kumins explained that the gospel he represented was his entire life, and he did not have to premeditate or choose his words because they came from within. Brother Kumins sensed that Arvids was deeply impressed, and he continued, "You know, Mr. Keikulis, let's have a meeting in your town."

Arvids became somewhat alarmed but had no courage to offer an objection to the bold suggestion.

"You have a public hall we could obtain, don't you?" the man continued. "I will bring the ministers and singers, and you get the meeting place."

The two agreed on a date, and the matter was settled.

The next day Arvids and Cilite took the train home. They rode approximately 43 miles by train, with 12 more to go by horse and carriage. They made the entire trip in silence, since Arvids was under conviction of the Holy Spirit. This statement kept ringing in his conscience: "Woe to me. I know the truth and do not do it."

Nervously, he chain-smoked. The next day when he opened the store and customers had not yet arrived, he paced the floor, saying to himself as he continued to smoke, "Woe to me. I know the truth and do not do it."

Finally he stopped walking and blurted out, "How can I do it, when I can't even stop smoking this cigarette that is damaging my health?"

Again he felt as if he heard a voice inside him, this time saying, "Do you want me to take it out of your mouth?"

He understood who was speaking and answered, "No, Lord, I will do it myself."

He threw down the cigarette and opened the door of the apartment to tell Cilite. "The Lord has delivered me from the cigarettes," he said.

Then he climbed a ladder and put his last pack on the top shelf. Prior to having the Lord in his life, he had tried many times to quit, only to pick it up again. This time he knew he had conquered the habit because the Lord was with him. From this time forward Arvids read the Bible for hours each day. He was hungry to know more.

Before the week was over, he had read the Bible, once again, from cover to cover.

* * * * * * * * * * *

The year was 1932.

During the weeks leading up to the spiritual meetings, the townspeople noticed the change that had taken place in Arvids' and Cilite's lives.

Arvids began to think about a location for Brother Kumins' gatherings. The town had a hall that could be leased, so he went to the government office, made the necessary arrangements, and rented the hall for the dates needed.

News of the meetings spread – through leaflets that had been distributed and by word-of-mouth. When the day of the first meeting arrived, folks from the country started coming into town in horse-drawn buggies to witness the special event.

That afternoon when Arvids went to the government office, he was told he would not be given the keys to the hall. In spite of his pleas, the answer was the same. It turned out that those who frequently used the town hall held considerable influence; they believed that "too much religion" would be harmful and did not want their community's lifestyles disturbed.

Word traveled fast about the denial of use of the town hall as people from miles around continued to arrive. Arvids had no plans for an alternate location.

In the same building as the Keikulis apartment was a saloon at the other end. The saloonkeeper was an atheist who liked to brag about his unbelief. Whenever he had an opportunity, he talked against God in a brazen manner. He had a bad reputation in other ways, too.

On this day, the saloonkeeper came into Arvids' store.

"What do I hear?" he asked. "Won't the hypocrites give you the keys to the town hall? Come on and have your preaching in my saloon. I will clean out all the bottles and tables. My sons and I can build benches, and for three days you can have my place for your preaching, rent free. I will have the place ready in an hour."

Arvids was not convinced that the substitute venue was a good idea, but there was no other option. As promised, the saloonkeeper went to work at once to prepare the facility, even whitewashing the walls to get rid of the smell of alcohol. His sons helped out by building benches, and the new meeting place became a sensational topic of conversation throughout the town.

The entrance to the saloonkeeper's apartment was directly behind where the preachers and choir stood, and a table was placed by that door to serve as a lectern. While preparations were taking place, Brother Kumins arrived with two additional ministers and a choir. The place filled up quickly. People were crammed in wall to wall, with an equal number standing outside.

Isn't God wonderful! He can even use one of his enemies, Arvids thought. This was a new experience for him, personally witnessing God's use of those against Him to further His kingdom.

Evening came, and the opening service finally got underway, with songs of faith filling the time between speakers. The Word of God was proclaimed with unaffected zeal, and it was evident the people had never heard this kind of preaching before – as a gale-force wind bringing in fresh air to stir the spiritual atmosphere. Each minister was unique in his own way, all speaking with conviction and authority, preaching the gospel with power that was new to the hearers. When Brother Kumins preached, he was as forceful as thunder and could be heard out in the street. Every message told the good news of the gospel: Jesus had come to earth to live, had died, and was resurrected to bring eternal life to all mankind. The net was being drawn. The choir sang with inspiration, and young people in the audience soon found themselves joining in. The meetings were off to a good start – in spite of the unusual setting.

After the meeting ended, the ministers came to Arvids' and Cilite's apartment to pray for the upcoming services. Each person found a place on his knees to voice a supplication to God. Arvids joined the prayers and wept softly as he cried out to the Lord, confessing Jesus Christ as his Savior. One of the preachers came over to him and said, "I witness that you have been saved!"

"I do not know that I am," Arvids replied, still unsure as to what was taking place in his life.

"But I can see that you are," the minister continued.

And so it began to dawn on Arvids that God was working in his life, even before he knew how to explain it.

In the next evening's service the saloonkeeper and his family were watching through the glass in their apartment door. The saloonkeeper stuck his hand through the open door and pulled on Brother Kumins' coat, whispering furtively, "Sir, you had better all run in here to save your lives. See, out there are ruffians who have come here to kill you!"

"We are not leaving!" Brother Kumins replied firmly.

Noticing the saloonkeeper whispering to Brother Kumins, Arvids turned around to see four large men with clubs in their hands squeezed in against the back wall. The faces of the men had turned as pale as the wall behind them, and they seemed to be frozen in place.

Suddenly, Brother Kumins announced, "Arvids Keikulis, who has just been converted, will come forward and give his testimony."

Arvids had not anticipated this. He became frightened, not knowing if he could speak to a crowd of people. As he stood up and began to walk forward, he had no idea what he would say. Then he heard a voice in his mind saying, "You fool, stop. You will never be able to fulfill that."

Even though it was his first experience of this kind, he recognized Satan speaking to him. When he reached the table at the front, an indescribable peace came over him, and he began to speak words not premeditated.

"From this day forward, I only have one Lord," he began, with calm assurance. "In His hands I place everything which is dear to me. My life, my family, and all of my life's goals now belong to Him, and with my whole heart I want to be faithful to Him."

"Young man, don't be so sure lest you fall," an older minister seated nearby whispered as he tugged on Arvids' coat.

Arvids turned and replied, "If I could say to my wife, who is only human, that I will be faithful until death, how much more should I be able to say it to my Lord!"

He did not fully understand that his spirit had been ignited by the Holy Spirit. He only knew that the Lord heard his affirmation and held him to the words he had shared before many witnesses. He also knew that by God's immeasurable grace, He would enable his servant to fulfill this promise.

Arvids was given a promise that would take him through long years of testing that lay ahead. He would experience the truth of Isaiah 54:11, which says, "Oh, you afflicted, tossed with tempest and not comforted, behold, I will lay your stones with colorful gems and lay your foundations with sapphires."

The services normally lasted about four hours. On this night the ruffians stood as if frozen the entire time. They looked like soldiers on guard duty, unable to flex a muscle. As the meeting drew to a close, one of the ministers handed Arvids a basket to pass through the crowd to collect an offering. The people were so tightly seated that Arvids literally had to squeeze through the crowd. He pressed against the stiff thugs, who remained standing with clubs in their hands.

When the service was over, the ministers again returned to the Keikulis' apartment. They could hear clubs being beaten against empty benches. Released from their dazed state, the would-be troublemakers were taking their anger out on the furniture.

Through these evangelistic services a church was born to which Arvids began ministering. During the coming years God would lead this new flock in the midst of heavy trials as the promise of Isaiah was experienced – along with some unexpected blessings on the journey.

* * * * * * * * * * *

Soon Arvids and Cilite learned how much they needed daily prayer time. They desired to grow in faith and help others who were seeking God. Already there were new believers who were like-minded and wanted to follow Christ, requesting help from the ministers who had brought the special meetings to Pampali.

"We don't have anyone that can come and teach you," the evangelists had sadly answered, so they sent literature instead.

The God who had recruited this flock would lovingly train them in His school of faith.

Chapter 2

Basic Training –
The School of Faith

When the revival services were over, Arvids and Cilite continued to rejoice in the truth they had received and the lives that were changed by the power of God.

Thus they were taken off-guard when Cilite's father and her cousin's husband came to their apartment with beer bottles in hand and began to curse and accuse them vociferously. The hostility – especially at this time – made them uncertain about their faith, because they had just chosen to fear the Lord and serve Him. Why then should those closest to them become angry and swear at them?

These actions were followed by several angry customers coming into the store and yelling profanity.

Arvids and Cilite knew no recourse other than to pray and seek God's will. They began to understand Matthew 10:34-39, which says:

> *Do not think that I came to bring peace on earth. I did not come to bring peace but a sword. For I have come to set a man against his father, a daughter against her mother and a daughter-in-law against her mother-in-law; and a man's enemies will be of his own household. He who loves father or mother more than me is not worthy of me. He who finds his life will lose it, and he who loses his life for my sake will find it.*

In spite of a few discouraging incidents, Arvids and Cilite knew many hearts had been stirred in the recent meetings. As soon as the store opened in the morning, people started to come in asking spiritual questions and sharing their heartfelt needs. Now, in addition to his responsibility as a merchant, Arvids was exercising his newly found faith by answering questions and praying with those in need. Brother Kumins had left gospel literature with the Keikulises, and they were distributing it as fast as new shipments arrived.

About a week after the final revival service, Cilite went to visit her mother in Liepaja. One evening after he had closed the store, Arvids became increasingly aware of God's presence and the realization that he was truly one of His own. The truth was so real and personal to him that he was flooded with joy and freedom. He wanted to hug someone or something to express his deep gratitude for God's grace. He felt like he could embrace the whole world. His heart was bursting with love. He began thanking the Lord and praising His name. This joy was unspeakable and full of glory. He was not aware of how many hours passed while he basked in this blissful state.

* * * * * * * * * * * *

Ten years earlier, Latvia had experienced a true revival among Baptists. There were real conversions and changed lives. Also, a prophecy had spread that a red dragon was to take over the country soon. A large number of Christians left for South America, as God led them. There they continued to grow in faith, starting churches, schools, and orphanages. The Holy Spirit poured out in revival fires in South America.

Those ministries continue to grow in Brazil and Bolivia at the present time in the 21st century.

The aftermath of the revival also saw the springing up of small cults and sects that had adopted false doctrines and practices. From the beginning there were questions about the Keikulises' beliefs and whether they followed any of the extreme practices, so Arvids and Cilite devoted themselves to diligent study of God's Word and spent time in fasting and prayer. They desired to stand firm to be able to give those who asked a reason for the hope that was within them, according to I Peter 3:15:

*Always be prepared to give an answer to everyone who asks you
to give the reason for the hope that you have. But do this with
gentleness and respect.*

In February 1933 Cilite traveled to see her mother again to attend
a week of special services at Paulina's church. Arvids had remained
at home to look after the business of the store. The Liepaja services
included fasting and prayer, preaching of the Word, and testimonies.
These were also times of soul searching before the Lord. Farmers and
other laborers helped each other with transportation to the meetings.

"After a week of these sanctifying services, I feel as if I have been to
the bathhouse and thoroughly washed clean," one sister proclaimed.

Throughout the week Cilite's heart was moved to follow the Lord in
obedience and discipleship. Then she heard messages about the believer's baptism. As the scriptures teach, those who have repented should
be baptized as an outward sign of the finished work of Christ within.
Cilite was in agreement within her soul, but she was distressed when
she learned there would be a baptismal service in the Baltic Sea at the
end of the week. How shocking that was to her young heart! She knew
the sea well and knew there would be ice on the shores. That evening
she talked it over with her mother. It seemed impractical during the
month of February. She could postpone it until the next time.

"The brethren are on fire," Paulina said. "I am sure you could wait
until spring."

At the next service, however, there was more preaching on baptism.
One of the speakers related a testimony from a previous baptism that
winter. When there was a new group of converts, a baptismal service
was held to seal the commitment. Fourteen new Christians had made
professions of faith and desired water baptism. Also, an elderly crippled
woman – believed to be more than 70 years of age – requested to be
baptized with the group. The preacher had tried to dissuade her, saying
that the Lord saw her condition.

"Do you want to just baptize the 14?" the woman insisted. "If I die,
what will I tell the Lord about obeying Him in baptism?"

Because of her strong conviction, the brethren carried her over the
ice and into the Baltic Sea. After she was immersed in the name of the

Father, the Son, and the Holy Spirit, she emerged from the water and walked out unassisted. The minister went on to say that he himself had remained in the water through all 15 baptisms. God's presence was evident, and he never got sick or even had a sniffle.

Upon hearing this testimony, Cilite's heart was convicted, and she knew she must not postpone her baptism. She could not wait to tell her mother her decision.

Paulina met her at the door.

"Dearest daughter," she said, "the Lord has convicted me that I gave you the wrong advice. He said to me, 'Are you going to teach her or am I?' Darling, you must do what He tells you to do."

What a glorious day when the congregation came together again! As each believer walked across the ice to the water, those gathered could hear huge blocks of ice shift and crack. The Baltic Sea was indeed cold, but the fire Cilite felt burning within was more intense than the icy waters. When Brother Kumins lifted his hand toward heaven and said, "I baptize you in the name of the Father and of the Son and of the Holy Spirit," she could hear a big bubble moving upward as she went down.

As she rose from the water, she felt warm and victorious. A Jewish lady who had been watching curiously followed Cilite around that day, asking, "Are you alright, dear?"

Everything was alright indeed because Cilite knew she had obeyed the Lord. As a result, the Jewess felt the presence of God and made a decision to follow Christ, her newfound Messiah.

Cilite returned home, confident in her own choice to follow Christ in baptism.

* * * * * * * * * * *

So much was happening that Arvids and Cilite had forgotten things of former importance.

One day as Arvids reached to get items from a high shelf, he suddenly realized that his chest was not hurting. It had been many months since he could lift his arms without sharp pains in his chest. He mentioned this to Cilite, and it occurred to them that he was no longer perspiring and his sleep was not disturbed at night. With considerable wonder and cautious young faith, they began to realize that God was doing a work

42

in his body and began telling this to their friends.

In time, one of the preachers came by and invited Arvids to attend a special three-day sanctifying service. At these meetings the believers got together for three or more days for fasting, prayer, and seeking the Lord. All day they would pray and study God's Word, late into the night hours. After three days of fasting, there followed a time of rejoicing in God's grace.

The preacher had suggested they bicycle the 75 miles to the special service. Still uncertain of his condition, Arvids did not feel his body could withstand that level of physical exertion. It had been several years since he had been able to engage in even moderate physical activity, so he offered to purchase train tickets instead. However, after pedaling 12 miles and arriving at the train station, they were told that another train would not come until the next day. The two were disappointed, and Arvids wondered why the Lord allowed this to happen.

"I want to go on bicycle," the preacher said. "You do what you think is best."

Reluctantly, Arvids agreed to go along on his bike. As they pedaled all day and through the night on a bumpy country road – even trudging through a snowstorm – Arvids' muscles ached because they were not accustomed to the strenuous activity. He kept wondering why the Lord was permitting this. Many times he lagged behind, and the preacher waited for him to catch up.

By morning they arrived at the farmhouse that was hosting the special meeting. When the time of fasting and prayer was over, the group heard memorable testimonies. During the first one, a lady told how she had died and gone to heaven. In fact, Cilite's mother had been present when the incident occurred.

Paulina told about the church's persecutions and said they had been called fanatics. False rumors about what happened at the meetings had also run rampant. The sister had apparently fallen over dead in her pew. Frightened church members thought of the accusations that would start if they carried her body out of the church. They decided to gather around her and pray. No one left, and they prayed over her for six hours.

Then the woman awoke and, hearing crying, asked, "Why did you call me back?"

Immediately she began to describe what she had seen in heaven. She said that the arches and buildings were so high they seemed to disappear into the sky. Although she had finished music conservatory, she lacked words to adequately describe the celestial music she had heard. She spoke of blooms, flowers, and fragrant scents unlike anything she had experienced on earth.

For weeks after this incident the lady wept because she felt she had to return from heaven. As Arvids listened to this testimony, he realized that God had brought him to this place to strengthen his weak faith. It was no mistake that he and his friend had missed the last train – so God could prove to him that he was healed of tuberculosis. His muscles ached, but he reasoned that pedaling against the wind for hours proved his breathing and lungs were actually strong. In fact, as he thought about it, he had not remembered any pain since he had believed on the Lord and accepted His salvation.

The services were exceptional. After the testimonies came a baptismal service for those who had made a commitment to follow the Lord. Arvids was baptized on Pentecost Sunday in June 1933.

From the beginning of his walk with the Lord, Arvids was aware of God's presence in his life. He was also tested with each progression of faith. He and Cilite experienced severe trials and were learning to overcome through the power of Christ, but during those early difficulties Cilite felt weak in her faith. She wondered why people became antagonistic toward them and why accusations continued. The editor of the newspaper had written terrible lies about the Keikulises in her column, and this was heartbreaking for Cilite. The cross indeed seemed heavy, and it was difficult to avoid giving in to disappointment. She knew, however, to bring her heartaches to the Lord.

One day she was lying in bed after crying out in prayer. As she meditated on the Lord, the words from Isaiah 30:15 came to her. She grabbed a pencil and wrote them on the wall, where they remained through many more trials to encourage the entire family.

"By calming and quieting yourself before God, you will find His strength," Cilite had penned from memory, from the old King James Latvian Bible.

As they began to follow the Lord in their new walk of faith, Arvids and Cilite endeavored to obey His Word in all things. In the first year they felt led to observe Sunday as a time of worship, prayer, and rest. However, Sunday had been the biggest day at the store, bringing in the largest profit. It was the one day that farmers could leave their work and come to town to buy supplies. So the couple prayed for God to help them in their efforts to honor Him on Sunday.

They called Nathan Kiels, Arvids' boss, who was a kind man.

"You know it is the biggest day for business," Mr. Kiels said, "and, besides, your competitor across town will take all the business on Sunday."

Arvids and Cilite felt they could not insist on their way without the boss's approval. However, a short time later they received an unexpected phone call.

It was their competitor.

"You know, we should not have to work as slaves seven days a week," he said. "How about it if we both agree to close shop on Sunday?"

Arvids and Cilite were gratified to watch the Lord take care of the circumstances. Upon their decision to comply with the request of their competitor, one of Mr. Kiels' assistants came to inquire about their plans. Cilite had been praying a long time about this, and she gently told him, "Dear Luftschitz, we fear the Lord, and we are committed to following His commandments. We have prayed for His will to be done, and we see our competitor's request as the finger of God."

* * * * * * * * * * *

March 1, 1934, brought with it a blizzard and high, boisterous winds. Arvids and Cilite heard banging on the windows of their apartment, which they thought was from the storm. Then it became clear that someone was breaking through the shutters, and they assumed it to be bandits or drunks. Due to the storm, Arvids had not been able to send the store money to his boss, and he feared thieves might be coming in after it. Finally he went out to try to determine what was happening and saw black smoke.

The entire building was in flames.

45

The Keikulises and the saloonkeeper had the same landlord. The couple had heard many accusations from the saloonkeeper. Also, in his rent lease the man had agreed to make certain building repairs and improvements, which he had not completed even though he was a builder. The lease was now up, and he would be in trouble.

He has finally done it! Arvids and Cilite thought.

They had also heard of a possible conspiracy of the saloonkeeper with others in town who thought they could get rid of the "sectarian," as they called Arvids, and their debts at the same time. People bought things on consignment, and their bills were past due. Because they were in the same building, the saloonkeeper thought he would never be suspected of arson. Gasoline had been poured around the Keikulises' apartment and store. Compassionate neighbors tried to help get the family out of the burning building.

Cilite was in her last month of pregnancy, and this ordeal was especially trying for her.

The fire burned quickly. Arvids knew the top ceiling was made of mortar for insulation, so he figured he had some time before the ceiling would collapse. Pausing to pray, he asked God for mercy and guidance. After carrying Janis and Cilite – covered in blankets – through the flames, he walked back into the burning building to call Nathan Kiels in Liepaja. The call was difficult in the storm, but Arvids was finally able to get through to tell his boss the store was on fire and to please come at once. Mr. Kiels tried to decline because of the weather, but Arvids pleaded with him. Then he took all the store's cash and stuffed it into his pockets. Out of concern for his family and his responsibility as store manager, Arvids did not think about personal belongings.

Arvids was worried that the oil and kerosene drums inside could explode. Upon his arrival, the store owner said everything in the store was insured and they should not worry about it. He then asked Arvids if their apartment and belongings were insured. Arvids said they were not.

"Oh, that is too bad," Mr. Kiels sighed.

However, some trustworthy Baptist neighbors had been busy taking things out before the fire spread. There, out in the snow, lay most of their belongings except for heavy furniture.

Cilite remembered that smoked meats were in the wall cabinet and murmured, "I guess the meats will be well cooked."

The neighbors pointed to meats they had also brought out, and Arvids and Cilite were grateful for these acts of kindness in the midst of chaos. The smoke had filled the rooms before the flames ignited, and some men had even brought out the oil drums. The heavy wooden barrels were charred black but had not burned through.

There was a flurry of activity and confusion. While some were trying to help and save things, others were looting. The saloonkeeper and a few others were actually throwing and smashing things that could have been saved. It looked like a violent temper tantrum. Arvids tried to calm him down. Then another saloonkeeper came with a bottle in hand and began to shout accusations, as if the Keikulises did not have enough anguish thrust upon them.

"We need to get rid of this man!" the troublemaker yelled. Not one of the onlookers called him down.

Actually, because of severe winds, flames blew to the end of the building, and the fire ignited the saloon and the saloonkeeper's apartment. His family had to jump out the windows, some breaking their legs. When it was over, the saloonkeeper lost much more property than the Keikulises did.

Arvids, Cilite, and Janis spent the night at the blacksmith's home. One particular man was of significant help to the Keikulis family during this time. He had obtained keys to a public warehouse and helped them carry store goods and personal belongings there for safe storage. He also helped find a room in town where they could move store items to open up shop while another facility was being built.

Many years later the man was found to be a Communist, but Arvids and Cilite never forgot his compassion during an agonizing time in their lives.

In the back of the storeroom was a small cleared area where the couple managed to squeeze in a couch and bed. Cilite said it was more like a corner than a room. Their personal belongings were piled into the remaining amount of space. Janis slept on the couch, Cilite on the bed, and Arvids found a place on the floor. The arrangement was not entirely comfortable, but under the circumstances they had to manage. Cilite

Arvids, Cilite, Janis & Anna, 1934.

tried to cook on a tiny petroleum stove. In a few days they were able to resume business in the room the kindhearted man had helped locate.

* * * * * * * * * * *

The burning of the store was just the beginning of a period of fiery trials, such as those described in I Peter 1:6-7 and I Peter 4:12-13:

> *In this you greatly rejoice, though now for a little while, if need be, you have been grieved by various trials...Beloved, do not think it strange concerning the fiery trial which is to try you, as though some strange thing happened to you; but rejoice to the extent that you partake of Christ's sufferings, that when His glory is revealed, you may also be glad with exceeding joy.*

Cilite had stayed outdoors too long in the freezing weather the night of the fire, and her face was frostbitten. Her cheeks and chin became discolored, and her lips were swollen. She was unable to assist Arvids in their new cramped quarters in the store as she awaited the arrival of the baby. Then on March 23, 1934, she delivered a baby girl, which they named Anna. It was difficult to bring a newborn into the tight quarters, with no convenient place for washing and hanging diapers; but they felt blessed that Anna was a quiet, contented baby.

In the following weeks and months the Keikulises learned the meaning of Matthew 3:11-12 as they experienced the baptism of fire that John the Baptist spoke about:

I indeed baptize you with water unto repentance, but He who is coming after me is mightier than I, whose sandals I am not worthy to carry. He will baptize you with the Holy Spirit and fire. His winnowing fan is in His hand, and He will thoroughly clean out His threshing floor and gather His wheat into the barn: but He will burn up the chaff with unquenchable fire.

Arvids reasoned that in order for Jesus to make His children fit for His service and for Himself, He sends the Holy Spirit to purge and clean out the dross – those things in their character which do not please Him. The process is not easy and takes a lifetime.

In the fire some glass stored in boxes had been broken, and one day Arvids stepped on a sliver while working. The glass pierced his foot up to his ankle bone. He was able to remove it, and at the time it seemed to be nothing more than an inconvenience – a small, clean wound that would quickly heal.

Still reeling from the disruption caused by the fire and added work of starting business again, he did not bother to keep a close eye on the wound. A few days later, the area became discolored, and blue lines spread up his leg. As the lines continued upward, the area around his right hip bone started to swell. Still later, Arvids saw the infection spread toward his chest. He managed to keep working in the store, for the most part remaining behind the counter so that customers were not aware of his pain and discomfort.

Then one day two men came into the store and sat down to talk. One mentioned a relative who had stepped on something that did not seem to amount to much at first. He had put off going to the doctor. When the man finally went, the physician said it was too late and the leg would have to be amputated. From that conversation Arvids realized that he himself had blood poisoning, evidenced by the blue lines on his legs.

The reality was frightening and difficult to accept.

A small group of believers regularly met with Arvids and Cilite. They were all new converts, and Arvids never wanted to burden them with his physical needs. Cilite had carried the load.

In the midst of their stressful trial with the blood poisoning they were distracted by a man who was determined to destroy them. His mother and sister had been converted and started attending church services. He was overcome with a spirit of bitterness and jealousy. He opened a small store and underpriced his stock, claiming that Arvids was known to cheat people and had not been weighing goods properly. Suddenly, customers started to ask Arvids why he was overcharging, and they double-checked to see that he was not cheating on the scales.

The Keikulises' cup of suffering was already full, and this seemed to make it overflow.

Once, upon seeing this man approaching in the street, Arvids started to turn into a store to avoid an unpleasant confrontation. It was then that Arvids felt the Lord speaking to him from Isaiah 7:4, "Take heed and be quiet; do not fear or be fainthearted for these two stubs of smoking fire brands." It seemed as if the Lord was telling him that he was merely facing a lot of smoke.

The scriptures tell believers to come out from among the world and be separate. From the beginning of their walk of faith, Arvids and Cilite had been ostracized and looked upon with scorn. In their small community, everyone was aware of their commitment to Jesus Christ, so the people concluded that they were foolish fanatics. The town doctor, who was an immoral person, had openly condemned them, blaspheming God and bragging, "I will see what the Christians will do when their children are sick and come to me. I will ask them, 'Well, where is your God?'"

Arvids and Cilite had prayed and fasted as they trusted God throughout this test. In each trial they knew they had only the Lord to depend on, along with the small group of believers.

Although he tried to keep going day after day, Arvids' strength was failing fast. He was near collapse, and Cilite recognized the seriousness of his condition. In a moment of inspiration, she spoke these words firmly: "Go rest, my child."

At last her husband submitted and fell down on his mattress, immediately slipping into a deep sleep that lasted for hours. His underarm was badly swollen, and he knew the poison had reached its last barrier.

After closing the store that night, he dropped again to the mattress and cried out to God. Their new landlord's quarters were close to theirs, and he too was an immoral person. Arvids covered his face with a pillow so his cries would be heard only by God. Satan had unleashed all his forces, it seemed, because people continuously screamed accusations and obscenities through the windows.

Out in the street the town drunks mockingly sang hymns – substituting blasphemy for words – and tried to break through the door. This was a miserable, humiliating experience, and Cilite fell apart, sinking into despair. Arvids called out to her, "Read the 73rd Psalm."

She grabbed her Bible as a drowning person would grasp a life raft and began reading the chapter aloud so they both could hear. These were truly words of life; and after she finished the chapter, peace returned to her, and she stood like a soldier of Christ.

Psalm 73, the words that comforted Arvids and Cilite, reads as follows:

Truly God is good to Israel, to such as are pure in heart.

But as for me, my feet had almost stumbled; my steps had nearly slipped.

For I was envious of the boastful, when I saw the prosperity of the wicked.

For there are no pangs in their death. But their strength is firm.

They are not in trouble as other men, nor are they plagued like other men.

Therefore pride serves as their necklace; violence covers them like a garment.

Their eyes bulge with abundance; they have more than heart could wish.

They scoff and speak wickedly concerning oppression; they speak loftily.

They set their mouth against the heavens, and their tongue walks through the earth.

Therefore his people return here, and waters of a full cup are drained by them.

And they say, "How does God know? And is there knowledge in the Most High?"

Behold, these are the ungodly, who are always at ease; they increase in riches.

Surely I have cleansed my heart in vain, and washed my hands in innocence,

For all day long I have been plagued, and chastened every morning.

If I had said, "I will speak thus," behold, I would have been untrue to the generation of Your children.

When I thought how to understand this, it was too painful for me –

Until I went into the sanctuary of God; then I understood their end.

Surely You set them in slippery places; You cast them down to destruction.

Oh, how they are brought to desolation, as in a moment!

They are utterly consumed with terrors.

As a dream when one awakes, so, Lord, when You awake, You shall despise their image.

Thus my heart was grieved, and I was vexed in my mind.

I was so foolish and ignorant; I was like a beast before You.

Nevertheless I am continually with You; You hold me by my right hand.

You will guide me with Your counsel, and afterward receive me to glory.

Whom have I in heaven but You?

And there is none upon earth that I desire besides You.

My flesh and my heart fail; but God is the strength of my heart and my portion forever.

For indeed, those who are far from You shall perish;

You have destroyed all those who desert You for harlotry.

But it is good for me to draw near to God! I have put my trust in the Lord God, that I may declare all Your works.

Arvids felt the agony of the valley of the shadow of death. After the intense pain and pressure, it seemed like he let go, and his head fell backward. He no longer felt pain but slipped into a coma, his body seeming to float upward. There was no fear – only peace and darkness.

Then he sensed a hand coming out to stop his journey in the darkness. He heard in his conscience, "You must go back. Eat and go back to work."

When he awoke, he saw Cilite standing over him, praying with her hand on his forehead. Everything was calm and peaceful, and it was quiet outside. They noticed that the swelling and blue lines were gone.

Arvids had drunk the entire bitter cup. The reward he received was that he not only believed in God but he now knew Him. He had laid hold of God and trusted Him with his very life and found Him faithful. He had been called on to exercise all his faith, though it seemed small. He was learning that faith was the realization of God's power. He thought of Hebrews 11:1, which says,

Faith is the assurance of the things we hope for, the evidence of the things not seen.

Thus Arvids was learning that faith is also the realization of God's power – and the way one gets to know God.

Several weeks after he had recovered, Arvids heard that his competitor was found to have picked up another merchant's shipment at the railroad and stolen it. The thief was facing a subpoena to appear in court, with his store closed and his goods being sold at auction. Mr. Kiels bought the merchandise and gave Arvids the keys to the competitor's building so the goods could be moved to their own store. One day as Arvids went to get the supplies, he ran into the former merchant in the street. The man sheepishly asked for mercy and inquired if he could please get some food for his baby.

Arvids handed him the keys and told him to get whatever he needed.

* * * * * * * * * * *

The Keikulis family eventually moved from the tiny room in the warehouse, renting a small apartment and space for the store until construction of the new facilities was completed, which took several years. Arvids had gradually converted their living space into three small rooms.

There was one bedroom with a dresser, bed, and glass case with shelves. Arvids made most of the furniture, as time and need determined. The sitting room had a fireplace with an alcove in the corner for wood and an extension with a built-in seat of mortar. Opposite the fireplace sat a couch and small table with a lamp. There was a narrow path for walking through the rooms. The kitchen's furnishings consisted of a tiny stove and a table against the wall with chairs around it. The toilet was more like a wooden outhouse indoors, situated at the right exterior wall and entrance to the kitchen. There was no light except for a hanging oil lamp. Behind the kitchen was a larger room for the temporary store. It seemed like people were always coming through the store and into the apartment. The little church met in the living room, using chairs brought in from the kitchen.

The small group of believers that congregated in the Keikulis home was an intermingling of simple folk. A number of the women worked as maids at large farms in the community. They said that wherever they went, people were discussing or arguing about the Keikulises. According to the women, most of the gossipers were fired up and angry, saying Arvids must be a rascal and dishonest, but a few would counter with, "We are supposed to be Christians, too, but I wonder if we could stand as they have stood."

Sometimes the local farmers went to the county seat to buy large amounts of feed from Arvids' boss, and they had been heard saying, "You know that Keikulis runs that store like it was his own."

"That is our agreement," Mr. Kiels always replied. He consistently demonstrated his trust in Arvids, and the two had a good relationship.

Mr. Kiels once confided to Arvids that his family had difficulty keeping a maid. His wife was nervous and impatient and his children a bit rowdy. He asked if perhaps someone in their church would be able to handle the job. Arvids and Cilite recommended a sweet, young German girl from their congregation. She worked out well, and the Kiels family fell in love with her. A few weeks after she started to work, Mr. Kiels called Arvids to express his appreciation.

"Where in the world could you find another person like this girl?" he said. "Our whole family loves her. Whenever I want to find the children, they are always in her room."

* * * * * * * * * * *

Anna Keikulis was born when Arvids and Cilite were learning how to take the reproach of Christ. They were experiencing drastic times of opposition, hostility, and ridicule. Still, the Lord blessed them through baby Anna's soft, yet bubbly and lively, personality. Wide-eyed with curiosity and enthusiasm, she put all her energy into every task. When just beginning to eat table food, she would often sit in Arvids' lap and grab a fistful of food from his plate that should have been too hot to handle, but she refused to release it from her fist. With trembling hands and excitement, she stuffed it all into her mouth, wincing and gobbling it down.

When Anna began walking, she soon figured out how to open doors and cabinets. Arvids installed latches out of her reach. One day the toddler cleverly took a tall broom handle and jiggled it against the latch on the door. Then she walked triumphantly into the store.

"And how did you get in here, little girl?" Arvids asked, with merriment in his eyes.

Feeling reprimanded instead of welcomed, Anna turned and ran to her mother in the kitchen. With grief and dismay on her face, she tried to explain the scolding as "Papa, blah, blah, blah, blah! Papa, blah, blah, blah, blah!"

On another day Anna came up with an idea. After studying by the oil lamp in the bathroom, she came into the kitchen holding a glass chimney with trembling hands. With bright-eyed expression she said, "All we need is matches and the glass to make light."

Arvids often said if it had not been for the children's endearing ways, they could not have made it through the rough times. God used their little girl's daily antics to lighten the atmosphere with joy and laughter. The couple found that their Lord was bringing a "way of escape" in the midst of heaviness or trials, and He used the little ones to relieve burdens. They recalled the promise in I Corinthians 10:13, which says:

> *The temptations in your life are no different from what others experience. And God is faithful. He will not allow the temptations to be more than you can stand. When you are tempted, He will show you a way out so that you can endure.* (New Living Translation).

Arvids' enthusiasm for merchandising was waning because he now knew he had a higher calling. Mr. Kiels noticed this and gave him a substantial raise, including back pay to make up for an increase in wages for the previous two years. Arvids and Cilite were glad to finally move into their new living quarters and place of business during this time.

As the business prospered in the new location, so did the persecutions. Every unbelieving husband whose wife attended the Keikulises' services could go to the sheriff and complain that they were confusing his wife. The sheriff would summon Arvids to his office, which involved waiting for several hours. Finally, as if proud to carry out his duty, the sheriff would read accusations and file a report with the court.

The visits to the sheriff's office reminded Arvids of John 15:20, "The servant is not greater than his master. If they persecuted Me, they will also persecute you."

House Church at Pampali, Latvia.

On the surface it seemed they were harassed unjustly, since Latvia's constitution granted religious freedom; yet Arvids and Cilite believed they were required to walk in the same way their Savior had. This was never easy, but they knew they were called and that He was leading. At times, in the flesh, Arvids wondered, Why do we have to put up with this? We are not breaking the law.

Then he began to understand Matthew 10:16-19:

Behold, I send you out as sheep in the midst of wolves.

Therefore, be wise as serpents and harmless as doves. But beware of men, for they will deliver you up to councils and scourge you in their synagogues. You will be brought before governors and kings for My sake, as a testimony to them and to the Gentiles. But when they deliver you up, do not worry about how or what you should speak. For it will be given to you in that hour what you should speak (New King James).

Arvids felt that they were called to bear testimony before councils and authorities, so he never hired an attorney.

After several weeks, he was subpoenaed to appear in court. On that day he waited in the courtroom for his case to be called. While he waited, he heard things about the accused in other cases that involved robberies, embezzlement, and immoralities. The judge conducted his court in a routine, dignified manner. However, when he came to Arvids' case, he became angry and emotional, even foaming at the mouth and not allowing Arvids to defend himself. The penalty was finally pronounced: a choice between spending two weeks in jail or paying a large fine.

This happened twice. Arvids had prayed a lot about the circumstances and was dissatisfied with their outcomes. The question he had been asked was, "Do you admit to holding religious services?" He could not understand his indictment since he had not broken any law.

The third time, he was summoned for an investigation. As he waited to be called into the judge's chambers, countless thoughts raced through his mind – but he kept praying, "Father, your name be glorified."

When the doors opened, he again saw the hateful face of the judge. The man's appearance made it clear that he had spent the previous night partying and suffered from lack of sleep. While looking over the papers, Arvids noticed that the chamber walls were lined with portraits and statements made by Latvia's president and leaders. The judge bellowed out accusations at Arvids as though he were the worst criminal he had ever faced, concluding with the question, "Do you admit to holding these illegal meetings?"

The Holy Spirit came upon Arvids, and he prophesied with strong conviction as he pointed to the wall hangings depicting Latvia's leaders and symbols: "A storm is coming upon Latvia and Europe, and all these will fall like autumn leaves."

"I dare you to say that again!" yelled the angry judge.

"A storm is coming upon Latvia and Europe, and all these will be carried off like manure," Arvids said a second time.

The judge's countenance crumbled, and then in a soft, trembling voice, he said, "Repeat that again."

Arvids said it one more time. By this time the court secretary was weeping uncontrollably. The judge began to shuffle papers and murmur, "Let us just say you never had a church service."

"Judge, do not sear your conscience," Arvids replied. "I held services which were not secret but public, as our constitution permits."

The judge mumbled and continued moving papers around. The case was dismissed for lack of evidence. Arvids had no idea what the prophecy meant.

The accusations continued, and two more times Arvids was called to court – but was dismissed. After one of these times, the sheriff walked into the store when it was filled with customers. He held out a piece of paper and said, "Here, read this and sign it!"

Arvids could see that it was the previous report on the case that had been dismissed for lack of evidence. The sheriff yelled at Arvids, shaking his finger in his face and said, "See to it that you do not do it again!"

"And see to it that you do not put your nose in my business," Arvids called back. "You know very well that there was no evidence against me."

The times when Arvids was summoned to court seemed worrisome to the children. They could not understand why their papa was going to court; they just knew it was an injustice. The accusations were false and absurd. However, when he returned home, the children sensed that the burden was lifted, and everything was fine again. God had intervened and delivered. Arvids came home a victor; his feet were light.

Many years later, when the family was in a displaced persons (DP) camp in Germany, Arvids served as an administrator of the camp with a Latvian judge who had heard about the court trials of the "sectarian," as Arvids had been called. The judge told one of the other administrators, "I am just thankful that I did not put my hand to this man!"

* * * * * * * * * * *

Ansis Kasparovics' hatred toward his wife, Paulina, and daughter, Cilite, had continued to grow because of their newfound faith. He was determined to destroy their inner peace. After a drinking binge, he was often emotionally and physically abusive. Sometimes when there had been severe physical mistreatment, Cilite and Arvids brought Paulina to their home for a reprieve. To Cilite's father, this came across as interference in his family's affairs, and it made him angry. Ansis was a tall man who was big with his words and opinion of himself; in other words, when he spoke, people had better listen.

One day a policeman came and handed Cilite a citation to appear before him on charges her father had made. Cilite was naturally upset that her father would go to the police, but she immediately took her heartache to the Lord. After her prayer session, she felt as if the burden was released and the peace of God controlled her.

She went to the police station in a spirit of meekness and trust.

She sat quietly as the accusations were read, the policeman becoming as angry as her father had been when making them. The accusations – all untrue – charged Cilite with stirring up trouble and influencing people religiously. When the reading was over, the policeman said, "See, your own father says you are a troublemaker."

"You know my father drinks and talks brashly under the influence of alcohol," Cilite responded, quietly but firmly. "You have not given me a chance to reply to the accusations and hear me out. I ask you to complete your report after you hear me, but do not add anger to the truth for your conscience's sake."

She noticed the back door to the office was ajar, and two eyes were looking in.

"See, even my wife is upset about this and warned me not to interfere with the saints," the policeman blurted out. "Maybe our daughter is sick because of this."

Cilite realized it must be his wife behind the door. The policeman then took time to listen to Cilite, recorded what she said for his report, and dismissed the case against her.

Cilite was acutely aware that God was with her.

Once Arvids and Cilite were invited to hold a service in the home of a converted woman whose husband seemed to be moved toward following Christ. He did not yield, however; and an evil spirit came over him, and he was determined to kill Arvids. He came to their home with a knife in hand, trying to enter through the window to attack. However, the rage suddenly left him, and he ran to the sheriff, throwing the knife to the floor and admitting he had intended murder. Instead of dealing with the vindictive man, the sheriff picked up the knife and came to see the Keikulises, waving the weapon in their faces with more accusations.

"See how your religion gets people so mad that they want to kill!" he yelled.

Indeed, the sheriff himself seemed angry enough to commit a crime.

* * * * * * * * * * *

Arvids' Jewish boss had given him absolute trust in carrying out the business of the store. Approximately every two years Mr. Kiels would come in with auditors to take inventory. During this time the store remained closed for three days.

At this year's audit, after using the abacus and checking the records twice, the auditors claimed there was a large deficit of funds. Arvids was shaken up, since he was sure he had been accurate in his accounting. Still a new Christian, he was respectful and wanted everything to be in order. As he checked the figures again, they looked correct. According to the auditors, the deficit could not be reconciled.

"Could you possibly have made a mistake?" Arvids queried.

"Young man, I do not make mistakes," the accountant curtly replied.

In a further attempt to resolve the discrepancy, Arvids traveled to the firm's office in Liepaja and arrived at the same conclusion – a deficit. When he left the office, he went for a lonely stroll along the beach. The wind was blowing and howling, and he cried out to God in his need.

Finally, before returning home, Arvids put his thoughts aside and purchased gifts to take to the children. He knew they had felt the seriousness and tension that had been present during the inventory and accounting, and he wanted to cheer them up. However, when he arrived home with the gifts, Cilite seemed upset.

"We are in such stress and accused of a deficit, and you come home with presents?" she asked, wondering how to justify the expense.

"That is our burden, and I do not want the children to carry it," her husband replied.

The next day as Arvids was going up the stairs to their apartment, the Lord gave him an answer that showed the miscalculation. He immediately wrote it on the stairwell. It was 500 lats that the auditor had failed to carry. When Arvids called the accountant to report that he had found the error, the man said impatiently, "Didn't I tell you that you had the mistake?"

"No, sir," Arvids countered. "It is your mistake, and you will find it in these calculations." He explained that the discrepancy was due to adding some unused old goods to the newly arrived goods.

He bowed his head and thanked the Lord for helping him resolve the situation.

* * * * * * * * * * * *

On another occasion God sent help from an unexpected source – the enemy camp – and used a non-Christian to aid Arvids.

The former saloonkeeper came into the store – drunk again – and began to shout accusations. The man had never been charged with arson in burning their building. He owed the store some back debts, and his hatred grew. As he bellowed lies and accusations, customers stepped away to avoid involvement. It appeared that the enraged man was going to physically attack, and Arvids began praying for wisdom.

Suddenly a large farmer known for his strength came to the rescue and addressed the raging saloonkeeper.

"Get off, you rascal!" he shouted. "All of our sins in this room could not stack up as high as yours. We all know you cheat at your card games and business matters. If you lay a finger on this man, I will crack every one of your ribs!"

The incident reminded Arvids of Proverbs 16:7, "When a man's ways please the Lord, He makes even his enemies to be at peace with him."

* * * * * * * * * * *

Sometime later, when Brother Kumins notified Arvids that he would be preaching less than 20 miles from the store, he asked if Arvids could come to see him. The two men seldom had an opportunity to visit, with Arvids' job keeping him busy and their residences located nearly 45 miles apart. Arvids was eager to see his spiritual father and began making arrangements.

When the men got together, their hearts were warmed as they talked about things not of this world. As they knelt to pray, Arvids could not help noticing a large hole through his friend's shoe and sock, revealing a bare foot.

How could this man who has finished a university and given up his professional career to preach the gospel be required to live this way? Arvids thought. He could not fully comprehend.

"It is your fault!" he heard the Lord speak to him.

My fault? How could it be my fault? Arvids was puzzled.

"You have not been paying your tithes," he heard God's answer within his heart.

Although he had no one to teach him the basic Christian principles of life, Arvids had learned them gradually by studying the Bible and trusting in God. Now he realized that tithing was something he needed to pursue further. He promised the Lord that as soon as he could, he would take care of it.

"How do you know I will bless you that much?" he heard the Lord speaking to him again.

Arvids got the message. He knew then he had to deal with the matter immediately. Upon returning to the store, he calculated his profits and salary from the previous two years and sent tithes to Brother Kumins. It was a relief to take care of the matter – in obedience to his Lord.

Soon after, Arvids and Cilite noticed a marked increase in business and profits. They were learning that God is true to His Word, as written in Malachi 3:10:

"Bring all the tithes into the storehouse, that there may be food in my house. And try me now in this, says the Lord of hosts, if I will not open for you the windows of heaven and pour out for you such blessing that there will not be room enough to receive it."

In those beginning years the tests were intense, but the Lord was close, and the young Christian couple could hear the words He spoke to them. While growing in faith, those times became more infrequent as they were called on to exercise that faith and discernment according to what they had learned from His Word and their daily walk with Him.

Brother Kumins endured persecutions parallel to theirs. He was jailed for preaching and fined 500 lats, which was more than his friends could raise. Then a woman from another congregation heard about it and said she would pay the fine. The believers were thankful that this Christian sister could identify with their bonds and care to that extent. However, before she sent the payment, skeptics began to talk to her and dissuaded her from getting involved with "fanatics." Brother Kumins called Arvids and Cilite asking for prayer. The very next day, he received a letter from America with the exact amount of the fine enclosed. He did not recognize the name on the envelope, and the believers were astounded at how God accomplished His work across the miles – even continents – and at just the right time.

* * * * * * * * * * *

During the holidays Arvids rode his bicycle to preach and testify in nearby towns. As he returned from one of these trips, he stopped at a restaurant for a meal. As he waited for his order, a gypsy woman carrying a baby – and looking very tired – approached his table and said, "Let me tell your fortune."

"I will not permit it," Arvids replied.

"Let me tell you just one thing," the stranger implored.

"I will not permit it," he repeated.

Just then his dinner arrived, and he looked at the ill-prepared pork chop. He heard the gypsy murmuring to herself, "All day I have served him [Satan], and he does not even give me food to eat."

"Here, you eat it," Arvids said, shoving his plate across the table.

The proprietress noticed the gypsy eating from the plate and said to Arvids, "Now she should tell your fortune since she is eating your supper."

"This man will not listen to fortunes as he serves only God," the gypsy said.

"Why do you not leave your master, who does not even feed you, and come to Jesus Christ?" Arvids asked.

"I cannot come to Him," the weary woman replied sadly, with real tragedy in her voice. "I have gone much too far."

* * * * * * * * * * *

During this time there was a man who seemed to particularly enjoy taunting Cilite. Mr. Lacits (Lahtseets) – or "Mr. Bear" – would find a time when Arvids was not around and ask questions such as "What if one of your children dies or gets killed? How will you trust your God then? You talk about everything in the Bible being true. What if you would lose your hand; then what?"

He continued to plague Cilite with his what-ifs, and it was difficult for her to answer these kinds of presuppositions. She dreaded seeing him coming to the store only to harass her with the persistent questions. She had to pray diligently to be able to face him.

Then Arvids and Cilite heard one day that Mr. Lacits had been dynamiting two large stumps and blew off his entire hand. They shuddered to think that the thing about which he had taunted Cilite had happened to him.

* * * * * * * * * * *

In the beginning years God had often spoken to Arvids and Cilite through His Holy Spirit, confirming the promise of John 16:13, "He (the Spirit) will guide you into all truth." They clung to the words of John 14:17, which teach that the Holy Spirit would come to be with His children and then in His children: "...the Spirit of truth, whom the world cannot receive, because it neither sees Him nor knows Him; but you know Him, for He dwells with you and will be in you." At times God would teach and warn them through words they heard distinctly. Sometimes they heard within and other times audibly, and on occasion

He spoke to them through dreams.

As they became known in their community as Christians, Arvids and Cilite had visits from people who called themselves Christians but followed false doctrines and practices. At times when the couple heard knocking at the door, the Holy Spirit would warn Arvids, "He is not of mine. Do not receive him." Cilite was shocked at her husband's lack of hospitality, since he usually did not have time at the moment to explain. Later, Arvids would point out that the scriptures warn of false preachers that will come, and II John 10 tells believers not to receive them into their homes.

The couple was ever thankful for the Holy Spirit's aid when they were still young Christians. Once a man came in through the back door of the apartment and, taking Cilite's hand, began to prophesy with words that sounded scriptural. Arvids knew in his spirit that this man was not from the Lord and, as he came in from the store, told the visitor to leave. Cilite had been uncomfortable, but she was surprised at her husband's abruptness. In his studies of the Bible, Arvids had learned that he could not be kind and polite when dealing with a false spirit. The Lord was teaching them discernment.

Matthew 7:15 warns of false prophets coming in disguised as something else:

> Beware of false prophets, who come to you in sheep's clothing, but inwardly they are ravenous wolves.

Verse 21 of that chapter states,

> Not everyone who says 'Lord, Lord,' will enter into the kingdom of heaven, but he who does the will of My Father in heaven.

In a similar instance, Arvids and Cilite had tried to help an acquaintance receive Christ and commit her life to Him. Over a period of a year she made no progress but continued to be confused. At Brother Kumins' advice, they discontinued fellowship with her and turned the matter over to God. Then one day the woman entered through the kitchen door, took hold of Cilite, and began to prophesy in a loud voice about how they needed to humble themselves and receive her as sent from God. If they followed her advice, she said, God would use them mightily. Her words flowed like a stream, and Cilite wondered if perhaps she was sent by the Lord.

Upon hearing her from the store, Arvids came upstairs and walked into the room.

"I stand on Christ; on whom do you stand?" he spoke with firmness and authority.

At this the woman fell limp and began crying.

"I do not know where I got this spirit," she wailed. "It drives me day and night. Why has this happened to me?"

The Holy Spirit continued to speak through Arvids, and he explained that she was hiding sin, which he identified. The woman could never make restitution and was finally sent to a mental institution.

Arvids and Cilite were grateful to the Lord for giving them the discernment not to receive everything and everyone that came to them.

* * * * * * * * * * * *

In 1934 Arvids had a vivid dream in which he saw old palatial buildings and towers. In the dream he entered through a large gate and then through the doors of a massive building. He saw what appeared to be government leaders and the public inside expansive rooms. As he looked around, he heard a voice speaking, "This is hell's portals and Satan's receiving room."

When he awoke, he wondered what he had seen. The building and rooms seemed vaguely familiar. Picking up a history book, he leafed through until he came to a page about Moscow. Pictured there was the building he had seen, the Kremlin. Once the seat of Orthodox religion, many had ruled from its large halls over the centuries, claiming to be God, as written in the Bible in II Thessalonians 2:4. Verses 7-10 of the second chapter warn of the lying wonders and deceitfulness of unrighteousness.

It would be much later when Arvids realized how all the nations of the world seemed powerless against the constant lies of Communism.

Years afterward, when the family had escaped the horrors of war and Communism and came to freedom in the United States, it was in Arvids' heart to warn American Christians of the power behind Communism. People smiled and looked at him as if he were taking things too seriously. He felt like the prophet in Isaiah 53:1, who said,

Who has believed our report? And to whom has the arm of the Lord been revealed?

* * * * * * * * * * *

One evening in the fall of 1936 Arvids was walking to a house where prayer meetings were being held. Dark came early in autumn, and he carried a lantern. The thought came to him that he could save time by cutting through a field. As he did, he noticed in the distance some lights and a commotion on the road. Not knowing what was happening, he turned off his lantern and walked on in the dark. Upon arrival at the home, the host seemed surprised to see him and said the sheriff had rounded up a posse of men to arrest him.

Arvids wondered why they would hide in the dark to try to arrest him when he worked openly in the public all day. Then he recalled that scripture says the work of darkness is carried out in the dark, as recorded in John 3:19,

And this is the condemnation, that the light has come into the world, and men loved darkness rather than light, because their deeds were evil.

* * * * * * * * * * *

On Aug. 31, 1936, Arvids and Cilite had been blessed again – with the birth of their second daughter, Judite. The following May, when the baby was nine months old, Cilite placed her in a carriage and told Janis, seven years old, and Anna, a toddler of two-and-a-half, to rock the carriage in the sun while she went back into the store. The children enjoyed pushing the baby and soon ventured down the garden path to the other side of the river bank. It was an exceptionally fine spring day, with the crystal water bubbling as if it were talking. Janis felt the river beckoning and told his sister to watch the carriage while he went down to catch some fish. After a while Anna became bored and decided to go down the bank to join her brother.

"Here I come, Janis!" she called.

Seeing the bank was too steep to push the carriage down, she sat in front and tried to pull it as she shimmied on her bottom. The bank was treacherous, and soon the carriage rolled over poor Anna. Little Judite's body hurled through the air and into the river, narrowly missing tall pines that grew along the side. Anna screamed in fright, while Judite laughed in sheer delight, not realizing the danger. The landlord's daughter, Sylvia, was at the river bank and quickly jumped in and rescued the baby. A photographer who happened to be taking pictures of the scenic landscape dropped his bulky camera and jumped in to retrieve the carriage and pillow.

In the excitement of bringing Judite into the house, Anna was totally overlooked. By the time she walked back into the apartment, the place was full of people running and shouting, crowding and talking all at once. From her vantage point peering up at the tall adults, she could not see that her sister was fine, dry, and cheerful – barely even wet.

Everyone continued talking loudly. In the commotion, Cilite had patted Anna on the head but did not realize the trauma that was going on in her little girl's mind.

"The baby is dead, and it is all my fault," Anna thought. Suddenly the sunshine turned into darkness, and she crawled into the safe, warm space on the fireplace, pulling her legs up to her face. The voices began to fade – far, far away.

When Cilite tried to comfort Anna, the little girl still did not see the baby. She sat in the alcove next to the wood bin feeling sad and lonely.

As a result of her confusion and fright, she went into shock. This was a profound experience for her little heart. First came trembling, then convulsing. It appeared as if Anna was a little candle on the verge of flickering out. The Keikulis home was filled with despair.

For two weeks the child grew worse and convulsed almost without ceasing.

"Where is your God?" the doctor mocked. Some villagers were sympathetic, some predicted certain death, but the new believers prayed.

"Your Name be glorified, O Father!" Arvids and Cilite prayed.

Arvids, who had to continue working through the long days, was forced to listen to predictions from people who came into the store with anything but comfort. However, previous trials had taught Arvids and Cilite to seek help from God and draw closer to Him. They had learned through prayer and fasting to depend on God in everything, even sickness, according to James 5:14-15:

Is anyone among you sick? Let him call for the elders of the church and let them pray over him, anointing him with oil in the name of the Lord. And the prayer of faith will save the sick, and the Lord will raise him up.

In the beginning their dependence upon the Lord did not require so much struggle in obtaining victory, as mentioned in Luke 18:7-8:

And shall God not avenge His own elect who cry out day and night to Him, though He bears long with them? I tell you that He will avenge them speedily. Nevertheless, when the Son of Man comes, will He really find faith on the earth?

They read about the spiritual warfare described in Ephesians 6:12 and II Corinthians 10:4:

For we do not wrestle against flesh and blood but against principalities, against powers, against the rulers of the darkness. For the weapons of our warfare are not carnal but mighty in God for pulling down strongholds.

They had learned to quiet the flesh and wait on God for His resources and strength. Yet in order to grow in faith, they were now required to wait longer and hope only in Him. Hebrews 6:11-12 and Hebrews 10:35-36 teach that through faith and patience, believers inherit God's promises. This couple were experiencing a struggle in their walk of faith.

And we desire that each one of you show the same diligence to the full assurance of hope until the end, that you do not become sluggish, but imitate those who through faith and patience inherit the promises. Hebrews 6:11

Therefore, do not cast away your confidence, which has great reward. For you have need of endurance, so that after you have done the will of God, you may receive the promise. Hebrews 10:35,36

So Arvids and Cilite waited – in humility and trust – and kept a close vigil on their daughter.

In an effort to lift Anna's spirits and stimulate her recovery, her father brought in a glass showcase from the store and set it beside her bed. With every spoonful of broth she could swallow, the parents lifted her head so she could see a new toy placed in the case, offering visible hope that she would play again. They made sure she felt secure in their caring for her. Her body had virtually stopped functioning, so she could only lie still. Others came and went, staying a while to join in prayer. Even in her feeble state, Anna tried to show gratitude that people were brokenhearted for her. She drifted in and out of consciousness; but when she awoke, the toys in the glass case were a reminder that she had eaten and would be getting strong.

During this time the atmosphere in the Keikulis home was heavy. They could only pray and weep in anguish as they saw Anna suffer. Her skin was taut and drawn, almost transparent. Janis did not like to look at her and sometimes ran to the river to get away. The family observed the child's illness continuing before their eyes – over several weeks that dragged on endlessly. She looked like a small candle that was soon to flicker out. This test required them to wait in prayer and fasting before God and endure many sleepless nights.

In one such time of heaviness, Arvids and Cilite were engaging in quiet conversation, acknowledging a shared concern. If our little daughter should die, would we be able to continue to stand in faith as we have until now? they wondered.

They had felt the pressure and agony of Gethsemane and with broken hearts surrendered their will to God's. Then, in a moment of inspiration, Arvids lifted his Bible and took Cilite's hand. Together they remembered Peter's words in John 6:68 and with a deep breath said aloud, "Lord, to whom shall we go? You have the words of eternal life."

There was no other way.

Still facing them was the struggle of their child's life or death. Arvids fell to the floor and cried out, "Lord, I will not get up, but I will die if you do not answer." His body was weak from restless nights and fasting.

It was then that Arvids and Cilite experienced the highest occurrence – the "mountaintop" – of their spiritual lives. The Holy Spirit came over them and flooded the entire room. They spoke to God and He to them in words that cannot be uttered, as described in II Corinthians 12:4, how Paul was caught up into Paradise and heard inexpressible words which were not lawful for a man to utter. They temporarily forgot their despair and circumstances, even their dying daughter. God's glory surrounded them and filled their hearts. They felt themselves drifting beyond earthly physical laws; their spirits communed with God and He with them.

Cilite's teenaged sister, Anna, had come down the hall and started to enter the room when she stepped back and cried, "What is going on? What is happening?" She fell to her knees in the hallway. She was aware that something holy was taking place, and she did not dare disturb.

Arvids and Cilite lost track of time in this sacred moment. When it was over, they "awoke" to their usual surroundings, but a transforming peace had come over them. They remembered little Anna and went to her. She was sleeping restfully and content. The presence of death was no longer upon her, and they knew she was healed. The storm had finally passed, and they praised God's holy name.

When Anna awoke, it seemed to her that the sun had come back into the room. Her mamin and papin – affectionate names the children sometimes called their parents – looked relaxed and peaceful. She asked her mother to pray that she could walk again. Gaining confidence, she wanted to get out of bed; but when trying to walk, she collapsed and fell to the floor. As they scooped up the frail body, she said, "God did not hear. I cannot walk!"

Arvids and Cilite pointed to her skinny legs, too weak to support her after being in bed for weeks. She would have to gradually gain back her strength. She wore two or three stockings to hide the protruding bones. Until she was strong again, she was pushed around in the carriage alongside Judite, where she could be heard whispering sadly, "I am not a baby."

She had overheard some villagers saying, "Look at those skinny legs.

She'll never walk again!"

However, in a relatively short time, Anna was running and bouncing about. She was full of energy and did her best to make up for lost time.

After a few weeks, Arvids' Jewish boss came to visit, and the two men sat down at a table to take care of business matters regarding the store. Several times Anna came running happily through the room, and Arvids felt that he needed to explain the interruptions – that the child had been seriously ill and since recuperating had been spoiled a bit.

"Yes, I heard about the sickness and how you did not seek medical help but trusted the Lord," said Mr. Kiels. "I respect you, Mr. Keikulis, as a Christian and an honest man. I, too, love and read the Old Testament; but, Mr. Keikulis, God does not require this kind of sacrifice."

Mr. Kiels spoke in the manner of a temperamental Jew. Arvids prayed to himself and hesitated before interrupting.

"Still, Mr. Kiels, God asked Abraham to sacrifice his only son, Isaac," he finally said.

"Yes, but Abraham received his son back!" the employer answered heatedly.

"I, too, received my daughter back, Mr. Kiels," Arvids said.

The answer surprised Mr. Kiels, and he remained quiet for some time. Then, as if talking to himself in a hushed voice, he said, "If only my mother could hear this. She still believes in the God of Abraham."

His mother was old and blind from advanced age. She had a good reputation in Latvia as a God-fearing woman who had raised her sons into honest men. Arvids had never met her.

A month passed, and business continued as usual – and so did the spiritual tests. Arvids forgot about the incident with his boss. His own countrymen had persecuted him because of his faith. Throughout Anna's illness the family had been taunted, accused, and ridiculed. The family had received anything but comfort; but the Jewish man, Mr. Kiels, continued to show faith in Arvids in business and personal matters.

Shortly thereafter, Arvids was called to Mr. Kiels' office for a business meeting. When they finished their work, Mr. Kiels invited Arvids to join him for dinner at his house. Upon arrival, Arvids found the family already in the dining room. For the first time, he saw Mr. Kiels' mother, a gentle, elderly lady with white hair flowing down her back. She had heard them enter and had extended her hands, gently calling, "Where is that man? Where is that man?"

Without saying a word, Arvids walked over to her, and in her blindness she slowly fingered his face, lips, and eyes. Arvids experienced a tender feeling as if he were receiving a blessing from their mutual spiritual father, Abraham. After this introduction the old woman did not say anything but turned and left for her room. As she departed, she whispered, "My spiritual eyes have seen him who worships the God of Abraham, Isaac, and Jacob."

Here, for a brief moment, they had met – two sojourners of faith within the bond of Abraham, their father. Still separating them was the barrier of ceremonial law, but in the spirit they were united. The rest of the family had stood quietly and reverently. Only after the door closed behind their matriarch could they all sit down to eat.

* * * * * * * * * * * *

One day Mr. Kiels was at the Keikulis home on business, and he said he would like Arvids to transfer ownership of the store to his name, taking as long as needed to pay off the debt. Arvids did not jump at the chance; but over the next three days Mr. Kiels kept bringing it up, reasoning that the store was like Arvids' anyway. They would change the title, and he would like Arvids to continue buying goods from his firm. He persisted in explaining why the deal should be made.

Finally, Arvids gave in.

But that night he could not sleep, feeling that the Lord was dealing with him and asking the question, "What have you done?"

"I agreed to buy the store," Arvids said, and then he began to make excuses. "Nothing will really change. Everyone calls it Keikulis' store, and I have been running it like my own."

"You may do it, but you will become like this minister," he heard the Lord answer, naming a popular cleric.

"There is really not much difference," Arvids reasoned again. "I will just have the title now."

Again the Lord spoke to him, "You can do it, but then you will become like this minister."

Three more times Arvids gave excuses, and each time the Lord pointed out another popular minister, saying, "You will have the world's smile upon you, but you will not have mine."

"Lord, I already gave him my word!" Arvids finally cried out.

"Go, humble yourself and beg him to release you," was the Master's reply.

Arvids recalled having read similar words in Proverbs 6:3:

So do this, my son, and deliver yourself; for you have come into the hand of your friend; go humble yourself; plead with your friend.

The next morning as dawn was breaking, Arvids got on his bicycle and rode 56 miles to see Mr. Kiels. When he asked to be released from the agreement, Mr. Kiels was surprised and asked why.

"The Lord will not allow me to own it," Arvids replied.

Years later, when Communists invaded Latvia, store owners were some of the first to be seized and sent to the horrific prison camp in Siberia. Also, over the years, the ministers about whom God had warned were found to have slipped into apostasy and did not stand true to the Word they had proclaimed.

* * * * * * * * * * *

By the age of two, Judite was a lively, energetic child. She loved to run and explore, climbing on anything in sight to satisfy her curiosity. On an occasion when Mr. Kiels was again visiting Arvids on business, Judite had climbed up on top of the door in the adjoining room and began pushing it in a swinging motion. Suddenly there was a crash to the floor, then a moment of silence, followed by loud crying. Arvids and Cilite rushed to check on the little girl, and they saw a long gash in her scalp and blood flowing furiously. Calmly, Arvids told Cilite to wash the wound, trim the hair around it, and bind it. Without a word, the mother picked up the child and took care of her. Moments later, the crying ceased. In less than half-an-hour, Judite, with her head bandaged, was running and playing again, even singing hymns.

Mr. Kiels could not hide his astonishment.

"If that had happened at my house," he said, "I would have called three doctors, my wife and child would have been hysterical, and the climate in our house would be ruined for the next week. You have such a calm and peace. How do you maintain that kind of peace?"

At every opportunity Arvids and Cilite had tried to share their faith with this kind man. He was honest, intelligent, and adept in his business. He owned a chain of stores and a large warehouse. They had heard of Hitler's invasion of neighboring countries and of his hatred toward Jews. Arvids advised Mr. Kiels that this was serious and that he should think about his family.

"Mr. Keikulis, I respect you, but Hitler will never go too far," Mr. Kiels smiled and said. "America will not permit him."

* * * * * * * * * * *

When construction of the store and apartment was finally completed, Arvids and Cilite had been elated to move into the new living quarters. As before, the store was downstairs and the apartment upstairs. Now they had two bedrooms with adjoining fireplaces.

Furnishings for the home consisted mostly of an assortment of handmade pieces. One bedroom was lined with beds that Arvids had made. With each new arrival, the infant got the crib and the growing child a new bed. The other bedroom had a bed for guests, as well as a desk where Arvids studied for sermons. He had also made an armoire and a dresser.

In the living room, or "zalite" (zah'-lee-te), was a large green "velvet" couch inherited from Arvids' mother. The piece was actually made of horsehair and had a high back with an oblong mirror attached. Each side was adorned with cabinets of beveled glass displaying stemware and hand-cut glass pitchers.

The kitchen was the gathering place for the family. Arvids had built a large table with cabinets underneath. The family had also inherited 20 tufted chairs that matched the couch. When the dining table was used for guests, it was moved away from the wall to make room for chairs brought in to accommodate the crowd.

The only heat in the living room came from the back side of the wood stove in the kitchen. Ovens took up one side of the large stove, and the other side was used for cooking on the top. The stone wall behind the kitchen stove kept the living room warm during the long, cold winter days.

A metal washstand with a white porcelain-covered wash basin stood next to the stove. Racks on either side held pressed linen towels, which the whole family used. Next to the washstand was a wooden stool which held a bucket of water that had been carried from the well.

The children were assigned chores of refilling the wood bin for the stove, taking out the slop bucket, and bringing in fresh water. The same basin was used for washing hands and dishes. The children helped with washing and drying dishes after mealtime.

Every week Arvids rolled a heavy wooden half-barrel into the kitchen. Large pots of water were heated for baths. The younger children bathed first, and hot water was added to keep the bath warm for the next person. Homemade soap was made from pig's fat and lye. The older kids complained about soap scum when their turn came to bathe. Before bathing, Janis would first scoop up the scum from the edge of the tub, grumbling under his breath, "It's not fair!"

Once a month the women and girls took a turn going to the public bathhouse, where large rocks were arranged with a glowing fire underneath. The men had built the fire and carried water from the river in wooden buckets. Wooden benches encircled the pit, providing seating for the women and girls in the hot, steamy rooms. They greeted each other and carried on pleasant conversations. All the bathers – young and old – splashed water on the rocks to create the steam, or sauna, and they washed their warm bodies with the cold water, passing around lye soap.

Everyone cherished the time spent relaxing in the sauna. This exercise had a stimulating effect and was thought to be healthy. After mother and child washed from the bucket, they washed their hair and kept splashing the rocks. The glowing wet rocks cast dancing shadows on the wall. When returning home in the winter, it was dark, and the moonlight danced on the glistening snow. They felt light-footed and clean as they walked back home. Upon entering the apartment, Arvids would exclaim, "You look so clean that you light up the whole room!"

The following night would be the men and boys' turn in the bathhouse.

The interior hallway of the apartment was located between the living room and bedrooms. On the left were hooks for hanging coats and a hand-built closet. Under the hooks sat a large chest for storing blankets. At the end of the hallway was cold storage for smoked meats, and at the opposite end of the hall was the toilet. The waste pipe was a long way down, so there was no unpleasant smell, and it was sprinkled daily with a chemical. Family members took turns cutting and placing strips of newspaper on a hook on the wall to use as toilet tissue. The hall door led to the steps going downstairs to the exterior door.

On Saturday nights, the children placed their clean-pressed clothes, socks, and shoes at the end of their beds in preparation for the Lord's Day. In their hearts was eager anticipation for the fellowship, special meals, and activities.

Sundays were always special, and the entire family participated in preparing for the coming together of the church. Arvids and Cilite rose early, and the children had a late breakfast of hot chocolate, canned sardines, and boiled eggs. Sometimes there was white bread on that day instead of the usual black bread, or dark rye.

It was customary for the congregation to stay together after church services on Sundays for meals, fellowship, prayer, and ministering to each other. Early in the morning Cilite would typically start a large pot of soup or stewed meat for the afternoon meal. In winter, they mostly ate soups or stews made from dried vegetables. Sometimes the farmers brought homemade sausages or a portion of whatever they were butchering or harvesting.

Services began at noon, and afterward Cilite would bring out the food – usually serving 20 to 30 guests. Looking back, the children sometimes wondered how a small pot of stew was always sufficient for the large crowds or how the meatloaf was sliced to accommodate so many. They were never concerned if there was enough, and Cilite – blessed with the gift of hospitality – found joy in serving. She liked to have a clean, pressed cloth on the table and fresh flowers as a centerpiece when available. She arranged the food creatively to stimulate the appetite.

The warmth of Christian love and fellowship during these gatherings was such a blessing that the preparations were well worthwhile. The Keikulises had learned that they could never out-give the Lord, and as faithful servants give, there would always be a sufficient supply for their needs.

Verses in both the Old and New Testaments had confirmed their faith in God to provide, including Proverbs 11:25, which says, "The generous soul will be made rich, and he who waters will also be watered himself" and restated in II Corinthians 9:6, "He who sows sparingly will also reap sparingly, and he who sows bountifully will also reap bountifully."

The worshipers arrived at different times according to their farm responsibilities. Most of the farmers traveled long distances, the early arrivals entering quietly and starting to pray. Their faces revealed an anticipation of entering the presence of the Lord as they prepared to worship with like-minded believers.

There was a time of testimony of God's working in their lives in the midst of trials and persecutions. The congregation would utter "amen" to show agreement and support, acknowledging their faith and oneness. It was true "koinonia," or communion, as described in Acts 2:42:

"And they continued steadfastly in the apostles' doctrine and fellowship, in the breaking of bread and in prayers."

Hymns that encouraged faith and trust were sung. Hearts were lifted above difficult circumstances to a higher heavenly calling. Their trials – considered in the context of the Bible – increased their reliance on the Lord, away from the flesh and things of the world. Arvids preached from God's Word, the things the Lord had taught him and things that he had been able to apply to his own life. He often said that one cannot preach what he had not experienced.

Over the years the country church grew to approximately 80 members.

One of the worshipers was a dear lady who lived in the village in a house that was half-burned down. Her husband was not a believer and adamantly opposed her newfound faith and fellowship. The wife often sneaked out when she could and came in late. With happy eyes and shining face, she nodded and greeted others as she found a seat. Another worshiper was a milkmaid who had rough hands, whom Anna liked to sit beside. To the little girl, the roughness of the woman's hands was comforting as they gently rubbed her own small hands, with drowsiness slowly descending upon her.

Arvids had taught the children to listen closely because God might speak to them in a specific way. To ensure that they all paid close attention, he was known to pause in the middle of a sermon to say something like, "Anna, what did God just say from His Word?"

"Jesus was feeding the 5,000," the child answered, relieved that she knew the story. The children knew if their papa paused without saying anything, someone was playing and not being attentive. They were also well aware that there would be a reprimand later, so the young ones in the Keikulis family froze at their father's sudden silence.

In addition to his roles as pastor and store manager, Arvids stayed involved with family matters. He frequently built things that would make his wife's life easier. He helped with preparations for guests and in the cleanup that followed. Arvids and Cilite worked as a team, and they were good examples for new believers. Women noticed Arvids' attentiveness and often made comments to Cilite that reflected their respect, saying things such as, "If I had a husband like yours, I would live just one day and then die happy."

Weddings and funerals usually involved three days of celebration. Women and children slept on straw mattresses side-by-side in the two bedrooms. The men took blankets and camped out in the hayloft high up in the barn. This barn behind the house was shared by renters and held spaces for chickens and other animals. There were also small garden plots. The well was outdoors, and all water was carried upstairs in buckets.

One of their most beloved brothers in Christ was an older gentleman named Mr. Lielsvager. When his wife found Christ, he had brought her to the meetings and waited outside, listening through the window. They had had a good life together, and he loved and respected his spouse. However, her new relationship with Christ baffled him. He came into the store one day and said to Arvids, "You are not doing a good thing, sir. We have been happily married for all these years and going to church. Now my wife is all excited about God, and it is coming between our marriage."

"Lielsvager, sir, her relationship with Christ can only improve your marriage because it now rests on an eternal foundation," Arvids replied.

The man was still upset and worried when he walked out.

Like Arvids had done, Mr. Lielsvager began to read the scriptures secretly. One day he was in the forest chopping down a large pine tree. When his ax struck the bark, the pine needles showered down, covering him. He felt as if the Holy Spirit was revealing that in the same manner his sins covered him. Conviction gripped his heart, and he fell to his knees confessing his need to God. He came with his wife to the next service and gave a stirring testimony of the change in his heart and life.

Mr. Lielsvager began experiencing persecution from his grown children. When the church held meetings in his home, the children summoned the National Guard, who came and surrounded the house as if something dangerous was going to happen. As owner of the house he was accused falsely and called to court. Arvids' and Cilite's hearts ached to see this gentle soul in his mid-70s tested in his newfound faith. The day he went to court they prayed diligently that God would enable and strengthen him.

When Mr. Lielsvager returned home, he was beaming. Eagerly his friends asked if the ordeal had been difficult.

"Why, I would be willing to die for my Lord!" he smiled and said. "The judge gave me a fine, and my own son who accused me paid the fee."

Arvids and Cilite continued to witness to people who came into the store. They conducted solemn assembly church services and were growing accustomed to persecution. When they had these special sanctifying services, they spread the word secretly to Christians to avoid disturbances. Gradually more of the meetings became underground. Many times at the sanctification services the brethren prayed that Arvids would be filled with the Holy Spirit. Arvids was not comfortable with emotional worship, and others praying around him were sometimes distracting. He wanted all that God had for him, but he wanted to dig deep and could not be satisfied with something that simply stirred his emotions. He firmly believed in the words from Joel 1:14 and 2:15 that say, "Sanctify a fast, call a solemn assembly...and cry out to the Lord."

* * * * * * * * * * *

On June 16, 1938, which was Pentecost Sunday, Arvids was riding his
bike to attend a service when the Holy Spirit spoke to him, "Today you
will receive what your heart has longed for."

According to the order of services, the first few days would be spent
entirely in prayer and waiting on the Lord. When Arvids arrived, he
found his place at prayer and joined the other worshipers. The new-
comers had brought baskets of food and at mealtime would leave the
prayer room to eat. The old-timers continued praying through this
time.

Whenever believers separate themselves to pray, it often seems like
the accuser is there also, attempting to prevent them from reaching the
throne of God. Arvids encountered a woman in whom he recognized
an evil spirit. As if knowing what he was seeking, she said, "You cannot
receive the Holy Spirit's fullness. Your hands are unclean."

Arvids ignored her and continued praying, and the hour grew late.

"Brothers and sisters, it is already 11 p.m.," an elderly minister said
to the group, rising from his place in prayer. "Let us retire and come
together again in the morning."

As the group dispersed, Arvids felt the taunting of Satan, "See, the
night is over and you did not get your promise."

"There is still one hour left," Arvids said.

The hostess passed out blankets as the men walked to the barn to
sleep.

Arvids dug out a little place in the hay, fell to his knees, and covered
his head with a blanket. Immediately the Holy Spirit came upon him,
and he began to worship the Lord. He experienced the promise that
Jesus spoke of in Luke 24:49 and John 7:38:

"Behold, I send the promise of my Father upon you; but tarry in the
city of Jerusalem until you are endued with power from on high."

"He who believes in me, as the scripture has said, out of his heart will
flow rivers of living water."

Throughout the night Arvids continued to praise God without ceasing. He never became tired but felt blessed. The river from within had

satisfied his thirsty soul and was truly refreshing.

From this time, Arvids knew the Holy Spirit was in him, empowering and teaching him. Previously He had felt His holy presence as in John 14: 16-17:

"And I will pray to the Father and He will give you another Helper that He may abide with you forever, the Spirit of Truth, whom the world cannot receive, because it neither sees Him nor knows Him, but you know Him, for He dwells with you and will be in you."

Arvids had enjoyed the earlier period in his Christian journey when the Lord spoke frequently to him, teaching him. Now the Lord seemed to expect him to grow and exercise what he had been learning at His feet. Arvids knew that Hebrews 5:14 and 6:1-3 instruct the believer to go on to maturity, not to remain in foundational teachings. He had experienced the closeness and tenderness of God, but now – like David in Psalm 131 – he was being weaned. It was time to learn to walk in another level of trust. Jeremiah 15:16-20 tells how believers cry and seek the Lord with all their hearts. Arvids had to learn a higher level of faith that did not come easy. Hebrews 11:13-16 describes the saints who were sustained by faith and looked for their real country, their heavenly home. God was teaching Arvids and Cilite to place their values and their lives on Christ Himself – and eternity.

Acts 1:8 teaches that believers will become witnesses after the Holy Spirit has come upon them. To be a witness, one must declare what he knows and has personally experienced, as I John 1:1 says, "That which was from the beginning, which we have heard, which we have seen with our eyes, which we have looked upon and our hands have handled, concerning the Word of Life." In Revelation 19:10, the angel said that they are fellow servants who have the testimony of Jesus. To have this testimony, they must walk as He walked and suffer as He suffered.

As in the days of Jesus, many followed Him to be fed and to experience signs and wonders; yet how many had gone on to drink of the bitter cup, as in Mark 10:38, which says, "Are you able to drink the cup that I drink and be baptized with the baptism that I am baptized with?" Also, II Timothy 2:12 teaches, "If we suffer with Him, we shall also reign with Him." A witness can tell only what he knows, not what he thinks. One must be able to tell how he has held onto God's Word, waited on it, and trusted his life on it – and then how he has experienced resurrection life through God's Word.

* * * * * * * * * * *

In the summer the business of the store slowed considerably, and Arvids could leave its running to Cilite and another worker while he rode his bike to surrounding areas to preach and testify. He had heard about a community of believers that lived separately from other people, far back in the woods in Dundaga, about 125 miles away. The men wore long beards and carried large, thick Bibles under their arms. This group scorned the newer King James translation and said that small Bibles were false. People talked about this group, and Arvids desired to seek them out and find out for himself what they believed.

Sturits (Stew'-reets), a close friend who was also a minister, agreed to go with him to find these people. As they went down the long, narrow path in the forest toward the community, they were apprehensive and wondered how they would be received. Arvids had thought perhaps Sturits would do the talking.

However, Sturits had another idea.

"Arvids, whatever you say, I will be right behind you all the way," he offered.

When they came to the settlement, they saw that the ground was sandy, much like that found close to the seashore, and the indigenous trees were mostly pine. The little farms appeared to be incapable of producing plentiful crops. As Arvids and Sturits continued walking slowly, some of the residents gradually began to congregate around them. The two introduced themselves as fellow Christians, and the people stared suspiciously.

At last, someone spoke.

"We would like to hear what you have to say," one of the men in the group ventured.

Arvids was uncomfortable as he stepped forward to address the small crowd that looked mostly skeptical. Not an emotional person, he was aware that Sturits was behind him praying, and the anointing was so strong that he held onto the lectern with all his might as the Word of Truth flowed freely from his mouth. He saw the faces before him change into intense hunger, and he could see the Lord feeding their souls.

At the conclusion of the message, Arvids and Sturits were greeted with sincere warmth and hospitality. The group ate a meal together, experiencing close Christian fellowship.

* * * * * * * * * * *

Trips on bicycles were not easy. As they faced the wind, the men tired quickly, and the towns were a considerable distance apart. In the rain, the clay became mush, and they had to carry their bikes to keep going. At times, when Arvids returned home from such a trip, he would collapse; yet the love of Christ compelled his heart to go and share the message as much as possible. He did not have lessons from seminary training or commentaries from which to study, and his fellowship with other ministers was infrequent. His preparation included reading the Word, meditating on it, and praying. He liked to walk through the forest as he pondered the scripture. Often it was there that he received a sermon from the Lord.

Another time Arvids and Sturits had traveled more than 100 miles by bicycle to witness. They met a man who told them they needed to go 30 miles farther to visit a deacon from a lukewarm church who was discouraged and needed to hear their message. By now they were already weary, so they were not enthusiastic as they continued their journey. They debated which one would do the talking. Nearing the farm, they saw it was surrounded by a neat fence, and in the front was a gate. They knocked until a man came out.

From behind the closed gate the farmer carefully surveyed the two standing before him.

"We preach the whole gospel," Arvids began – and then hesitated waiting for a response. The silence was deafening – and awkward.

"We are evangelists," Arvids added. The farmer's stoic expression remained unchanged.

"Not only do we preach the whole gospel, but we keep it," Arvids said. That statement transformed the day. The man turned and ran up the path to his house – leaving his visitors behind the closed gate, not certain of what to expect. He opened the door to his house and suddenly, as if remembering the guests, he turned and ran back down the path and unfastened the gate.

"Where have you been so long?" he asked, bowing low.

Leading the two into his home, he seated them at a table. They watched as he ran to get his wife, his brother and sister-in-law, and his children. He sat them down saying, "Now we will listen to what God will say to us."

This man, who had introduced himself as Brother Ziedins, was so hungry for truth that when Arvids or Sturits finished pouring out his heart, he would quickly say to the other, "Now you tell us" and so on back and forth. He had complete trust in them, and they could tell he was hearing every word.

After this, they visited Brother Ziedins often. His farm was secluded enough that underground sanctification meetings could be held there without disruption. This brother grew in faith and love.

After the Germans occupied Latvia during World War II, farmers had to register all their animals and could not slaughter any for themselves except for chickens and rabbits. During this time when the church held special meetings at Brother Ziedins' house, as many as 200 people attended. The home was spacious, and the host liked to prepare a large feast for the crowd. When the believers saw the big, delicious roasts on the table, they asked incredulously, "How did you keep this meat from the Germans? Did you hide it from the rest of your herd?"

"No," Brother Ziedins would explain matter-of-factly. "I just dedicated one cow and one hog to the Lord, and when the German soldiers came to take count, I watched them count carefully and they wrote down one less cow and hog. They had not counted those I dedicated to the Lord so, you see, the Lord provided this meal for us!"

Later, when the Russians came in and Latvia became a battlefield between Russia and Germany, a Russian plane crashed on Brother Ziedins' land. In pure love – like the Good Samaritan in the biblical story – Brother Ziedins lifted out the injured pilot and brought him into his house. Shortly after, German soldiers arrived on the scene and shot Brother Ziedins on the spot for harboring the enemy. However, the situation reversed when Communists took over the country. The Ziedins family was treated better than other Christians because it was known that the father had been shot for aiding a Communist pilot. The family members ultimately received many blessings as a result of the incident, experiencing kindnesses that made their lives easier.

* * * * * * * * * * *

The Keikulises tried their best to maintain peace in the midst of persecutions and trials. It seemed most difficult, however, to watch their own children suffer. Worse than physical suffering was the persecution Janis had to endure between ages 10 and 13. Children pick up attitudes from their parents, and Janis was verbally and physically persecuted almost daily. Many times when he came home from school, his clothes were torn and his body bruised from having been beaten by other youths. He often vomited on himself out of panic. Even worse was the attitude of his teacher, who seemed to delight in shaming him in front of the class.

A Jewish family reported to Arvids and Cilite that the children had ganged up on Janis and were trying to crucify him on a tree, like Jesus Christ. The Jewish family wondered with skepticism, "If you are Christians and they are Christians, then why are you being treated so badly?"

One day some boys dunked Janis in a creek, holding him under for several minutes. Janis knew he was in trouble, so he stiffened his body and faked being dead, remaining in that position for some time. When the boys realized what was happening, they let go and ran off in fear. Then Janis swam underwater and got out into the bushes. He knew he had been under water a little too long when he could feel the blood pressure inside his head pulsating, and he felt pain in his temples. After resting about 20 minutes, he was able to go home. Later that evening the boys were shocked to see Janis walking around and wondered how he had managed to escape. They seemed to be frightened, thinking Janis would squeal to their parents or teachers, but Janis did not tell anyone at the time what had happened.

Janis had very few friends except for some gypsy children. The boys either ganged up on him or, pretending to be friendly, tried to entice him into compromising situations to shame his parents. Once when the boys had broken some exquisite stained glass windows in the local state church, Janis was blamed as being part of the gang. He had not been; but rather than argue, Arvids paid a significant share of the cost to repair the windows.

As a typical boy, Janis wanted to stand up to his tormentors, but he was also concerned about his Christian witness. There was a lake close to a lumberyard that was a favorite place for boys to play. Often they would get a large plank, lie on it face down, and paddle with their hands in the water. Once Janis saw one of his persecutors out on a plank paddling. Janis, a good swimmer, dove in and swam up behind the boy, who failed to recognize at first who was splashing and swimming. Janis reached the back of the board and rolled it over, dunking its rider. Every time the boy tried to reach the board, Janis would dunk him until the boy began to apologize and promise to treat Janis better.

Although Janis had probably not used the best Christian judgment by taking the matter into his own hands, from that day on the boy left him alone.

Many times Arvids and Cilite would have loved to intervene and protect their son from abuse, but they decided to leave their enemies for the Lord to judge. I Peter 2:21-23 says that Jesus did not revile but committed Himself to God, who judges righteously. They, too, had to learn to trust their Heavenly Father, just as their Master had done.

For to this you were called, because Christ also suffered for us, leaving us an example, that you should follow His steps: Who committed no sin, nor was deceit found in His mouth; who when He was reviled did not revile in return; when He suffered, He did not threaten but committed Himself to Him who judges righteously.

Anna was not persecuted because she had told the other children, "If you think I am going to put up with what Janis puts up with, you have got another thing coming!" She was a highly spirited child, and there was five-and-a-half years' difference between her and her brother. When teachers tried to ridicule her, she would stand up and say, "My daddy is not a fanatic, and you are not going to make fun of him!" When the class came to the study of religion, the teacher was known to say to Anna, "You had better go out," to which the girl firmly replied,

"No, I am not!"

Sadly, the family realized that most persecution was the result of adult attitudes passed down to children.

* * * * * * * * * * *

Arvids' walk with God was that of a prophet. He made decisions like a prophet. Even though he was gloomy at times, he was decisive. There was no bending. Cilite's faith was just as strong, but she was more emotional. She cried over disappointments, and Arvids sometimes gently reprimanded her for not trusting God completely. When the persecution was particularly severe, there was heaviness in their home. It strained their relationship, which was actually a result of their individual approach to stress and the way they responded to trials. Though they both sought God, they were each responsible for their own choices in coming to a place of surrender and trust.

Once Cilite was carrying a bucket of dishwater to throw on the garden plot. Anna, who was six at the time, was helping her mother carry the bucket. Cilite's heart was heavy with burdens. Standing in the middle of the garden, she noticed that her neighbor's garden looked lush and green while her own was withering. From the burden in her heart she cried out to the Lord, "Why is it that everything that is mine just withers?" Then the Holy Spirit within reminded her of the words of the psalmist in Psalm 73:16-17. She recited the words aloud, "When I pondered to understand this, it was too troublesome in my sight, until I went into the sanctuary of God; then I understood their end."

Anna looked up and saw big tears rolling down her mother's cheeks. Crying became Cilite's quiet response to God's lordship, as verses 21-24 of Psalm 73 describe:

"Thus my heart was grieved, and I was vexed in my mind. I was so foolish and ignorant; I was like a beast before you. Nevertheless, I am continually with you; you hold me by my right hand. You will guide me with your counsel and afterward receive me to glory."

Cilite realized that she had been grieved, and her thinking had become foolish and ignorant. Once again she recognized that God was always with her and would guide her all the way to His glory. The circumstances had not changed, but her outlook was relieved. She was settled in the presence of the Lord. With the peace of God restored, Cilite and Anna walked back to the house, which was called "Asaros," meaning "tears" or "among tears" – their home having been given a name according to Latvian custom.

And so Cilite learned how to release her burdens to God. She had a wonderful relationship with her Lord where she could express a concern from the depths of her soul in weeping and prayer and then enter back into His sanctuary and be comforted again. In that private place, she found that she could be completely honest with her emotions. The children remember her as a great intercessor, not only for her family but also for her extended spiritual family and lost souls who needed to be saved. It was not unusual for the children to see tears streaming down their mother's face while she stirred a pot on the stove. She wept frequently over her loved ones until she "prayed through," leaving them at the throne of God.

"Mama, are you alright?" one of the children would ask when they saw her tears.

"Oh, yes, I am just talking to the Lord," she would reply.

Her heart was tender and pliable, broken over the things that break God's heart. She knew the heartbreak and devastation of sin and had put her hope in the One who heals and restores. After praying for specific burdens and needs, she often commented, "I have perfect peace. God is working, and He is almighty!"

* * * * * * * * * * *

It was difficult to raise children under the constant pressure of accusing words and reactions, but most often the children provided so much joy that their amusing comments and antics would divert Arvids and Cilite from their burdens.

Little Judite was always investigating and climbing, sometimes wandering off without realizing it. One day Cilite had called and called her – with no response. The family started looking through the store, in the apartment, and then outside. Along with some neighbors, Arvids began to search the nearby fields – but still no Judite. Finally, Cilite came back inside with Anna, wondering where to go next. Suddenly they heard a little voice singing from the bedroom. They ran into a seemingly unoccupied room with sounds coming from under the bed.

Having explored and played under the bed, Judite had gotten tired and taken a nap. When she awoke, she had begun singing one of her favorite hymns: "I do not have to worry, I do not want to complain, just to be with Jesus my heart only longs. Sorrows and worries want to overwhelm me, then I trust in Jesus and joy fills my heart."

Everyone had to laugh. Judite had been oblivious to their concern, and after enjoying a secluded rest she woke up singing about trusting in the Lord. At that time she was missing her front teeth and pronounced "r's" as "l's," but that did not dampen her enthusiasm for singing. Anna had been working with Judite to teach her to pronounce "r's" correctly. When the day came that she was able to roll the "r's" distinctly, she ran into the store and pulled up a chair next to her mother. Standing on the chair and turning her mother's face directly to hers, she sang her favorite hymn again, this time loud and clear, noticeably rolling each "r."

* * * * * * * * * * * *

Feeding the family was sometimes a challenge for Arvids and Cilite – and they could not have imagined how it would become an even greater concern in their future with the approach of World War II.

At this time in their lives, however, they were in the process of refining their own methods of disciplining the children, whether it occurred at the dinner table or elsewhere. Through it all, they developed close relationships with each child and cherished every moment as they followed God's lead in molding and guiding their young hearts.

Their daily menu did not always represent a complete, delectable meal or a balanced diet because the seasons dictated what was available. In the winter the family often ate dried green peas cooked with bacon, if available, and served with clabber (buttermilk). Cilite had a number of hearty soups in her repertoire. If one of the kids started to complain, she would take the wooden spoon in her hand and tap the child on the head, saying, "Be thankful!" In fact, she could reach all the way across the big table and administer that firm reminder. In the children's eyes the spoon was huge, and they tried to duck.

With Cilite there was no time for discussion or instruction because that was the way she was made. What might be missing in verbal instruction was never missing in her devotion to the Lord and in her tender heart – not only for her own family but for others. She always prayed for the Lord to instruct her children, that they would have listening ears to obey Him. When the kids started to squabble, out came the spoon with a loud whack.

Arvids' method of discipline was structured. He picked up his Bible, opened it to an appropriate passage, and showed the child where the sin was against God's commandment. Whether it was "Children, obey your parents" or God's view of rebellion, they did not question the truth and authority of the Bible. They knew they had sinned but that God also provides for forgiveness and restoration.

Arvids instructed his children to confess their sins in prayer and to thank the Lord for His gift of eternal life and forgiveness through Jesus Christ. He taught them that confessed sins are forgiven and gone, according to I John 1:9: "If we confess our sins, He is faithful and just to forgive us our sins and to cleanse us from all unrighteousness."

After the discipline, there were hugs and it was over. The guilt was gone. As the children grew older, they understood their responsibility and voiced their own prayer. Their papa usually had an instrument for discipline, such as a cloth-woven belt, that hung in a conspicuous spot as a reminder it would be used when necessary. After the prayer of confession, a few whacks were administered, and there was immediate restoration. Because of human nature, the children never stopped sinning, but after each confession they found grace and a new start, a clean slate. Over time, the younger Keikulises matured and grew in the knowledge and wisdom of the Lord.

When the children were toddlers and just beginning to understand the meaning of "no," they liked to test the boundaries to see if they could get away with small temptations. Arvids would place his hand over a little hand or diaper and swat himself as a reprimand. The toddler would cry as if in pain. Actually, the child's feelings were hurt, since their papa had taken the blow himself, demonstrating a picture of the Heavenly Father. In sending Christ to pay for the sins of the world,

He took the blow so mankind could be cleansed and restored to His family, as stated in II Corinthians 5:19:

God was in Christ reconciling the world to Himself, not imputing their trespasses to them, and has committed to us the word of reconciliation.

At mealtime, events of the day or things to come in the future might be discussed. So, too, were burdens and needs of others. Usually the mealtime blessing included gratefulness for God's provisions and prayer for those with special needs, with Arvids expressing his prophet's heart. He was consumed with God's honor and righteousness, and he viewed current events and world politics in light of God's authority and His eternal kingdom. Arvids and Cilite were motivated by their relationship with the Lord, from a heavenly perspective. Arvids was known to preach a sermon at the meals, expressing spiritual concerns for his country and the condition of the human race. If he needed to stop any loud talking or squabbling during the meal, he would hit his forefinger loudly in rhythm on the table's edge. Everyone would freeze and look at him. Sometimes he had a reprimand; other times he just wanted them to listen.

In the body of Christ, all are one; so burdens, joys, and victories are shared. Prayers for each other were fervent since God, through the Spirit, had knitted them together in His love. Persecutions and trials had drawn the flock of believers close to God and to each other.

The Keikulis family knew a woman who was converted and subsequently went and confessed her wrongdoings to the judge. She was given a six-month jail sentence. She had six young children, and Cilite took them in and cared for them during their mother's absence. It became evident that the visitors had not been consistently disciplined, and sometimes they got the Keikulis children into trouble. When Arvids asked, "Who did this?" his children remembered their stories about little elves who sometimes played mischief, so they replied, "The elves did it."

Arvids had a gentle, soft side to his nature, always pointing out God's handiwork to the children. He had placed birdhouses in the branches of a tree growing outside the kitchen window. He often pointed to them, saying, "Look how God has provided food for the little bird, and see how it is preening and grooming itself. Now it knows to sing praises to its maker. In the same way God takes care of us, His children, and we, too, can praise Him."

The children's hearts were kept tender and their consciences sensitive. They not only wanted to please their earthly father but also learned about the love of their Heavenly Father. Increasingly, the children were learning to see God in everything and to seek His perspective in things great or small. This Latvian children's poem by an unknown author illustrates their reverent attitude:

> *I placed the ladybug back on the blade of grass*
>
> *And God said "Thank you."*
>
> *I put a baby bird back in its nest*
>
> *And God said "Thank you."*
>
> *Then I lay down in the grass and turned my eyes toward heaven*

And I said "Thank you" to God.

The children loved and honored their parents. At the time, the young ones may not have understood the deep waters they were going through or the seriousness of their lives, but they respected their parents' stand for the Lord and His truth. They heard their names called out in daily prayers. The parents prayed that the children would have hearts to love and know God. Cilite's prayers were like those Jeremiah expressed in Lamentations 2:19:

> *Pour out your heart like water before the face of the Lord. Lift your hands toward Him for the life of your young children.*

The children were often awakened to the sound of their mother praying. After a time of intercession Cilite usually ended her prayer time with songs of worship to the Lord. Sometimes the songs were hymns and other times were those the Holy Spirit inspired at that moment. She did not know that someone outside the walls of her home was touched by her supplications.

"That woman's prayers drew me like a magnet," a man in the village remarked. "I would sit under her window to listen to her praying and singing. At times I would think of agreeing with the other people's troublemaking against the Keikulises, but I couldn't. I was always drawn to listen to Mrs. Keikulis' prayers. They made me think of heaven."

Arvids' and Cilite's selfless service to the Lord for lost and troubled souls had a long-lasting influence on the children. The family always made room to house, feed, and clothe those in need. There was no private pastoral office for counseling and prayers with seekers or new believers, so the children regularly viewed lives being changed and born into God's kingdom. Arvids usually went right to the point with sinners; if they did not confess their sins, he might name the sin. There were encouraging words and comfort for the hurting, and prayers voiced at any time of day. The children's daily routines and playing were never seen as interruptions in God's work. The kids had their squabbles and accidents, but the parents knew everything was working together for good in God's eternal plan. They also knew they were on holy ground and that God was in it all.

Arvids prayed in conversational tones, addressing and speaking to God personally. Sometimes it was tender and grateful, calling his Heavenly Father "Abba, Tetin (Teh'-tin) (Abba Daddy)." In times of trial he called out from his heart.

* * * * * * * * * * *

As the little church grew, so too were constant pressures. To provide the family a much-needed reprieve, Arvids liked to scout out a place of refuge, usually in the surrounding forests.

Latvian forests were filled with a variety of trees. The tall pines were covered with a medium-brown bark, their long branches cascading downward. Groves of birch trees provided a stark contrast with their shimmering white bark. Finding weeds or branches lying on the ground was rare, since local residents gathered small brush to use as tinder for starting fires in stoves and fireplaces. In the summer the forest floor was covered with a luscious carpet of green moss and ferns, and walking through the wooded areas was a favorite pastime in the area. It was good exercise – and therapeutic.

On such outings led by Arvids, the Keikulises anticipated an adventure of discovery. Their papa had a special call to announce a unique place or spectacle in nature: "Ahaha vota!"

Then they all ran as one to see the surprise that awaited them.

Arvids recognized the importance of teaching his children to take time to think about how God takes care of His vast, detailed creation, down to the tiniest ant, and that He is also mindful of and will always provide for His children. He might point out how God had covered a rock with a soft, delicate moss, a special formation in a tree, a nest or underground den for an animal, or an unusual wildflower. The children would gather up close and in a chorus express their "oohs" and "wows." Arvids pointed out that moss always grows on the north side of a tree. He instructed the children to put their forefinger in their mouth and then hold their hand high.

"This is how we can know which way the wind is blowing," he said. "God always leaves His mark in the woods to give direction so we can know which way to go. So, also, God's Word gives us instructions on the direction for our lives. He points us to the right way."

Arvids was following scriptural admonition, from Psalm 119:105, "Your Word is a lamp to my feet and a light to my path" and Deuteronomy 6:6-7, "And these words which I command you today shall be in your heart. You shall teach them diligently to your children, and shall talk of them when you sit in your house, when you walk by the way, when you lie down, and when you rise up."

Once when Arvids and Anna went out to the shed to get sauerkraut for dinner, Anna spotted their gander as they walked toward the building. The children had named the animal "the ruler of the barnyard." Had it not been for her papa at her side, the large bird would have chased and nipped at the girl's heels, but he respected Arvids. Suddenly a small frog hopped by, much too close for escape. Stretching his long neck, the gander quickly swallowed his prey. Then he bent his ear to the lump he had swallowed, following it down his long neck to listen.

As usual, Arvids used this opportunity for a teaching moment, saying, "Look, he is listening." He continued teaching how Jesus promises to give us His peace when we are afraid and how we must put our spiritual ear to our heart, where Jesus lives, and listen. All through the scariest times of the war and imprisonments, Anna remembered her papa's instruction and was comforted.

These teachable moments were pleasant and reassuring. To the children, this was when their papa was at his best. Often in the living quarters there was an atmosphere of pressure, and Arvids' voice was firm and authoritative. Arvids and Cilite had to be attentive to God and watchful in prayer. Sometimes it seemed as if they were back in the trenches. Drunks banged on the windows and threw rocks. In the forest Arvids was free, even merry, and his voice was soft, filled with excitement. The family thought those special places in the forests were created especially for them. The tender moments were a sanctuary from which the family returned home refreshed and invigorated.

Another kind of family outing provided pleasurable entertainment as well. In Latvia picking berries and mushrooms was a national pastime, and children were taught these skills at a young age. Arvids gave each child a basket or bucket made from old cans with a wire for a handle, vessels appropriate for their size. Filling the containers provided hours of fun, and they returned home with berries for their mother to make into delicious jam – or mushrooms to be cooked for dinner. The younger children usually ate more berries than they put in their baskets, as evidenced by the red stains around their mouths.

Arvids was creative and resourceful, using his infrequent spare time to build furniture and household aids. He loved to surprise the family with his crafts. When a high chair was needed, he turned one chair upside-down on another and placed a large belt around the legs to serve as safety rails to confine the toddler. He also created playthings for the children, such as wooden "clickety-clack" shoes that had hinges in the soles so that they bent with the movement of little feet.

* * * * * * * * * * * *

During this time the church was preparing for a wedding with a large number of guests, anticipating the joy that surrounds such an occasion. As the wedding date approached, Arvids began to make out the long list of food that would be needed from the store for the days of services while guests were present.

"This is quite a large list," he remarked to Anna Kasparovics, Cilite's sister who assisted in the store. "I hope I will be able to pay it back quick enough."

"I am sure there will be a lot more business next week, and we will be kept hopping in the store," Anna replied. The more they shared, they more the business came in.

And so it always was.

The wedding celebrations always included time for singing, testimonies, and preaching. Six ministers took turns at preaching the Word. A young minister from Estonia delivered a sermon using as his text the three Hebrew children in the fiery furnace, from Daniel 3. The speaker was eloquent in his description, and the audience sat on the edges of their chairs in suspense as he closed in on the climax of the story. He told of the courage of Shadrach, Meshach, and Abednego as they stood before King Nebuchadnezzar (Daniel 3:17-18).

"Then when the boys were hurled into the furnace," continued the preacher, "not a thing was burned, not the men, not their clothes, not a hair of their heads was singed nor had the smell of fire passed on them!"

In the middle of the exciting passage an elderly minister who was known for his serious nature spoke up abruptly from the back of the room.

"What do you mean, nothing was burned?" he asked. "Something indeed had burned!"

A hush fell over the congregation as they waited for an explanation.

"The ropes that bound them had burned, and they were walking around loose!" he exclaimed.

To the spellbound listeners, that statement was a bold affirmation of the power of God. Cilite had been so involved in listening to this sermon on God's mighty deliverance that she lifted her hands and shouted "hurrah!" She meant to say "hallelujah," but it came out "hurrah." She was embarrassed, but the brothers and sisters were blessed by her enthusiasm.

Arvids later consoled his wife, explaining that the origin of the word "hurrah" came from the Turks going off to war, willing to die. They would shout "hurrah," which meant "off to paradise."

So Cilite's word was appropriate after all.

Chapter 3

The Occupation Period

In 1939 the Russian Communists occupied the three Baltic States – Estonia, Latvia, and Lithuania. One of the first things the Communists did was to confiscate private business, liquidating most of the stores. All this was done with lies. They said they came to help the people avoid war and would return their properties later. Later they said that the nations had asked them to help.

History revealed that the Germans and Russians had agreed who would take over which countries, and thus Eastern Europe was divided between the two powers. It was not long before the truth was revealed, and gradually more arrests of government leaders and intellectuals were made in Latvia. Many tried to hide in the forests to escape arrest. The Communists had come in with big plans on how to improve the economy, but they were unrealistic and always failed.

The village state church was confiscated, and the minister and his family were thrown out of their home, which was a nice-looking farmhouse representing a good standard of living. The minister had never approved of Arvids and the small church in their home, and it was said that he often referred to Arvids as the anti-Christ in his sermons. Arvids now heard that the minister and his family were hiding and had moved in with friends, so it was a surprise to see the man come into the store one day. No other customers were present at the time. The minister's face was grave. He stretched out his arm and shook Arvids' hand, looking him straight in the eye but never speaking. Then he turned and left quietly. Arvids presumed that this was the man's way of making things right between them. The Keikulises never saw him again. They learned later that he had been arrested and died while being tortured.

The store was confiscated. Because Arvids was the manager and not the owner, he was permitted to sell whatever was left and bring the profits to a government office every day. The Communists had decided that the forestry industry would bring in considerable revenue and had sent their officers to accomplish the task. As usual, mismanagement and lack of expertise prevailed, so the goal was not achieved.

Arvids' name was mentioned as one who was experienced in forestry and could get the ball rolling, and a conflict ensued between the political secretary and the job supervisor. The argument became so heated that the noise could be heard outside, and Arvids' friend overheard them arguing about him. The supervisor needed Arvids to accomplish the job, and the party secretary said he could not trust the "sectarian." Arvids knew that all the ministers and religious leaders were black-listed, and the sending of exiles to Siberia was just a matter of time.

Arvids soon received news that he could not possibly get the job. However, he knew he had been assured by the Lord that he would have a position as forest administrator, so he said, "The whole Communist Party cannot prevent me from having that job." He had even purchased leather boots and a pouch in which to carry the papers. Several days later the party secretary came to Arvids and handed him a paper to sign, looking the other way. The document stated that Arvids was to supervise the work of the forestry.

During the Russian occupation there was an election that was a farce. Everyone was required to vote, but only one candidate's name was on the ballot – and therefore no choice. Word spread that those who did not vote would be exiled. Arvids was told to vote, but he refused since he knew it was just a show. He was threatened repeatedly, but still he refused. On the morning of the election Arvids and Cilite were instructed by local authorities that they were required to vote. They paid no attention to the reminder. That evening they were having family prayers when armed soldiers barged in shouting that it was almost closing time and they had better come and vote.

"I am a grown man, and I know where the election booth is," Arvids told them, matter-of-factly.

Taking them by the shoulders, he led them into the dark hallway outside the apartment and shut the door behind them. The family heard them stumbling down the stairs. The soldiers remained in the yard for some time, talking about what to do.

Finally they left. Nothing happened.

Perhaps Arvids was needed in the forestry job.

Conditions rapidly deteriorated. Gunshots could be heard as dissenters were shot. The Communists tried to annihilate all the leaders, intellectuals, and thinkers. These were gloomy days. One day Arvids saw the old sheriff who had been the source of much of his heartache. The sheriff ran over and grabbed him as if they were old friends.

"Mr. Keikulis, tell me what's going to happen!" said the sheriff. "What will happen?"

"You are asking me?" Arvids answered.

"Do not talk like that," the sheriff stammered. "I have always honored you highly."

"What you are seeing is only the beginning," Arvids said. "The worst is before us."

Many were trying to hide to keep from being arrested, and as far as Arvids knew, the sheriff stayed out of sight in the forest. Eventually the Communists began to drive around using a loud speaker to call for the fugitives. They called the sheriff's name, warning, "If you want to see your family alive, you had better come out." The man finally came out and surrendered. Soon he and his family were exiled separately to Siberia.

These were times when everyone was threatened in one way or another. Some became Communists. Most were afraid to say anything against the Communists and by their silence appeared to condone the actions.

Arvids noticed that his fellow countrymen were more humble under the new circumstances. He was walking in the forest one day with some former Latvian army officers, who began questioning him.

"Everyone is afraid of the Communists and cannot resist them," they said. "We have noticed that you and your family are the only ones that are not intimidated by them. Even your children seem brave. Where do you get that kind of courage?"

* * * * * * * * * * *

On Sunday afternoon, June 14, 1940, as Arvids looked out the window of their home, he saw large trucks loaded with people driving past. Their faces were familiar – leaders, businessmen, and landowners – families and children included. All the faces were downcast, many crying hysterically.

This was one of Latvia's darkest days, when 36,000 people were exiled to Siberia.

Shortly thereafter a Russian party leader came to Arvids and began to threaten him.

"What is this I hear that you are brash enough to hold services still?" he yelled. "All the churches are closed, and the priests have been sent away. How then do you dare to conduct church services?"

Arvids began to testify to the party leader. He spoke with authority given by the Holy Spirit, proclaiming, "I am not a priest or clergyman, but I am a Christian who preaches a living Christ." Other words flowed out that were not premeditated.

Finally the officer nodded his head and then shook Arvids' hand respectfully, stammering, "Yes, yes, I see you do have an idea!" and hurried off.

On July 30, 1940, Cilite was in hard labor with her fourth child. As he had done during the births of the other children, Arvids decided to stay on his knees in the adjoining room until he heard the baby's cry and the midwife calling him. As he prayed, he heard Satan's words, "You might as well quit praying. The cord is wrapped around her neck three times, and she will not make it."

"Get thee behind me, Satan," Arvids said. "Lord, only you have the power of life and death." He lifted up his hands, continuing to pray and wait on God.

Presently he heard the midwife spanking the newborn five times, followed by a robust cry. Soon the midwife called him in. She started to speak, "If you only knew—"

"I know," Arvids interrupted. "The umbilical cord was wrapped around her neck three times."

The midwife seemed surprised that Arvids was already aware of the circumstances of the birth. They had almost lost this little Modra, whose name meant "bright, shining, and alert," but the Lord had spared her. She became an unusually healthy, fair-skinned, lovely child.

As before, Arvids made a larger bed for Janis, Anna moved up into his bed, and Judite was to move into Anna's bed to make room for the new little sister. Sticking her face against the rungs of the crib, Judite realized what was happening and announced with all the authority she could muster, "Get that living doll out of my bed!" Startled, the family burst into hearty laughter. Looking somewhat defeated, Judite climbed into her new bed.

Soon after the birth of Modra, Arvids received notice that he needed a physical examination to continue in his government work as a forester. The doctor, who knew Arvids well and had heard his witness that he had been healed, was skeptical. His wife was more sympathetic, perhaps because the Keikulises had given her a Bible. When Arvids saw the physician, he realized this man was intent upon destroying his testimony.

The doctor's examination was meticulous and careful. Finally he threw down his stethoscope and said in anger, "Either I don't know anything about medicine, or you never had tuberculosis. You have the lungs of a newborn baby. TB always leaves a scar, and I can't find anything!"

"You know the director at the sanatorium, and you can call him to check my records," Arvids answered. The sanatorium where he had stayed was less than 12 miles away.

Without another word, the doctor filled out the papers, giving his patient a clean bill of health.

* * * * * * * * * * *

In the first Russian occupation there were nightly arrests. Black cars were seen stopping, and Russian soldiers went into homes to arrest mothers, fathers, teachers, and anyone else they could find. No one knew who would be next. There were rumors of abuse, and later evidence was found of atrocious torture having taken place. There was an atmosphere of extraordinary uncertainty and insecurity. Children did not feel safe to go outside and play, preferring instead to be within sight of their parents. Educators and civic leaders had been exiled to Siberia; others were selected for no known reason. The country was in a prolonged period of despair, and there was a black cloud over Latvia.

Anna felt uneasiness in her heart. The older children remembered hearing that their father could be arrested for being a pastor. Arvids had prayed and kissed his family goodbye. When Russian soldiers arrived to arrest him, Cilite gathered the children together in the living room to pray for their papa's safety. Everyone knelt. Without sobbing, this burdened mother expressed to their Heavenly Father her concerns for her husband and children. Big drops of tears welled up and fell on her chest – plop, plop, plop. Arvids went out to meet the soldiers, who were coming up the stairs. The family heard the noisy arrest – shouting, grabbing, and pushing – sounds of intimidation and horror.

Then Arvids came back in, smiling calmly.

"They must have seen the angel of the Lord standing beside me because they ran all over each other to get back down the steps," he said.

What a relief it was to be reunited again!

Later a list was found that showed Arvids was to be on the second deportation to Siberia.

* * * * * * * * * * *

During the Communist occupation Latvia was cut off from the outside world. After the 36,000 were exiled, the Keikulises heard rumors that the Germans were coming. Finally, in 1941, bombing and shooting could be heard, and the German army pushed out the Russians. The Germans came in on main roads. They knew they would be welcomed. People were relieved to see the Russians leave and looked to the Nazis as their deliverers. The Nazis allowed workers to continue in their current occupations, so Arvids remained in the forestry job. It seemed the Germans, too, were in need of lumber and were appreciative of the forestry industry.

In the coming years the Keikulises were able to work and live with little disturbance. It was a welcome reprieve, though temporary.

Janis, then 14, was given a job in the forestry industry keeping a lookout for possible forest fires. He gladly accompanied his dad each day and reveled in the responsibility of watching for fires. Later he was given the job of herding cattle.

Then, along with other young men, he was assigned to digging foxholes – a strenuous job, especially for a young teen. During the week the boys slept in a barn close to the job and then walked the six miles home on weekends. It was a grueling job, and the boys soon found a way to outsmart the officer in charge.

In the mornings workers were taken to a long trench and ordered to start digging. They were expected to continue all day. Janis and two friends picked up their tools and began to dig. They knew it would take the soldier some time to walk to the end of the trench before returning. When the soldier turned his back and was 50 yards away headed in the other direction, the boys dashed off into the woods taking their tools with them. They were not missed and were able to sneak off to a roadhouse every day.

The roadhouse was an aluminum building used by the road engineer to store equipment. Inside were a few bunks for workers to rest. One of the boys, an electronic whiz, wired up the outside of the door so that if anyone tried to open it, he would get an electric shock. The friends rested and played here during the day and were never discovered. Between the hours of 4 p.m. and 5 p.m. they would sneak back into their foxholes and dig hard.

In spite of the Germans' occupying the country and trying to run it, people continued to work and plant crops. The harvesting of crops seemed to come all at once, as daylight hours were long. Farmers hired teenagers to perform the extra work that was required. One such young woman lived with the Keikulises for a brief time and was much loved by the family, including the children. She was more like a daughter and older sister, helping the Keikulises with household chores and minding the children. At harvest time a wealthy farmer hired her as a maid. It was rumored that this man had been unfaithful to his wife and had relationships with other women. In time he seduced this young lady.

She arrived home grief stricken and ashamed that she had sinned against the Lord and the church. Arvids and Cilite were heartbroken and prayed for God's guidance in discerning the best way to unravel a situation that could damage this girl's reputation and bring intense pain to the church. They sought healing and closure for their friend and for the Christian community.

With a heavy heart and after much weeping and prayer, Arvids fell into an exhausted sleep. He dreamed that he saw a butterfly trying to exit its cocoon. Sympathizing with the laboring butterfly, he retrieved his pocketknife and was preparing to free the creature. It was at that moment he heard a clear voice saying, "If you cut the cocoon to free her from her struggle, she will never fly."

Immediately upon awakening Arvids knew God had spoken concerning the conflict their friend was enduring. Through the consequences of the experience she would gain maturity and stability. Arvids and Cilite supported her wholeheartedly while she made things right with the offended family and church, resulting in restoration and healing.

Arvids and Cilite were learning that God's ways are higher than man's ways. They realized through this experience that sometimes it seems kindest to intervene to make a difficult situation end without painful consequences; yet it is best to seek God's will and allow His maturing process, which is critical for gaining wisdom. God's methods keep believers humble to enable them to better discern situations and minister to one another. He does restore and make things new, but the process is as important as the result.

It was the struggle that enabled the butterfly to soar.

* * * * * * * * * * * *

The small country of Latvia had been caught between two world powers. First the Russian army came in, forcing young men into their army. When the Germans arrived, they treated the Latvians in the Red Army as traitors and shot them. Then the Nazis took the next group of men to serve in their army. In God's providence, one of the boys taken would later become a deliverer for the Keikulis family.

These were the most peaceful years spiritually. Arvids' supervisor was congenial, and he granted his employee time off for special services. The believers could preach and congregate in the open, and there was a sense of freedom of worship. Only one incident occurred.

The shoemaker across the street had been unfaithful to his wife. In her sorrow the wife came to the Keikulises for counsel and spiritual guidance. The husband, a heavyset man, became angry and in a rage met Arvids as he came home from work. The man picked up a large log and came forward, gasping and breathing hard. Arvids tried to reason with him, and the log fell out of the man's hand. Then he picked up a big rock and lunged again, while the Keikulis family watched from the apartment window. The children thought their papa might be killed. Anna saw that the shoemaker, who was head-and-shoulders taller than her father, was coming with a rock. Arvids was still ducking from the first attempt, and the panicked girl passed out. The shoemaker gasped and choked as though he might be having a heart attack. Arvids continued trying to settle him down. Finally, the man dropped the rock and managed a few weak blows. With that he nearly fainted, and Arvids continued trying to calm him.

Frustrated and disappointed that he had not clobbered his foe, the shoemaker tried another tactic. He wrote a letter to the German government office saying that Mr. Keikulis was preaching the faith of the Jews and used the Bible of the Jews. He thought that would surely indict Arvids. However, he received an answer stating that the German government did not interfere in a person's religion. Once again God's Word comforted the family, as they remembered Psalm 18:48-49:

> *He delivers me from my enemies. You also lift me up above those who rise up against me; you have delivered me from the violent man. I will give thanks to you, O Lord, among the Gentiles and sing praises to your name.*

* * * * * * * * * *

Anna was eight years old and reading aloud three chapters of the Bible at a time. Arvids occasionally helped her with the difficult Hebrew names.

"Papin, do I have to read all the begats?" the girl asked from time to time.

"Is the whole Bible God's Word, Anna?" Arvids said thoughtfully, asking his own questions. "Did God inspire all the begats?"

"Yes, Papin," Anna answered.

"Then what do you think?" her father pursued.

"I have to read them," she said.

"Alright, keep reading," Arvids said.

* * * * * * * * * * *

The Latvian industries had had labor unions prior to the war, which the Germans allowed to continue operating. However, the workers were periodically sent papers containing Nazi propaganda that they were required to sign. Sometimes the papers told of the American Army knowingly bombing hospitals or stated that the Jewish race needed to be annihilated. People signed these papers reluctantly, hoping to keep their jobs without harassment.

Each time Arvids was given one of these, he threw it down and refused to sign. The supervisor reasoned with him that everyone had to sign, whether he agreed or not.

"I cannot go against my conscience," Arvids replied, still refusing.

Union workers, particularly, were expected to sign. Later, when the authorities were investigating why Arvids did not oblige, the supervisor observed with curiosity, and Arvids heard him ask the secretary, "Did Keikulis sign the papers?" When she indicated he had not, he said, "I thought he would not."

The supervisor actually seemed pleased and showed Arvids respect.

When Arvids was questioned again, he explained that he had never joined any worldly organization, that the only organization he was part of was the Church of Jesus Christ.

He never heard about the matter again and was able to continue working.

After a period of calm came the slaughter of Jews that brought back the reality of being occupied. The people described it as "the same crab to bite you but with a different covering."

More and more the Jews were harassed. First, their jobs and property were confiscated, and they were kept under surveillance. A number of times Arvids visited his friend, Mr. Kiels, who disclosed where he had hidden his family's personal valuables. The man tried to give Arvids some items to hold onto, but Arvids refused to accept them. Arvids said that under the circumstances, he did not want to be found with someone else's belongings.

Increasingly news spread about the murdering of the Jews. One day when Arvids came home, Cilite's face was ghastly white in shock and she could not speak, only motioning to him. Finally she managed to whisper a few words. The Jewish couple across the street from their apartment – the doctor who had examined Arvids, along with his wife, who had accepted a Bible from them, and their child – had been machine-gunned to death. Their baby was still in the mother's arms, all lying in a pool of blood out in the street.

Cilite was so overwhelmed that she was pulling at her hair. She held her head in her hands, and fear shone through her glassy eyes. She could barely speak.

"How could God forget His own children?" she asked. Arvids began to speak firmly to her from the Bible.

"God is still sovereign and in control of men's deeds," he said. "Can we question Him or tell Him what to do? God has been pleading with His people for thousands of years, and they would not hear Him."

Embracing one another tightly, they wept out loud.

Arvids knew that the world sometimes sucks God's children in to destroy them, and they may become temporarily overwhelmed with sorrow, seeming to lose their direction. Arvids encouraged Cilite to find comfort in the Lord. Toward evening Cilite's expression changed as she leaned on her Heavenly Father in this perplexing time. The entire family fasted for the remainder of the day.

Showing friendship or sympathy in any way to Jews, even in the death of loved ones, was to jeopardize one's life. People seldom spoke of their Jewish friends. The day after the massacre of their neighbors, the Keikulis children secretly sneaked away to the sandy area where the family was buried. There was blood all over the ground. In their innocent love and sorrow for the tragedy that had taken place, the children gathered wildflowers and placed them on the graves. The risk involved was their way of protesting the sheer brutality. Even though the couple had once laughed at them for their faith, the Keikulises identified with them in their need and oppression, striving to remain sensitive and hate the sin but not the sinner.

As in many oppressions, the personal property of the victims was sold at cheap prices to degrade them even further. During both occupations, the Russians sold or gave away valuables belonging to the dead. There was an open market with the Jews' personal property peddled at low prices.

The Keikulises did not purchase any of the items.

"No matter how great our own need, we must not buy things stained with blood," Arvids said. "We must guard to keep our consciences tender."

During this German occupation and later in the war, the children were forced to pass bodies of the slain heaped in piles, sometimes as high as a building. Arvids always told them to turn their heads. They tried to maintain sanctity of life in a time when thousands upon thousands of lives were being lost. Millions were murdered in Europe, and 30,000 Jews were murdered in Latvia.

Over the next few years, virtually every known Jew was killed. Many were brought in from large European cities and murdered in the smaller rural communities. Nazis were known to get young Latvian boys drunk and order them to shoot the Jews. The boys were frightened, knowing that if they refused they would be executed. Sometimes the young men drank until they became sick enough to vomit. Then they were too ill to handle a rifle.

These were the most disgraceful years.

In the midst of the annihilation, the Keikulises were able to aid one Jewish family. Initially, those Jews who were Christians were exempt from execution. Later the Nazis ignored the Christianity aspect and killed them all. In Brother Kumins' church was a Christian couple who faced grim reality – a Latvian wife and a Jewish husband. The man's life was in danger, and it was difficult to conceal his identity in the city. They asked for help, and Arvids found a Christian brother living far out in the country who was willing to hide a fellow believer in the loft of his barn.

The man spent two years hiding in the barn. Arvids visited him often to offer encouragement. Living alone and hiding so long was trying, and the poor fellow came close to despair. Then the farmer heard rumors that anyone hiding Jews would be executed and everything within a radius of half-a-mile of that residence would be burned. So Arvids found a Christian family living in a cottage farther back in the forest, and they were willing to take in their Jewish brother. He lived there quite freely, as few people ever ventured so far out to visit. When the German occupation was over, the man was able to go to Belgium with his wife.

Life had become chaotic and abnormal. The suffering affected thousands of families. A Keikulis neighbor's son was taken by one of the armies. His mother wept uncontrollably because she did not know her son's whereabouts or what was happening to him. The young men were forced to obey orders from the occupiers as they were inducted into their armies.

Arvids and Cilite had sent Judite and Modra to Cilite's parents for an extended visit. Grandpa Kasparovics was a skilled craftsman who made beautiful carriages, wagons, and furniture in his shop. Although their grandfather was usually strict and hard on them, the children loved him and he them. When the children were in his lap talking and playing, his demeanor softened. As innocent children, they did not know how to be afraid of their grandpa, and they would immediately run to him and begin to play with his beard. He could not refuse this attention. In times when he was angry and had come to the Keikulis home to give the adults a piece of his mind, little Modra – not comprehending the meaning of his words – would playfully climb into his lap and distract him from his intentions. The children brought out the best in him.

During this particular visit, Paulina overheard her husband trying to influence the little girls to his philosophy. He was talking about Brother Kumins and mentioned that the best place for him would be in the stable with the horses. Modra, too young to understand the sting in his voice, answered sweetly, "Yes, Grandpa, and we will just put you with the pigs."

It shut him up for the moment, but later he told the girls, "Tell your father that if he comes here, the only thing left of him will be a puddle and two eyeballs on the floor!"

The girls repeated this to their papa as if it were a joke.

Knowing God was with him, Arvids felt compelled to face his father-in-law. When he arrived, the neighbors warned of this man's hatred for his daughter's husband. When Ansis Kasparovics was told Arvids was coming, he angrily slung his axe into the floor of his wagon shop.

"Hello, how are you, Ans?" Arvids said as he walked straight into the shop and extended his hand. The disheveled old man was so startled that he just stuck out his hand and mumbled.

On another of the children's visits to their grandparents' home, Arvids and Cilite received a phone call that Irma, Cilite's youngest sister, and Judite and Modra had become sick with diphtheria. Irma was already hospitalized, and there was a question about what Arvids and Cilite wanted to do about the girls. Arvids asked that they be placed on the train so he and Cilite could meet them at the station.

When the girls arrived home, their parents attended to them and spent much time in prayer. Judite bounced back quickly and did not seem affected, but Modra remained weak and feverish for several days. As was their practice, Arvids and Cilite stayed on their knees for hours at a time. It was not easy to see their young child suffer.

Their spiritual warfare through prayer had brought them to a time when they could heartily commit their child into God's hands and into His will. While praying, Arvids lifted his hands and said, "Lord, I give Modra to you."

Janis had been listening, and he thought this meant his papa was giving his sister up to die. He rushed in crying, "Papa, do not give her up. Do not give her up!"

Arvids comforted his son and explained that he was committing Modra to God, who loved her even more than they did. Ansis Kasparovics had been angry with them for not taking both girls to the hospital, but before the week was over Modra was completely well. Irma, who had the benefit of hospitalization, was severely sick for six weeks.

The Lord was always faithful when the couple put their trust wholly in Him.

* * * * * * * * * * *

Brother Lielsvager, the kind, elderly farmer, had a son who was an army commandant during the German occupation. He was a brusque, brutal person and enjoyed his authority. His wife had been under conviction for years but had struggled with her commitment to Christ. She saw how her in-laws and the Keikulises endured persecution, and she did not want that kind of life. She was aware of how Janis had been persecuted and said she could never stand for her children to go through that. She was an exceptionally beautiful, stately woman with long, blond hair. When she came down with tuberculosis and realized she was about to lose everything, she turned to the Lord in despair.

Her husband was outraged because she became a believer and attended church services. He had bragged that if the Keikulises ever put their feet on his property he would shoot them. He once rode his horse into the store as a gesture of his disdain for them. His wife remained weak in her faith and became seriously ill with the disease. Arvids and Cilite were concerned for her and hoped that her faith would not waver in her fiery baptism. In spite of her husband's warning, they knew they must visit her home to encourage and pray with her.

Arvids and Cilite had prayed and had peace in their hearts that they had to go to the sick woman in her hour of trial. Even Cilite showed unusual courage. When they entered the house, Brother Lielsvager's son was seated at the dining room table loading his rifle. They greeted him and walked past him to his wife's bedside. They were able to boldly minister the Word of God to her even while they heard her husband repeatedly loading and cocking his rifle.

They visited her numerous times until the Lord called her home. She had once requested that for the funeral her thick long braids that fell past her waist be placed over her chest. However, in the last few days of agony her hair was heavy and added to her difficulty in breathing, so she asked that the braids be cut. Later, after her death, when the Communists came in, her husband was sent to Siberia.

Brother Lielsvager had become one of the congregation's dearest and most faithful members. He could always be counted on and was a shining example to other Christians. He had stood by Arvids in countless tests with a humble, gentle spirit. One night Arvids and Cilite were called to his bedside, and they found him paralyzed on one side, apparently from a stroke. He was able to speak and comforted them saying, "Do not be sad for me. It is my time to go, but you all will have many sorrows and difficulties ahead of you."

Several days passed as they spent time with him, ministering to him and he to them. He asked them to look after his wife, as his children were ungodly. For days he drifted in and out of a coma. The family's maids were part of the congregation, so they cared for him and regularly reported on his condition. During the night he had asked one of them, "What time is it?"

"Three a.m.," she had answered.

"At seven I am going to die, but do not tell my wife," he said. He raised his paralyzed arm and kept it raised until 7 a.m. Then he lowered it and in peace went to be with his Lord.

His passing reminded the congregation of Psalm 116:15, which says, "Precious in the sight of the Lord is the death of His saints."

As requested by their faithful friend, the Keikulises brought Mrs. Lielsvager to live with them. She was a charming little lady and a delightful addition – much like having a grandmother in their home. At first her sons charged that the Keikulises wanted their wealth and were keeping her for that reason; however, they brought food and milk to the house for their mother. When Arvids learned what they were saying, he told them he did not want a crumb or a dime from them; their mother was staying with them only because they loved her.

After that, the sons humbled themselves and begged the Keikulises to accept support for their mother. Mrs. Lielsvager lived there for almost a year. Then she began to grow weaker and talked about joining her dear husband. She remembered the agony before his death and did not want to be alone when she died. Her bed was against the wall in the room adjoining Arvids' and Cilite's bedroom.

"When you hear me knocking on the wall, would you please come in?" she asked Arvids. Several times he went and ministered to her until she was again at peace.

One night Arvids awoke and heard her talking in the next room. In her sweet voice she was calling, "Beloved, beloved!" He jumped out of bed and went into her room. She was smiling peacefully and had already gone to be with her beloved.

As had become the custom, funeral services were a time of rejoicing and spiritual meetings, with the saints coming together for a kind of celebration. Three ministers each had a victorious message of the resurrection of Christ and His church. The meetings were long and open, and outsiders came out of curiosity. The police, who served as existing government agents during both occupations, did not dare disturb funeral services. A dark cloud had hung over Latvia since the extermination of Jews. Cilite sang "The Old Rugged Cross," as Mrs. Lielsvager had requested. It was a blessing for Arvids and Cilite to share in the victory of the cross and in the passing of a believer.

Some of the Keikulis family's fondest memories were the funeral services of dear saints of God.

＊ ＊ ＊ ＊ ＊ ＊ ＊ ＊ ＊ ＊ ＊

Before the occupation, the Keikulises became acquainted with a Russian widow and her teenaged daughter, Mariana. The father, a Latvian soldier, had died when the girl was four. Olga Greitans had enjoyed shopping at the store because Cilite and Arvids spoke Russian and were kind to her. When Mariana was about 16, she had worked for Brother Lielsvager's son and wife during harvest time. When church services were held at the elder Lielsvager's home, Mariana attended and heard Arvids preach the gospel. During one of the services, the Holy Spirit spoke to her thirsty heart, and she felt she had found the Spring of Living Water, the Lord Jesus Christ.

Her family was upset that she had joined the "sect," as the congregation was called. Several times Olga came to the Keikulises asking, "What has happened to my daughter? She has said no matter what, she must follow her new belief."

They witnessed to the distraught mother, and in time she, too, became a believer. Young people were being extradited to Germany by the Nazis for possible deportation. Mariana feared she might become one

117

of them. Olga asked if her daughter could come to live with the Keiku-lises and help with the family and household chores.

Arvids and Cilite agreed for Mariana to move in. Tearful and wring-ing her hands, the woman came to say goodbye. She asked that the Kei-kulises look after Mariana as their own and correct her when needed. The mother realized that this separation might be permanent, and she embraced Mariana, weeping.

"Maybe when this is all over we'll meet again," Mariana said, trying to be brave.

Olga Greitans went to live with her oldest daughter, Anastasia. Her son, who had been deported in 1941, returned after a few years. Mari-ana thought she would never see any of them again.

During the Cold War, when in the United States, Cilite wrote letters to every relative and Christian she could locate. Arvids' letters never reached their destination, since he was black-listed by the Communists. For 30 years Cilite faithfully prayed for and sent packages to everyone she knew or heard about.

Maryann's (Americanized name) siblings had persecuted her for her faith, so she did not know how to re-start a relationship with them. Ci-lite wrote to Anastasia as an old friend. Anastasia had a well-educated daughter, Leinite (Lay'-nee-teh), who had leukemia. Leinite was read-ing books on Eastern religions seeking comfort.

Cilite asked a pastor friend to visit Leinite and offer a "book."

Pastor Zvirgzdins went to visit, sharing the gospel and praying with Anastasia and her daughters. He left the Bible with them but said Leinite seemed confused and influenced by the Eastern philosophers.

However, after spending time reading the Bible, Leinite wrote with joyous conviction that she had met the Author. Soon she was baptized and joined a small underground church. God gave her two years of good health and then called her home.

Anastasia and her younger daughter, Ilze, were also saved. Anastasia made a request of her boss in the factory where she worked and was granted permission in 1977 to visit family in the United States. There was no time to write, so one day she appeared at Maryann's front door. Anastasia became everyone's surprise guest at Arvids' and Cilite's 50th wedding anniversary celebration and experienced the joy of being baptized by Arvids.

Anastasia said the Latvian believers wondered how the Keikulises had wound up in America, so Arvids took typed pages of his journal to share this story with them. Anastasia rolled the pages and sewed them into the hem of her coat for her return journey. She read the story to her church, where many old friends of the Keikulis family were members. The small congregation was amazed and said, "Cilite was our 'Esther' for such a time as this. Her packages helped us through our difficulties."

* * * * * * * * * * *

Mariana fit into the family well and proved to be of immense help. She assisted with household duties and cared for the children. She was adaptable as she observed and participated in prayer times and Bible reading. She grew in her faith and Christian walk, ever submissive in following spiritual guidance.

Times were unstable, and the believers felt the need to consistently pray and prepare their hearts before the Lord. In the Old Testament, Joshua 3:5, the children of Israel were called to special times of sanctifying, or separating themselves, before the Lord. Just like those believers, this small congregation had periods of soul searching and seeking God's face. They believed the promise in James 4:8, "Draw near to God, and He will draw near to you. Cleanse your hands, you sinners, and purify your hearts."

In one of the sanctification services several churches came together for a time of seeking the Lord. At the close of one of the meetings, a sister began to prophesy. They were strange words that remained in the hearers' hearts: "There are those among us who will go across many waters to distant lands. Others will be taken through tremendous fires of testing."

They all wondered what those words could mean.

"This sister must be in the flesh," Cilite thought to herself.

The believers were not quick to accept every prophetic utterance but tried to test the spirit as God's Word admonishes, so they hid these words in their hearts or "put them on a shelf," as it were.

Years later, when the Keikulis family was crossing the Atlantic Ocean, Cilite was seasick during the whole trip, and she remembered the words of the prophecy.

* * * * * * * * * * *

Modra was a talkative child who sometimes pushed a chair to the wall under the telephone, cranking the phone and announcing to the operator, "I want to talk to my papa."

"Who is your papa?" the operator would ask.

"My papa," replied the child indignantly.

"Where is your papa?" the operator probed.

"He is working in the forest," Modra would explain. "Tell him to pick strawberries, blackberries, and blueberries, and then I will eat re-e-al good."

Although it was not easy to raise children in the turmoil, these parents continued to see God using the children to bring equilibrium to an otherwise hopeless, unstable period. The children said delightful things in their innocence that diverted the adults from the heaviness of the moment. The young ones' expressions and mannerisms brought laughter and exuberance that lifted the spirits of those around them.

* * * * * * * * * * *

The supervisor in the forestry continued to be understanding when Arvids needed time off. His father, Karlis, was dying, and he wanted to see him. Also, Cilite was expecting their fifth child and was nearing the time of delivery.

"Your father must die anyhow, but you need to be with your wife when she gives birth," the supervisor said when he granted the leave.

Cilite insisted she was fine and encouraged her husband to go to his father, believing the baby would not arrive for another week. Arvids had tried to witness to Karlis, but his dad could not – or would not – listen. Karlis Keikulis had spent his time in the lust of living and had visited a number of fortunetellers. When Arvids began to talk about the Lord, Karlis would lift his hand and step backward pleading, "Oh, please, do not talk like that." Then he would start mumbling as if in a panic.

When Arvids walked into the room this time, he could tell his father was in death's agony. Not wishing to disturb him, the son quietly put his hand on the sick man and began praying silently.

"Please do not do that, son," Karlis said in a shaky voice as he opened his eyes. "It only torments me."

Arvids left the bedside grief stricken because the dying man could not respond to prayer. He wept for his father all the way home. Years of sin had hardened the old man's heart, and even at death he could not acknowledge God.

Karlis died soon after that visit.

* * * * * * * * * * *

On June 7, 1943, Arvids' and Cilite's fifth child, a girl they named Ilze, was born. Mariana was of invaluable help in caring for the new baby while Cilite recuperated. There were rumors of war, and Cilite felt despair at bringing a child into that kind of situation.

* * * * * * * * * * *

Arvids was paid for his work with German marks that were printed exclusively for the occupied countries, but the marks could not purchase anything since all stores had been shut down. To help out, the supervisors also paid the workers in brandy and cigarettes. Arvids would not accept his portions, although his co-workers offered to buy them.

These might have been peaceful times except for an outbreak of severe scabies, with a secondary bacterial infection. There had been an epidemic among the soldiers, and it spread rapidly among the public, including the Keikulis family. The sores and itching were severe, and eventually the children began to lose their fingernails as a result. There was no relief, and the family felt like they were experiencing Job's afflictions. They called Brother Kumins and lamented that they were undergoing Job's trials.

"So you think you are like Job?" Brother Kumins commented, sound-

121

ing surprised.

Cilite was particularly troubled when Ilze, now only six months old, began breaking out on her fingers. The rash was ugly and smelly. Days and nights seemed unmercifully long, with the entire family uncomfortable.

A week later Brother Kumins telephoned to say, "Yes, we, too, are in Job's afflictions."

It was disconcerting when they began to hear that Christians everywhere were stricken with scabies. Gradually believers came to understand that God was bringing them through another difficult test to teach them more dependence on Him.   This was a particularly humbling experience, since others looked down on those who had the dreaded disease. They clung to the words of James 4:6:

"He gives grace to the humble but resists the proud."

The family was grateful that while Cilite's hands were broken out and painful, Mariana could do the cooking and washing. Then when Cilite improved, Mariana came down with a worse case, and Cilite took over the workload. Some family members suffered with scabies for as long as three years.

In its early phases the disease was an itchy, dry infection. During the dry stage, itching was so intense that it could not be relieved by scratching, although the urge was constant. Scratching created large patches of skin that resembled raw meat. Cilite had made small mittens to put over the children's hands to keep them from scratching themselves bloody.

Next the skin became wet, with more infectious itching. Scratching was followed by liquid forming beneath the skin and blistering, accompanied by a burning sensation. At times they felt feverish. Their joints were sore and the inflammation severe. When the disease spread below the skin, it affected the movement of joints. Opening and closing one's hands and bending the elbows and knees were painful. Everyone felt restricted.

In the next stage, sores became boils over large, infected areas. Many of the boils had deep roots, which left large scars when finally healed.

In the blistering stage, when scratching caused rawness, the skin would peel off. The large boils became infected, and armpits were so swollen that a patient could not hold his arms next to his body. When the children were severely infected, Arvids, Cilite, and Mariana removed their clothing to keep it from adhering to their bodies. The only way to deal with the situation was to wrap the person in a sheet, like a large bandage. To remove the sheet, the child was submerged in a tub of water and the sheet gently unrolled.

Because of scabies, Anna was forced to miss an entire winter of school. During this time Cilite read her the Book of Job in its entirety at least three times. Soon to be nine years old, Anna understood the book from her young perspective. Many years later when reading Job, she had to concentrate to determine what was really happening. As a child, because of the prolonged suffering she was experiencing, she had completely related to it. Although she could not have understood the full implication of Job's relationship with God in the suffering, it seemed that God was not testing Job so much as perfecting him. Her own suffering was God's way of showing His love for her and His faithfulness in seeing her through. She could not fathom from an adult's point of view that all Christians were suffering. She was simply looking at it from her vantage point that God was caring for her just as he had taken care of Job. Seeing herself in the same position as Job made her feel important to God.

"Someday He is going to resurrect this body that is decaying," Anna thought. She memorized the verse in Job 19 that says, "Even though the worm eats my flesh, my Redeemer lives." She could see that her flesh looked terrible and was decaying. She was ashamed of her body, scarred and covered with boils. She had every reason to believe she would be disfigured. However, it was a comfort to see herself in the same predicament as Job in the Bible.

"What shall I read today, Anna?" Cilite would ask.

"How about reading about Job, Mama?" the little girl would answer.

Anna loved the part where God rebuked Job's friends for all the chatter they had made. Their "comfort" was all philosophy and not experience.

"There, those comforters were not very good and kind, and God rebuked that," was Cilite's comment.

Perhaps it was the way her mother had read it to her, but young Anna found Job's friends amusing. They certainly had a lot to say. She did not perceive them as mocking Job or that they did not understand him; it simply surprised her that for all those days they could sit there and talk, talk, talk, just discussing philosophies.

Job became Anna's hero. She loved the ending. In all his suffering, this man had remained faithful to the Lord. The Lord blessed him in the end with more family and more goods. It was a thrilling climax, and she knew it by heart. To Anna, the book was about this great man of God, and God had been with him. In a similar way, here she was in her suffering, and she knew God was ever present. She felt elevated to Job's place. She was enduring grueling tribulations, exercising the same faith in God.

As a child, it was comforting to have her mama and papa close by – not talking about "big" things. They cared for her with gentleness and understanding, knowing she was miserable. They would pick up her little body and gently stick it in the tub and wait for the soaking process so they could remove the sheet. Anna cried because it stung.

"We are so sorry," they said. "We know it hurts, but we have to get it off."

Although difficult, these were special moments for the family because they had drawn closer, spending many hours caring for and nursing each other in a personal way. It was a memorable, tender time.

Reading and memorizing verses from the Bible reassured them during this ordeal, and two favorites were Hebrews 2:10 and Hebrews 5:8:

> For it was fitting for Him, for whom are all things and by whom are all things, in bringing many sons to glory, to make the captain of their salvation perfect through sufferings...Though He was a Son, yet He learned obedience by the things which He suffered.

It was much later that the Keikulises could look back and realize God's grace in teaching them patience and endurance through this dreadful disease, character traits that helped them keep their composure and trust during the war and oppression in the Nazi and Communist camps. They were grateful to understand that their Father knows the end from the beginning, and He knows what to put into the curriculum to prepare and mold His children. If Christ, who was perfect and complete, had to endure suffering during His life on earth, how much more do believers need to learn to submit to the Potter's hands for His work in them?

The work of perfection to Christ's image takes a lifetime. His followers must be ever grateful for His continuous work in them. The book of Job brought comfort to the entire Keikulis family.

They learned to agree, in triumph, with the Old Testament hero, who said in the 19th chapter of the book in the Bible that bears his name: "I know that my Redeemer lives!"

* * * * * * * * * * *

After the war the family learned that the Ukrainian Christians had also suffered from an epidemic of scabies. Strangely enough, it seemed that only Christians were afflicted.

In one particular family everyone was tormented and anguished. One of the young boys became embittered after days of itching and misery. He screamed out, "If this is what it means to be a Christian, I do not want any part of it!" and stomped out of his house. Almost instantly the boy's skin began to heal, and he felt the presence of God leave him. It was such a frightening experience that the boy cried out in repentance and ran back home. The scabies returned, and the boy then had a gentle, quiet spirit.

Through this trial the Keikulises came to a more meaningful point of view concerning the struggles of earthly existence, and their response was one of renewed submission and deeper understanding. Who are humans to question the ways of God and the tools He uses to mold character into submission to His will!

* * * * * * * * * * *

During the German occupation, the Keikulises heard a personal testimony that inspired and moved them. A Mr. Pucits (Pooh' tseets), whose name meant "blossom," had been drafted the week after he had committed his life to Christ. Because he refused to bear arms, he was beaten and jailed for a year. He was constantly intimidated by others who said, "Are you not a man, that you are afraid to fight and face death?"

"I am not afraid of death," he said.

Eventually, Mr. Pucits was offered the opportunity to assist the medics in picking up the wounded and dead from the battlefront. He had prayed for courage to honor God.

God honored his faith, and he carried out his duties with integrity. He realized if he crawled on his belly he would be like the others, so he always walked erect. Daily he trudged through fires and shooting to find the wounded. Once, when looking for injured soldiers by following their cries, he realized he was caught in a crossfire and turned to face a Russian tank. A great peace came over him, and he continued his duty without being harmed.

Mr. Pucits grew accustomed to trusting the Lord amidst death and terror and paid little attention to the bombing and the enemy. It mattered not to him if he went into a Russian or German bunker to get the wounded out. During one search, when he was following the sounds of a soldier crying in pain, he suddenly walked up to a Russian pointing a machine gun directly at him. Instinctively he fell to the ground. In the next second, a bomb exploded, killing his enemy.

Winters during the war seemed especially bitter and cold. Soldiers on the battlefield found it difficult to keep their hands and feet from becoming frostbitten. Many became hysterical and delirious or froze to death in their bunkers. Mr. Pucits realized that God was his only resource, and he got down on his knees, raising his hands as he prayed for peace and strength. He had been praying for several hours when he realized he could not lower his hands, which had frozen. He then began praying for his hands. Gradually they warmed and the blood circulated, and he was able to move them again.

When Mr. Pucits' troop became completely surrounded by the enemy, the weary soldiers succumbed to panic and hysteria. It seemed as if there was no hope.

"What about the holy man?" someone said. "Can't he pray?"

The officer sought out Mr. Pucits and asked, "Can you help us in this despair?"

"Yes, I can," Mr. Pucits answered. After a brief prayer, he commanded, "Prepare. Get your wounded together, and be ready to leave."

With Mr. Pucits leading the way, the entire company of several hundred men began to follow, carrying their wounded. They walked across the trenches where the Russians were stationed. Russian soldiers, clutching their guns, looked startled, but no one made a move to attack or stop the procession. The company continued walking several miles until they reached the German front.

Prior to this incident, Mr. Pucits had been teased about his faith. Now orders were given that no one was to touch him or make fun of him. When he was on leave strolling down a sidewalk, an approaching officer would step down in respect, permitting him to pass.

Upon hearing this stirring testimony, the Christians were meaningfully strengthened. Mr. Pucits prayed for his home church. His heart yearned for the familiar place as a suckling babe desires its mother. In their hearts the Keikulises prayed, "Lord, enable us to stand as this young man stood in the midst of flames and death."

God heard their prayer.

* * * * * * * * * * *

Arvids and Cilite were in the habit of praying an hour each morning before starting the day. They knew that times were unstable and uncertain, and they needed to prepare themselves spiritually for whatever they were called to do. Often they sensed a spirit of intercession and supplication as they verbally poured out their hearts to their Heavenly Father. In the early hours, they covered themselves with a blanket to keep from waking the children. Mariana and Janis sometimes joined the prayer time, but in their innocence, they were not completely aware of the dangers ahead nor of the spiritual warfare involved. They prayed for a while and then dozed in and out of sleep.

The family was grateful for the strength gained through communion with their Lord, who knew what lay ahead and was preparing them for it.

* * * * * * * * * * *

127

The warfront returned, with Communists showing military strength that brought destruction all around. During the German occupation Latvians were forced to mobilize their army against the international treaties. Accustomed to occupations by both Russia and Germany, Latvians were not sympathetic to one power or the other. They were simply caught in the middle. Since the German army was already set up and had been functioning for three years, Latvians were forced to ally with the Nazis to hold back the Red Army. Most had hoped the United States would help keep a democratic form of government, but that did not happen.

In the summer of 1944 Arvids received an official notice to report for induction into the German army. He was not against serving in the military but was against the motives and purposes of Hitler's army. As a Christian he understood that he could not serve in an army that had performed mass slayings of the Jews and other people they did not like.

Arvids had several days from the time he received the notice until the time he was to report to the induction center. By now, fasting had become a regular discipline in Arvids' and Cilite's lives, as Isaiah 58:6-14 directs. So they fasted, prayed, and waited on the Lord. Others in the church joined them. Cilite did not attempt to persuade her husband to try to get out of the draft, nor did she give advice as to how to handle this circumstance. The state-owned radio and newspapers made it clear that dissenters would be shot. Cilite faced the reality of being left with a nursing infant and four other children; but the couple knew their hope was in the Lord, and they looked to Him for a solution.

The day arrived when Arvids was to report to the induction center. The Lord had not yet provided direction, so Arvids kissed Cilite goodbye, not knowing if he would return. When he arrived at the center, the hall was already filled with draftees. The induction committee was seated behind a table taking roll. A speech was given on the lofty goals of the Nazi army. Arvids stood in the back with his heart beating increasingly fast. He knew he would have to speak but did not know what he would say; he had learned from experience to not stress about words in circumstances like these. This always required a difficult inner struggle. He had memorized verses from Mark 13:11 and Luke 21:14-15:

But when they arrest you and deliver you up, do not worry beforehand or premeditate what you will speak. But whatever is given you in that hour, speak that for it is not you who speak, but the Holy Spirit ... Therefore, settle it in your hearts not to meditate beforehand on what you will answer; for I will give you a mouth and wisdom which all your adversaries will not be able to contradict or resist.

The Nazi officer announced that there would be no physical examinations, but everyone would be inducted. Arvids knew it was time for him to go forward, still not knowing what to say. He walked through the crowd to the commissioners' table and began with these words, which, under the circumstances, was the most risky thing he could have said: "I cannot accept the invitation. I am already called to another army."

The members of the committee were stunned, their eyes widening in amazement. They were clearly taken aback at this man's overconfidence.

"What other army?" the commissioner demanded.

"I am a soldier in the army of the Lord," Arvids continued confidently. "For 11 years God has called me to fight in His army, to fight with His weapons of love. Determine for yourselves: Can I take into my hands these weapons of death when I am called to carry the message of God's love?"

Arvids recognized that the Holy Spirit was upon him and that he had spoken with God's authority.

The commission officer looked frightened that Arvids could possibly confuse the whole induction procedure.

"Yes, yes, I see that it is entirely different with you," he answered. "You may go!"

With that he took Arvids' papers and stamped them "dismissed" and handed them back to him. The next commissioner sprang to his feet and yelled, "You must arrest him!"

But Arvids knew that he had already won the victory, and he turned and started to go out. The crowd of men in the room parted, making a path for him to walk through.

This faithful soldier of God marched slowly and deliberately out of the room.

Cilite had been anticipating the possibility of Arvids' returning home, and she spotted him walking freely with steps of joy and victory. Indeed, victory is glorious, but it requires a price.

Arvids had learned in his study of the Bible that Christians cannot hide, that believers must be in the forefront, as he had read in Matthew 5:14: "You are the light of the world. A city that is set on a hill cannot be hidden." How often one would rather run and hide, as the psalmist uttered in Psalm 55:6-8: "Oh, that I had wings like a dove! I would fly away and be at rest. Indeed I would wander far off and remain in the wilderness. I would hasten my escape from the windy storm and tempest."

When Arvids had received his induction notice, the whole town knew it and gossiped.

"It will be interesting to see the holy man toting a rifle," they jeered. "Oh, just wait and see, till this holy man totes his rifle; then none of his prayers will help."

The radio broadcast announced that 14 Christians in Germany had been shot because of their refusal to be inducted into the army. This message was a warning to others who might be looking for a way out. Now that Arvids had come through standing on his convictions, with God having delivered him from serving in the military, his former adversaries were quiet and respectful. Some even said, "We, too, did not want to join that army, but we did not have the courage the holy man did."

* * * * * * * * * * * *

Prior to the air raids, Mr. Kalejs, the blacksmith, had told his wife to take the Keikulises one of their cows. The Nazis had not counted one in their census. The blacksmith was concerned about the provision of food for the children. A lady who lived behind the Keikulis home kept the cow in her barn for them. The forestry department provided hay to feed the animal, and the cow was an important resource for the family's sustenance during the weeks to come.

Bombs began dropping on Latvia in November 1944. By this time the Keikulis family had become somewhat used to hearing bombs and had been preparing for possible flight. Mariana would walk outdoors to the stable to milk the cow, whistling as if in defiance of the shrapnel falling at her feet. However, when the area was directly attacked from the air, that was another story, and everyone ducked for safety.

Arvids talked to the family about the likelihood of leaving their house and following God's leading to a safer place. He made small suitcases for the older children and knapsacks for the young ones. They had been packed in readiness for weeks. Each satchel contained supplies for that child, a set of clothes, and some food. Money was sewn into the hems of clothing. They had rehearsed what they had in their luggage and what they should do if they became separated. Each older child, including Mariana, was in charge of a younger sibling. They would help each other dress, and leaving would be orderly and methodically carried out.

"Do not worry, Papa," four-year-old Modra commented matter-of-factly. "When we run out of food, there is plenty of firewood to eat."

On November 20 the artillery bombardment of Pampali began, continuous day and night. Unable to sleep, Arvids listened to the discharge of the battery followed by a screaming of the shell from the subsequent explosion. The children became acclimated to the noise and even managed to catch some sleep. When a close bomb rocked the house, shattering the window panes, the older ones sat up in bed and, seeing their papa calmly sitting there, went back to sleep. Persecutions and difficulties in the past had taught them to maintain tranquility.

During the First World War Arvids was young and carefree, not fearing danger and destruction. Now in the second war he was a man with a family – and the responsibility of their wellbeing upon him.

Their safety rested solely on his shoulders.

Chapter 4

The Warfront in Latvia

On November 22, 1944, a formation of bombers unloaded their deadly cargo on Pampali. The explosions were so close and violent that all the remaining windows in the Keikulis home shattered into a million pieces, and the family was thrown from one wall to the other as bombs detonated on either side of the house. Hundred-year-old trees were broken apart and swept several yards away from their original surroundings. Deep holes were left in the ground where stately trees had once flourished. As Arvids inspected the damage, he saw that only half of his neighbor's house remained.

The man stepped outside and, seeing Arvids, spoke.

"Keikulis, if we live through this hell, we will be the best of friends," he said, surveying the ruins of what had been his home. Normal circumstances had not prompted any kindness in him; but stripped of his home and security, he began to think of more permanent values.

Although the explosions had been close, Arvids could see no apparent damage to their house except for the windows. Nevertheless, he knew they could not live here any longer. The front line was close, and they could hear rifle and machine gun fire. Neighbors gathered in the Keikulis home that morning to seek counsel as to what they could do as a group. Many had already fled, among them those who had formerly opposed the Keikulises. When Arvids started giving advice, they had chosen to do the opposite.

Otherwise, it was a bright, sunny day.

Janis ventured out to look for bread possibly left by German soldiers. As he looked up in the sky, he could clearly see bomber planes approaching. Suddenly there was a rustling of leaves and a light wind, followed by the loud whining and scream of bombs. He turned around and dove into the hallway behind the heavy doors. As he tried to run up the steps to the apartment, glass from the skylight in the ceiling shattered, showering him with splinters. The explosions continued; and in panic, thinking the house was going to fall upon him, the boy ran into the vacant apartment next door, seeking to exit through the back. There he found black smoke and heaving earth, and the concussions of air were powerful hitting his face. Again he turned and ran to the stairwell and up the stairs.

The others stood behind the door upstairs in the stairwell. One of the neighbor ladies, thinking this was the end, kissed Arvids' hand and asked forgiveness for any unkindness she had rendered.

When things quieted down, Arvids opened the door slightly to look out on the street and skyward. The dread was there; airplanes were circling, so they braced themselves for another attack. They wondered if they would survive. In those short moments, Janis began to think about every wrong thing he had done in his short life and was preparing to meet his Lord.

Once again, the bombers unloaded their cargo and disappeared into the horizon. This second round was just as powerful as the first; but because all the windows had already shattered, there was less noise and destruction.

"God has always provided for us, and He will take care of us, no matter what!" Arvids had said during their most recent meal. He continued to be the children's window to trusting God. The togetherness and peace of God kept them from experiencing the widespread hysteria and fear that occurred during the war.

The family had taken Arvids' aged mother to live with them since she was not able to care for herself. She was not a believer and had become senile, no longer recognizing her son or other family members. It had been Anna's responsibility to dress her grandmother for the intended journey in the cold weather. However, when the girl tried to put on her shoes and coat, the old woman resisted, screaming, "Thief! Thief!"

thinking she was being robbed. To save the rest of his family, Arvids had no choice but to finally give up and leave her behind.

During times of war, ordinary people are forced to make extraordinary decisions, choices that are best for the majority and ones they would never consider under normal circumstances – and sometimes their actions may have seemed heartless, though necessary for survival.

Arvids proceeded to get the family together, rehearsing each one's job. They helped each other dress. Already prepared for such an eventuality, each child grasped the small suitcase or knapsack their papa had made. Cilite carried Ilze, the youngest. Just before this catastrophe had hit, Arvids had given the children a new puppy. Naturally they wanted to bring it along on their journey. Later that afternoon the family, along with Mariana, left their home in an effort to put some distance between themselves and the front line. They took a few items of clothing and other incidentals that could be carried by hand. Departure was orderly and methodically carried out.

Stepping outside, they saw that the bomb craters were larger than their building, one gigantic hole after another. Even the children realized God had protected them inside their house, and His hand had prevented the bombs' explosions from hitting them. Leaving their home, they walked to the barn to get Cherry, the cow. As they passed the large state church, they could see it had been demolished. Huge, old trees that had surrounded the structure were flattened. They soon came to a large open field, and shelling started coming directly toward them. Observing their calm demeanor, some of the neighbors had joined them.

Now with the shrieks and explosions of the bombs, these neighbors began to run and scream. The children panicked and attempted to bolt along with the others.

"Peace!" Arvids yelled in his loud sergeant's voice. The young ones stopped in their tracks.

"Children," he explained, amidst all the chaos, "if we step to the right, we may be killed. If we step to the left, we may also be killed. We are going to walk forward in the Lord. Our steps are ordered by Him, so let us walk with the Lord. If we stay within His path and do not panic but just walk, we can be sure to get through this field."

It was difficult to maintain this kind of composure because of the shelling and the confusion of screams and people running. Planes were still flying overhead and shooting. Judite, in shock, repeatedly dropped her suitcase. Her little hands kept opening, unable to grip. Arvids told the children to continue walking, and they followed. The family walked slowly and safely into a dense, wooded area. They almost walked into a bomb that was buried halfway into the ground, still undetonated. Arvids directed the family to walk gingerly around it, knowing that the slightest misstep could set it off. They noted the large size of the deadly weapon and the destruction it could cause, but fortunately this bomb remained dead.

As other bombs exploded, shrapnel scattered – but showered above them like bursts of light in an umbrella formation.

They entered the forest and felt momentarily safe, aware of the peace of God. Arvids realized how much his family depended on his conduct and assurance. He was thankful for the school of experiences and tests God had brought them through. He had learned to depend not on his feelings or circumstances but through faith grasp the promises of God's Word. Eventually faith becomes stronger than one's physical senses, and the family had learned to fully trust God. Arvids was able to transmit that trust to his children because of the training in years of persecution, sickness, and various trials. He had learned to submit his fears to the Lord, and the peace of God ruled his heart – the peace that surpasses man's understanding.

> Be anxious for nothing, but in everything by prayer and supplication, with thanksgiving, let your requests be made known to God, and the peace of God, which surpasses all understanding, will guard your hearts and minds through Christ Jesus (Philippians 4:6-7).

Now even the puppy and the cow seemed to obey Arvids' commands of "Peace!"

After hours of walking, they reached a farmhouse called Cepurnieki. The Bartusevics family, who were members of their church, lived and worked there, occupying a small room similar to servants' quarters at the back of the farmhouse. The Keikulises spent the night with their friends in the cramped room.

In the morning the group was surprised to learn that the front line had caught up with them, and they were cut off from all major roads.

The air raids and explosions had been so loud and severe that Mariana could only whisper over the next few days. She did not want to converse, avoiding any sounds or movement. To overcome her fear, she meditated on scripture from Hebrews 13:5, "I will never leave you nor forsake you." She thought, "What God has done for the heroes of the Bible, He can do for me."

The farmhouse quickly filled up with people seeking shelter. Medics were treating the wounded on the ground floor. The Keikulis family remained here in the vicinity of the front lines for 22 days, under constant artillery fire. Cilite and the children, along with other refugees, found shelter in a small cellar where potatoes were stored. For private times of prayer, Arvids went to the barn where they had placed their cow with the other cattle. He had stood firm through all their trials, seeking no help from anyone except the Lord.

The potato cellar provided practical protection, much like a bunker. The bombing and artillery continued without ceasing. When the noise of the explosions was close, the people huddled in the cellar, especially the Keikulis children, would glance at Arvids' face. He would proclaim with levelheaded resolve, "Peace!"

Even the puppy sitting between his feet would look up at his face as if searching to see if peace was there. The puppy had two light spots above his eyelids that seemed to rise when his eyes rolled upward. The children became accustomed to glancing not only at their papa's face but also at the puppy's. Arvids never changed his expression. From it, the others could read the assurance that everything would be fine.

They trusted God. Peace reigned.

Later, when they could not continue carrying the puppy with them, they gave him to a German soldier who needed a cheerful diversion.

Once they were surrounded in a siege. Bombs were exploding everywhere. Children living in this kind of situation have little entertainment, and sitting still and waiting for days on end is boring and difficult. They longed for something to happen to break the monotony of hiding underground while gunfire and bombs exploded all around. They were cold, hungry, and dirty; and nothing – except war – was going on.

During this time, no one removed their clothing but slept fully dressed, ready to run if necessary. The children were the only ones able to sleep at all. The cellar was usually so crowded that the adults had no room to lie down, so they tried to rest sitting or standing.

In the hours just before daybreak, war activities seemed to slow down. After a night of fitful sleep, Arvids seized a welcome opportunity to take a walk along the side of the barn and into the woods, where the Russians could not observe him. It was the third morning of living with constant shooting and bombing. They had run out of food. Even though there were potatoes in the cellar, they could not be used by refugees since the vegetables were confiscated for the German army. Arvids began to pray, as was his habit during walks in the forest.

"I have always trusted in You, and You have met all of my needs," he began. "Now, Lord, the children have no food. What am I to do?"

As he was speaking and walking, the early morning sunlight began to shine. Suddenly he looked down and saw a loaf of bread at the bottom of a tree! Thanking the Lord, he picked up the bread and ran back to the little cellar. This bread became the family's main staple. Along with milk from their cow, the Lord had supplied their need.

The next morning before daybreak Arvids awakened Janis and took him along on his walk. They passed the barn and entered the wooded area. They took turns praying and then found another loaf of bread in the same place. This continued for 22 days! They did not have time to stop and think about who was putting the bread in the forest; they only knew that their desperate need was being met.

Many years later, as they recounted God's guidance and His blessings, they would stop and remember the time they found bread in the forest. Then they would wonder how it got there. How was it that every day in the forest, on cold December mornings, a loaf of bread was waiting for them? They never understood how God supplied that need, but they were always thankful to Him, their supplier in everything. To the question in Psalm 78:19, "Can God prepare a table in the wilderness?" the Keikulis family could emphatically answer, "Yes, He can!"

Death and disaster loomed all around. Coming up to use the facility in the farmhouse, the people regularly saw dead bodies frozen in a tall heap due to the cold weather – 30 degrees below freezing. Arvids had again instructed the children never to look at the corpses so their compassion level would not harden and they could no longer weep for the suffering.

"Close your eyes to death so your soul does not get callous," he admonished.

There was no time for burying the dead, and wounded bodies were carried into the farmhouse on a daily basis. Once while all the family was in the cellar, a commotion erupted in the yard. A horse was bellowing loudly, so everyone knew it had been hit by shrapnel. Finally they heard a man screaming. Everyone ran to the door to see what was happening, and they saw blood gushing out of the man's head. He had been running and had taken a deadly hit.

"Cover your eyes, children, so that death will not become an everyday occurrence," Arvids spoke firmly to the children. "That is somebody's brother, son, or father. Each is precious to the Lord."

With all his might, Arvids endeavored to preserve a sensitive spirit within them so they could respond to those in need. Wartime can inflict things that, once so painful to see, become commonplace, and the human mind may cease dealing with them.

Several times during the first few days of living at the warfront, Arvids walked into town to see if there was any recent news of the war. On these trips he went back home to check on his mother and take her food. Usually she was bundled in layers of clothing and appeared to remain fairly warm. She never recognized him nor acknowledged his help or desire to evacuate her. On these trips he looked in the cupboard for canned goods or fruit preserves to take back to the family.

On one such trip, Arvids asked Mariana if she would like to come along and check on his mother and possibly find food. Mariana agreed and joined him. Still young in her faith, she leaned heavily on the Keikulises' advice and was quick to follow it. She did not feel strong in her own walk with God but diligently prayed, "Lord, honor Brother Arvids' faith as he has put his entire trust in you."

Deep in her heart she feared the Lord and wanted to do His will, but she saw it was easier to follow someone whom she knew trusted the Lord completely. She had observed that faith was not expressed so much in words as lived out in daily lives. The Apostle Paul had said, "Follow after me as I follow after Christ." Mariana knew her adopted family well and that death represented no threat for them. Each person held to the unshakable example set by the apostle: "I am ready to die for the name of the Lord." She recognized that severe trials had revealed to them that their most precious possession was life in Christ; they could count it joy that they had been tested and proven.

On their return trip, Arvids and Mariana emerged from a stretch of forest into a large, cleared field that they would cross – a little less than half-a-mile – to reach another wooded area. The Communists bombed this field continuously to discourage refugees in their escape efforts. The two stood at the edge of the clearing, watching bombs dig deep into the ground, slinging dirt and mud high into the air with each explosion.

"Will you go with me across the field?" Arvids asked.

"If you go, I will go," Mariana quietly replied, looking pale and serious.

Cautiously and deliberately they trudged across the field, never ducking or turning but pressing forward. Bombs fired and exploded all around. They reached the other side safely, not feeling at all like valiant heroes. They were keenly aware, once again, of the deep peace of God that passes all human understanding. His presence had enabled them to walk calmly across that terrifying field.

Several days later they learned that their house in Pampali had been bombed. Nothing was ever found of Arvids' mother.

In the mornings when things were quieter, the older people slowly crawled out of the cellar to use the bathroom in the servants' quarters. Everyone had dysentery. Nerves were frail as people stood in line. One old man slept in a dirty fur coat, and when he went out, he left it lying on the potatoes. The children ran to it to cuddle up and get warm. Unfortunately they picked up lice from the old coat. Cilite took them upstairs to the servants' quarters and with a candle tried to pick out the lice and burn them. While de-licing the girls, she witnessed to German soldiers hiding in the rooms.

During a lull in the bombing, the families ventured out of the cellar for fresh air and joined Arvids in the barn for prayer. Artillery firing would often start up and hit the stone foundation at the base of the barn. These times were frightening, and the group huddled together for safety.

"Papa, what would you do if one of our children were killed?" Cilite once asked after a loud explosion.

"That cannot happen because I have placed everything in the Lord's hands," Arvids replied with calm assurance.

On one particular day the families had again gathered in the barn for prayer. The frightful bombing began, with the entire yard around the barn seeming to be on fire. The group had been praying when they saw two German soldiers running to the barn door to escape the bombs. When the soldiers saw worshipers on their knees with their hands lifted, they drew back in respect.

"Quick, inside!" Arvids shouted in German military fashion.

Instinctively the two obeyed and leaped inside the door. Immediately the barn door was shot to pieces. Outside, a wagon full of grenades and ammunition caught on fire and appeared ready to explode any second, which would mean certain death for those in the barn. Mr. Bartusevics ran to the wagon, appearing to disregard the fact he could be killed. He grabbed the cover and began to beat the flames vehemently into the ground. A cloud of smoke was already rising.

Inside, Arvids ordered the families to join hands, and in single file they marched out the door, past the blazing wagon. Arvids knew that once the wagon exploded, so would the barn. In an orderly fashion the two families walked hand-in-hand across the yard. Visibility was poor due to the dense smoke. The wagon was just a few feet from the exit, so Arvids led the group back around the other side of the barn. Almost by habit, the children responded to their father's orders, so in a few short seconds the barn was evacuated. After leaving the women and children on that side, Arvids ran back to help Mr. Bartusevics.

Due to Mr. Bartusevics' quick action and bravery, none of the bombs exploded.

The people stayed hungry during the long days and nights in the potato cellar. The temptation was almost overwhelming to sample the potatoes on which they were forced to make their beds. The owner of the farmhouse was concerned for her own welfare and never offered a potato to any of the refugees, so no one dared to eat one. Preserved meat was stored in barrels nearby, there was plenty of butter, and several cows were in the barn; yet no food was offered to the hungry people. Again the families were forced to trust only in the Lord. They survived on the bread Arvids had found in the forest, milk from their cow, and the few jars of preserves that Arvids found on his infrequent trips back home.

When Sunday came, they met together for a church service.

"This is the Lord's Day, and we will gather for worship," said Arvids. "If anyone wants to join us, well and good. If anyone wants to mock us, let them mock, but we will worship the Lord."

They sang hymns, and Arvids preached as if they were worshipping in a traditional church sanctuary under normal circumstances. Whenever he proclaimed God's Word, he always spoke with authority and careful enunciation. Some refugees listened respectfully, while others shook their heads in disbelief, thinking the believers were fools.

One day a young German soldier came into the cellar and looked around. He did not appear to be more than 16 years of age but spoke with the authority of a man.

"How many men are here?" he demanded. As the men stood, he continued, "This is a war in which men are laying down their lives. Do you think you can just hide out here? Come with me. There is work to do!"

He took Arvids, Janis, and Mr. Bartusevics, along with other young men, to an open field within a mile of the front line and pointed to a small bathhouse that was part of the farm. He commanded them to tear it down so they could use the material to build a bunker. Arvids tried to reason with the young soldier that this was not an ideal place for a bunker, that it would be too visible to the Russians.

"I am giving the orders here!" the soldier shouted.

So the men began to follow his instructions, Janis getting onto the roof to rip open the shingles and boards. Arvids was walking away from the building when bombs began skipping across the field nearby. The soldier and others fell to the ground and yelled at Arvids to come back. He kept walking through the bombing to get some bread he had left in the tree for lunch.

When the shooting began, the soldier and young men dove into a square hole that had been dug for the bunker. There was little protection, because these kinds of shells exploded in the air before hitting the ground. Not finding protection in the hole, the boys then followed the soldier, who ran into the cellar of the house. They took turns making a dash for the house – the soldier opening the door for each one to dive in. When it was Janis's turn to run to the cellar, he was within a few yards of the door when a bomb exploded in front of him, splattering his face. He froze in fright, thinking he would be hit.

"Quick, inside!" the soldier screamed.

Although he was much closer to the door than to his dad, Janis quickly turned around and ran to Arvids. He grabbed his father by the hand, trying to hasten their steps to the cellar. Somehow he felt safer by his papa's side than without him in the cellar. He was so frightened and panicked that Arvids reprimanded him, "Don't ever let the devil know you are afraid."

Father and son continued to hold hands as they walked slowly and deliberately across the field. Janis needed further assurance to forge ahead in the midst of continued shooting.

"God has promised to protect those who put their trust in Him," Arvids said. "He has never let us down, and He never will."

Seconds stretched into minutes, and Janis began having flashbacks to times when as a young man he had grown weary in the long church services. Why can't Papa be like other ministers who do not take things so seriously and were not persecuted? he had wondered. His life had been made more difficult as a result of his parents' stance, and sometimes he resented the persecution he had endured. Thoughts raced through his mind. He remembered that in the sermons his papa would warn the flock that "now is the time to learn to be alert and pray, to take time to know God and be filled with His Holy Spirit." Arvids had said that when destruction and peril come, it is often too late to ask for wisdom and guidance because then the flesh reacts, and one loses control. All the admonitions the children had heard about putting their trust in the Lord sometimes had seemed vague to a young mind. Janis had heard them frequently.

Now under constant bombing and the presence of death, it was remarkable how enlightened he became to those spiritual truths he had heard over and over again. They had become a reality and were written on his heart.

I Corinthians 3:3 says that the Spirit of the living God writes on the tablets of human hearts. It takes the testing of agonizing trials to make it a reality.

The bombing continued for some time, and Arvids and Janis made it into the cellar. They had learned they could determine the close proximity of a bomb by the sound it made on impact.

Finally the bombing slackened, and the lieutenant decided they could try to leave. The soldier had lost interest in building a bunker, so the men walked back to their families. Occasionally while they walked, more bombs would fall. Janis kept walking with his dad instead of falling to the ground as the others did. He later told his papa that he felt safe close to him, knowing that God would protect them because his earthly father had put his entire trust in their Heavenly Father.

Numerous people had hidden in farmhouses. Sometimes these people would stand on cellar steps as if they wanted to come closer to safety but not hide with the believers. Cilite was accustomed to praying aloud; and once she began to intercede for all those hiding in the area, for their safety and wellbeing, and that they would recognize the Almighty God in these circumstances. She was praying in spirit and in truth, her prayer flowing like one of David's psalms in which he describes the power and attributes of God. Those listening stood in awe and reverence, commenting later that she must have written and memorized such powerful prayers.

Cilite continually prayed for the Lord's guidance and deliverance, sometimes to herself and sometimes audibly, and her words flowed loud and naturally. She knew Psalm 62:8 by heart and believed its promise: "Trust in Him at all times, you people; pour out your heart before Him; God is a refuge for us." Her testimony was like that of Psalm 59:16-17:

> But I will sing of your power; yes, I will sing aloud of your mercy in the morning; for you have been my defense and refuge in the day of my trouble. To you, O my strength, I will sing praises; for God is my defense, my God of mercy.

While the family was in the cellar, Cilite made a vow to God in prayer: "God, if you deliver our family with all our children out of this war, I will always witness of your faithfulness."

After the war, the passage in Psalm 66:8-14 and 16 was found underlined in her Bible. In the security of God's deliverance, Cilite kept her vow. She prayed for everyone she met and witnessed about God's faithfulness.

Prior to the war the Keikulises were called "holy ones" in mockery. Now under fire of the warfront they were called "holy ones" with reverence and respect. The family began to notice in the cellar and elsewhere that not only the children carefully watched Arvids' face to gain confidence from his faith and peace, but increasingly others watched him as if their lives depended on it. This put even greater pressure on Arvids to trust explicitly, and so he pressed harder.

Death was close and evident. One day the family had gone up to the attic of the farmhouse to get a better view of the battle. They could see rows upon rows of Russian soldiers in the trenches. Then they saw a soldier who stepped on a mine as he walked along. There was an explosion, and his body shot up in smoke. One of the little girls saw it and shrieked hysterically.

The children had become so accustomed to the various bombs that they, too, began to recognize them by the sound and knew how long to wait before bracing for the explosion.

On December 14, 1944, the farmhouse came under heavy artillery barrage from the Russian front. Shells fell so close that the cellar filled with cordite smoke, and explosions kept blowing out the kerosene lamp. The men tried using a rotten potato with a wick inserted for a light, and they also burned rancid butter and oil.

Even German soldiers sought shelter in the overcrowded cellar. Coming in from the front lines, they would drop to sleep anywhere. They were handsome young men, but their faces were pale and solemn in the midst of death's terror – not the usual masks under which sinful men may hide. Seeing the two families praying, they joined in. One, a Catholic, took out a crucifix and, crossing himself, began his prayers. The children held their ears during the loud explosions, and so did the soldiers.

The closer the soldiers came face-to-face with imminent death, the more the guises of defiance and superiority disappeared. The inhabitants of the cellar became one common people. The Nazi soldiers were no longer Nazis to the small group of believers; they were ordinary young men who spoke fondly of their mothers and sweethearts, even showing photos. They simply became human. The soldiers knew that these people could possibly end up in their homeland, and they gave their addresses with descriptions of the beauty of the land. A tenderness had emerged in them as if they knew there was no need for a superior race. Everyone was facing death, and that realization made them equal. The little ones were not considered merely children underfoot; when passing, the soldiers began to give them a gentle pat on the shoulder or a rub on the head. There was genuine softness now, under pressure.

During a brief letup in the bombing, some of the girls ventured upstairs in the farmhouse where the communication center for the warfront was installed. With great interest the children watched the switchboard operator calling out, "Achtung! Achtung! (Attention! Attention!)"

Noticing the visitors, the operator wheeled his chair around and with a twinkle in his eyes motioned for them to approach. He opened his wallet and showed them photos, smiling broadly.

"Mein mutter, mien liebchen (my mother, my sweetheart)," he said. The girls looked with keen interest, also smiling. They felt no fear of their captors.

One of the children's former schoolteachers from Pampali, who had been an extremely rude, arrogant person, came into the cellar. He had despised the Keikulises for their faith in Christ and had delighted in belittling the children of Christians in school. When the children saw him enter the bunker, they froze in fright, but they soon saw he was no longer an overconfident man. In fact, he did not appear to be completely stable. Slumping down next to Arvids, he asked what might be the outcome of the war. Arvids answered him kindly. They were no longer sectarian and educator but mere mortals preparing to face their maker. At times like these, even the atheist realizes that someone is in charge and everyone will have to give an account. The closer they came to the front and to death, the sinners' arrogance became less and less visible.

Their nature became gentle and more forgiving.

During these weeks, screams of panic had been heard repeatedly. However, in the presence of death, everyone was intensely somber. Arvids had joined his family in the cellar to help comfort and calm the children. He began seeking God and with a heavy heart questioned, "Lord, why must I go through this difficulty and despair with my family? I have not taken sides or been a part of this war."

Arvids and Cilite were prepared to be sent to Siberia for Christ's sake and therefore waited for the front to roll over so they might be sent to Russia, whose language they understood and spoke fluently. Early in their Christian walk the Lord had revealed to them that they would preach the gospel to Russians. Cilite had learned the language and culture in Moscow, and Arvids was conscripted in World War I to work for the Red Army. Cilite had spent time teaching her husband to improve his Russian skills before they had any idea how God was going to fulfill the call He had placed on their hearts.

Now on the warfront, as Arvids prayed, the answer came: "Your road to the east is closed. Take the one leading west."

"Lord, I will go, but let me remain here for the night," Arvids answered.

The heavy bombardment eventually subsided, and the families spent a relatively restful night. With the breaking of dawn on December 15, the Keikulises prepared to leave the cellar.

Just then, an attractive, well-dressed young woman came down the cellar steps. Arvids tried to speak to her about the seriousness of the time and whether she was prepared spiritually. She took one look at the group and grimaced, seeing that they were dirty, having spent nearly a month without baths or any convenience of normal living.

"You have a particular religion that adheres to suffering and sorrows," she said, eyeing them with scorn. "My philosophy is that everything will be just fine."

She was a cultured, intelligent woman and rambled on that she had packed her good clothes and new piano on a wagon and would wait till the front passed, and then she would go back to living as before. Surely this would all end soon, she supposed.

While making preparations to leave the area, Arvids and Cilite en-

147

couraged the others to come with them – to no avail.

So the Keikulis family and Mariana left the farm where they had suffered 22 days of indescribable difficulties, with death a constant threat. Although the weather had been cold, there had not been any snow. They took Cherry, the cow, and began walking through the side of the forest that seemed least exposed. However, for some time it seemed the shelling followed them. As they trudged through the woods, bullets pelted the trees like hard rain.

From years of practice they had learned to maintain calmness, and so they traveled on. Eventually, walking became easier, and they reached a small shelter in the forest where they stopped for a brief break. They were aware that they were covered by the grace of God, for they were never hit or even scratched.

As the family walked on through the trees, they came upon a loaf of bread lying on the ground. Then one of the children spotted another, then another. The bread was scattered about in a clearing several yards from the road, solidly frozen and intact, not decayed or dirty. They were so intent on walking to safety that no one seemed surprised at finding bread or wondering how it got there. Cilite passed around a pillowcase to hold the loaves.

Only later when they stopped for the night did they begin to contemplate how they had bread for 22 days in the potato cellar, and now on their journey, when there was no place to find or purchase food, they had been able to eat and remain alive due to an inexplicable provision. The bread was dark rye, the main supplement of a European diet, and it met their need for the next week of walking.

Along the way they were met by a wagon carrying German soldiers, who looked at the family in sympathy, trudging with a bunch of children and bundles on this cold winter day. Each child still had clothing and other items strapped in a pack on his back. In compassion, the soldiers gave them the wagon and horse. The children all wanted to jump on the wagon at once, but Arvids was concerned that they would freeze quicker if they stopped moving. They stared at their papa with wide eyes. In their little minds, traveling in a wagon would obviously be preferable to endless walking. Arvids could not persuade them all, and some jumped eagerly into the vehicle.

They soon found that riding was difficult over the bumpy, frozen ground. When they hit a stump, the wagon shook violently. Finally, a forceful jolt broke the axle, and the wheel fell off. More soldiers approached, attempting to clear the area of the many refugees seeking to escape the front.

The soldiers informed Arvids that they were on their way to evacuate their remaining guards and communication equipment from the farmhouse. The front had collapsed. Arvids related that some friends remained there, so the soldiers invited him to come along.

First Arvids took his own family to a safe area to await his return. Cilite removed her outer coat for the children to sit on until their papa came back.

In the potato cellar or wherever they stopped to camp, the family would recount God's faithfulness in stories from scripture. Taking turns, they told of what God did for the children of Israel and for Daniel in the lion's den. They recounted what God had done for Paul and Peter. The children nodded in agreement when their parents said, "Well, then God is still the same, and He is able to take care of us."

They also quoted their favorite promises. Thus they were strengthened and kept their minds on God as their fortress. They found that the words in Isaiah 26 proved true: "You will keep him in perfect peace, whose mind is stayed on you, because he trusts in you."

As Arvids and the soldiers approached the farmhouse, the bombing seemed to be directed at the compound. The place was caught in a crossfire. A large bomb had hit in front of the door, exploding horizontally, creating a large crater. It was almost unfathomable that the house had not been hit during 22 days of constant bombing, since the site was clearly visible. The people who had remained there were frightened and eager to evacuate.

As the soldiers and others busied themselves packing in preparation for leaving, Arvids hurried to get ready for a quick departure, and soon the two families reunited, grateful for God's protection. The Bartusevicses showed the Keikulises nine loaves of bread they had found on their way. They were the larger family, with seven children. It would take seven days to reach the port city of Liepaja. These loaves of bread would be their main sustenance to keep them alive until they reached the city.

The two families spent the next three nights in two different farm-houses that had been abandoned by their owners. At the first stop they learned that the house where they had spent 22 days had a direct hit and burned soon after Arvids' return trip with the soldiers. The same fate befell the other two farms after the families left. They heard that the intelligent young woman who had not taken the warfront seriously had been injured and crippled. They were told that she might have been saved had she been rushed to a hospital, but there was no possibility of rescue in the midst of the bombing.

The families were well aware that the hand of God was leading them one step ahead of destruction.

However, they realized they were still vulnerable to the danger of continued bombing. They had learned to interpret the initial sounds of various bombs and knew what could be expected to follow. Often they covered their ears and bent their heads. When explosions came close, the noise inside their heads felt like a pumpkin shattering from within. The brief lulls were fervently appreciated.

As they approached the third farmhouse, everyone was weary and exhausted, but Cilite's eyes lit up when she spotted a bathhouse. Like they had once enjoyed, most Latvian homes had outdoor buildings used as bathhouses, with a pile of large stones inside and water to be heated over a stove. The Keikulis family remembered the routine well: When the water and stones were hot, wooden buckets filled with cooler water were used to splash the hot rocks to create a sauna effect.

"Oh, I will get to wash all the children tonight!" Cilite exclaimed. They were all dirty from weeks of sleeping on potatoes or on the ground.

Just then a bomb hit the bathhouse, and the little building burst into flames. Cilite had been wearing two coats so she could use one to cover the children at night, and she was carrying Ilze. Seeing the destruction and the bathhouse going up in flames, she became disoriented. Acting swiftly, Arvids led her to sit on a tree stump nearby. In his commanding voice he told her to sit and not move. He then instructed the others to start marching toward the house and leave her and Ilze behind. It overwhelmed the girls, who did not understand how weary and perplexed their mother had become and that their papa was trying to prevent her from falling apart. At that point, she could not force herself to keep going.

Modra was especially upset to leave her mother behind. The only way she knew to vent her frustration was to say, "I cannot walk anymore, either."

"Modra, Papa wants you to carry this belt and the next time you decide you cannot walk anymore, you ask him to give you a spanking," Arvids said as he took off his belt.

Anna looked down at chubby little Modra, who was glancing tearfully back at her mother in fear and anguish. There she was, stumbling along on the frozen ground, sometimes sliding into the hard ruts. The children wore several layers of clothing, which added to their discomfort. Now the child was dragging a big belt behind her and a knapsack on her back, with two frightened eyes fighting back tears.

"Modra, would it be OK if I helped you with the belt?" Anna asked, waiting for her sister to catch up.

"Yes," the little one whispered.

Anna picked up one end of the belt, and they walked together. Pretty soon the fear left Modra's eyes. Anna recalled a scripture she had been taught, from Ecclesiastes 4:9-10: "Two are better than one, because they have a good reward for their labor; for if they fall, the one will lift up his companion."

Anna realized that her mother was not going to be left behind for nothing. We will always be together, she thought.

Arriving at the farmhouse, they walked into the barn and found a few animals left behind. Cherry could share a stall with the others. The straw was still warm, and it seemed that this was the best place for the children. It would be comfortable after a day of walking in the cold weather. Arvids settled the children inside the stalls and spoke reassuringly to them. He realized they were scared because this was the first time they had left their mama behind. After ensuring that they were all alright, he rehearsed their duties to each other.

"Who are you responsible for?" he asked each one, starting with Mariana and ending with Judite. The chain of responsibility created a close bond. Through that accountability, they knew they were not alone and that they would always take care of each other, no matter what happened.

Arvids then ran back about a mile to the edge of the woods. Needless to say, there was relief on everyone's faces when he returned with Cilite and baby Ilze. They were all together again and knew God would be with them.

He would never forsake them in this tragedy called war.

* * * * * * * * * * *

On December 19, 1944, the group finally reached Saldus, in central Latvia; its German name was Frauenburg. The railroad station was located here, and tents were set up to protect people from the bitter cold while they waited for the train. Cilite approached a Nazi officer to sell the cow. Cherry had traveled a long way with them, providing milk for the children. The officer gave Cilite a small amount of sugar and the bottom of a sack of farina (cereal grains). There was no bartering, just an exchange controlled by the officer. This little bit of food kept the families alive in the first internment camp, where no food was offered.

The next day the two families boarded a train that would take them to Liepaja, approximately 45 miles away. The only provision from the German troops was an unheated freight car. A trip that normally took three hours ended up being a 26-hour ordeal.

At one point artillery shells demolished the track ahead, leaving the train stranded in an open area for six hours. While the men tried to figure out how to repair the damaged rails, Cilite Keikulis, Madele Bartusevics, and their children sought shelter at a nearby home to keep from freezing.

A woman who answered the door was reluctant to allow them to enter – an understandable reaction, since they were a pathetic bunch.

"My children are sick, and we are freezing," Cilite implored. "Please let us in for the night."

The woman finally obliged, and the travelers settled on the floor around a stove in the kitchen. It was comforting to lie down close to one another.

All the time the men were working on the railroad, they were being shelled by artillery. They were also attacked by a single plane that dropped several bombs, damaging the railcars but leaving the freight car unscathed.

Upon returning to the freight car, the passengers saw an old man frozen to death, still sitting with his head on his knees. Arvids called for men to help bury him. A German soldier said there was no time for a burial and the ground was frozen anyway, to "put him in the ditch." Although they had seen hundreds killed at Cepurnieki, it was a shock to leave this body in a ditch.

Judite had been ill and wondered if she would be left that way if she died.

"Will I have to leave one of my children behind dead?" Arvids prayed.

God's answer was clear: "No, you will all reach your destination."

When the track was finally repaired, the train moved out of the dangerous open area.

These were agonizing hours. Everyone was tired, cold, and dirty. The children were sick. They could not remove their coats for fear of losing an extra layer that provided a bit of warmth. People were stuffed in railcars like the cattle that had previously occupied the space. Judite was running a high fever, and Arvids had to give up his overcoat to cover her. While she was in this condition, Arvids anointed her from the little bottle of oil that he carried in his pocket. Gathering around Judite's body, the family prayed that God would spare her. During the prayer, Judite opened her eyes and asked for water. Her lips were parched and dry. There was no water available, so with her fingernails Cilite scraped the frost off the inside of the train wall to moisten her daughter's mouth.

By the time they reached their destination, Judite had recovered.

Conditions in the freight car were overwhelming, even to a young mind. Anna had realized that Judite was not well. They were all hungry and uncomfortable. Few were able to lie down, for lack of room. A young mother was alone with her baby, who was crying from hunger and weariness. The mother tried to soothe the infant. As bomb explosions cast a light in the train, her taut face was revealed. She looked as if a part of her was not even there. She obviously heard the baby but was no longer able to respond to his cries. In the intermittent flashes of light, the travelers saw her remove her coat, dress, and slip. She then put her dress and coat back on and unwrapped the baby. As she took off the child's ragged clothes, steam rose from the wet body and soaked garments. The mother knew there was no way to change the baby except to use her slip, leaving less protection for herself. Finally the child quieted down and fell asleep.

As nine-year-old Anna closed her eyes, she could see in her mind the steam coming off that little wet body. She realized the situation was drastic. People were in despair. Without God they had no hope. At the same time, Anna knew she had hope. Her family had hope. Strangely enough, the children continued to place their hope in their parents' trust in God, and through them they knew they could trust, too. That is the way children learn and transmit. Arvids and Cilite shouldered a heavy responsibility to consistently direct their children's trust to a faithful Heavenly Father.

Among the refugees in the freight car was an atheist family whom the Keikulises knew well. All the travelers were near total mental and physical exhaustion but managed to stay composed, except for the atheists. At one point, they succumbed to the ever-present terror and began to scream hysterically. However, before reaching their destination, the atheist father came up to Arvids and, grabbing his hand, said, "We all would have perished here if it were not for you saints."

None of the bombs and artillery had hit their railcar.

When the train arrived in Liepaja at noon on December 21, 1944, the distraught refugees and their exhausted children – bundles and all – began stepping onto the platform at the station. Suddenly sirens started blowing, announcing an impending air raid, and people reacted by running and screaming. It was common knowledge that train stations were hit first because they were arteries of transportation. The two families finished gathering their few belongings out of the train, and they knew now by instinct that they would not run. They had learned that panic is an enemy.

Arvids directed them to put their bags in the middle of the platform floor. Seating the children on top of the luggage, he continued his instructions.

"Papa has no idea where there is a bunker," he said. "I have no idea where there is safety, so our only safety is to stay right here where God knows that we are. God knew that we would arrive right in the middle of this air raid, so we are just going to sit and wait it out."

Sometimes their father's orders seemed extreme, creating doubt among the family members. They felt an urge to run for shelter like the other passengers did; but as each looked at their papa's face, they saw that quiet, resolute peace again. Then they, too, felt calm, and fear began to dissipate.

After waiting for a period of time, the sirens announced that the air raid was over. There had been no bombs, to everyone's surprise and relief. At the train station soldiers were directing refugees to go directly to refugee camps. Because the Keikulises had family in Liepaja, they were permitted visits but had to report back to camps for lodging. The Keikulis family picked up their baggage and walked to Cilite's parents' home. Grandmother Paulina fed them warm food. For the first time in more than a month they ate well, took a bath, and changed their clothing.

"You know, a strange thing happened today at noon," Paulina said. "We did not have an air raid. For weeks now we have been having bombings in the mornings, at noon, and in the evenings at the same time. Maybe they are not going to bomb us anymore. They called it off!"

At first no one thought much about it; but for the next two weeks bombs fell at the same hours, three regular times a day, in Liepaja. The family realized that God had intervened the day they sat at the railroad station. What had seemed like a bad time to arrive was actually God's perfect timing.

I need to trust Papa, Anna thought to herself. He knew we would be OK.

By trusting her dad she was also trusting the Lord. It struck Anna's young heart and mind that because they belonged to the Lord, they were invincible. She had no doubt that He knew exactly where they were and had prevented the air raid that day. In every circumstance God is there, and He knows His children; He will never forsake them. The latest experience reminded her of Psalm 139:1-3 and 7-8:

O Lord, you have searched me and known me. You know my sitting down and my rising up; you understand my thoughts afar off. You comprehend my path and my lying down…
Where can I go from your Spirit, or where can I flee from your presence? If I ascend into heaven, you are there; if I make my bed in hell, behold, you are there.

* * * * * * * * * * *

For Christians, there are no surprises with God.

Yes, they were just as hungry or poor or deprived as the non-Christians, but they had confidence; and God proved Himself faithful, that He was there. He knew the problems they were experiencing and could hold back enemy planes or change adversaries' strategies – or work in other mysterious ways to accomplish His will for their lives.

In the evenings they knew to hurry suppertime because an air raid would come on schedule, so they prepared ahead of time to go into the bunker, everyone ducking down and huddling together. Liepaja was nearly flat, and everything was visible to enemy planes. Most people had bunkers where they could hide. German resistance was weak. It seemed like the Russians' bombing was a mere formality to show their power and that they were coming in.

After a few days, the families were temporarily separated and placed into refugee camps. The Bartusevicses and Mariana were placed on the third floor of one building, and the Keikulises ended up in a different camp not far away. Approximately 80 people occupied their large room, with no chairs or beds. Individuals and family groups placed bundles and luggage in a pile as a makeshift place to sit or recline. There was a daily roll call, and the Nazis began to select teens to separate from their families. People dreaded the worst of what might become of their youngsters. Rumors circulated about Nazi "so-called" experiments.

The Keikulises received permission to visit Cilite's parents, whose home was located across the street from a park separating the house from the beach. The park had been turned into anti-battery emplacements. When the anti-aircraft battery shot back at the planes, everyone

156

in the vicinity got the brunt end of the opposing sides, both noise and explosions. However, major military installations were targeted, not the city itself.

Russian bombers often flew over the city at night. First they would drop hundreds of flares attached to small parachutes that illuminated the area, making targets visible. It resembled a Christmas display, turning the darkness of night into brilliant daylight.

"Look at the pretty Christmas lights!" one of the children exclaimed, seeing flares all over the sky.

Then all hell broke loose.

The earth shook, buildings came down, and the noise from the anti-aircraft battery was almost unbearable. Back at the camps, when things quieted down, some of the refugees attempted to have a meager Christmas celebration.

No one was certain of the future.

A few days earlier, Arvids had been walking down the street and unexpectedly met a former colleague from the forestry department. The man said that their office had moved into the city and that Arvids could still draw his salary for the last several months, as well as receive special travel permits. In addition, all Latvians who worked had been required to have an identification (ID) card that was issued by the Nazis during the occupation period, and the man insisted that he be sure to get that as well, warning, "Never let go of these!"

Arvids declined at first, saying that "such things as money and paper have little value these days." Nevertheless, the man was persistent and persuaded his friend to drop by the forestry office.

Sure enough, Arvids was able to obtain travel permits not only for his wife and children, but also for the Bartusevicses, since he considered them his family in the Lord. He also asked for – and received – his ID card. The families would later board a ship to take them to Germany, where the papers and ID became invaluable.

Mariana, whose surname did not match either of the two families, was not given a permit to travel with the others. At 21 years of age and having a different last name, she had been placed in a separate camp with young people by this time. In the evenings she had visited the Keikulises to pray together. She feared she might be sent to a concentration camp in Germany.

Eventually she received papers to board a different ship than the families would travel on. She had begged for permission to join her friends but was denied. She came to them with the news, and after having prayer Arvids reassured her that God is able to change circumstances and encouraged her to see the authorities.

When Mariana pleaded with the officials for permission to travel with the Keikulises, she was turned down and ordered to take the ship to which she was assigned. Fighting disappointment, she recalled that all authority is given by God and that He has the final word.

Our lives are in God's hands, she thought. Men are not the ones to make the final decisions.

She continued to fast and pray.

Arvids and Cilite had connected with some believers in Liepaja and mentioned that they would be leaving for Germany on December 27. Plans were made to have a communion service for prayer, fellowship, and goodbyes. On the eve of their departure, the families met in an upstairs room with the congregation of the Liepaja church. They sang hymns and prayed for the journey of friends and loved ones, as well as for God's provision for the travelers and for those who remained.

As the communion cup was passed, air raid sirens started blowing. Lights went out, and the city went black. The believers continued their worship, commemorating their Savior's sacrifice for them in His suffering. They celebrated the sacrament of the Lord's Supper – one cup and a piece from the loaf of bread – tapping on the next person's shoulder as they passed it from one to another.

There was no heat, but no one seemed to mind the cold room. In their hearts they knew they might never meet again this side of heaven. The Pentecostals were in the habit of "greeting each other with a holy kiss" when a worship service was over. Women greeted women, and men greeted men. They were practicing this tradition in the dark when the lights came back on. A chubby old gentleman had bent down to kiss Anna and was embarrassed, but she just smiled.

The two families began getting ready to leave on the ship the next day. Mariana was crying, and two young soldiers who saw her asked why she was upset.

"My family is being sent to a different place, and I need permission to go," she tearfully replied.

That night, the ship to which Mariana had been assigned was destroyed in the port. Early the next morning – the day of the Keikulises' departure – came the announcement in her camp: "All people who are heading for Germany be prepared; a ship is waiting for you."

"Is it for singles, too, or only families?" Mariana questioned in surprise.

"Everyone," was the reply.

She was overjoyed, thanking the Lord that she would be able to go with her spiritual family.

Two days after Christmas the Keikulises said goodbye to their loved ones. Arvids stopped to see Brother Kumins and told him how the Lord had directed them to go west. Brother Kumins agreed that they must obey the Lord's leading.

"You will go far," he said. "I, too, would go, but the Lord has not pointed that way."

The two friends prayed together. Arvids Kumins had been an inspiration and spiritual father to Arvids Keikulis, and saying goodbye was poignant and heartrending.

For his faith, Brother Kumins was later arrested and served two seven-year terms in Siberia. He endured much suffering for Christ's sake, but the Lord used him there. He continued to be a blessing, preaching throughout Russia and in Latvia as soon as he was freed.

Chapter 5

Ship to German Prison Camps

On Wednesday afternoon, December 27, 1944, the Bartusevics and Keikulis families, along with Mariana, boarded a ship bound for Germany. The voyage was full of danger and uncertainties. The former battleship was escorted on either side by minesweepers, and the vessels moved out to sea slowly to avoid setting off mines. Russian submarines and planes patrolled the waters. The passengers had heard of Russian planes regularly attacking ships, having destroyed one the previous night.

"Papa, what if the Russian planes spot us?" Cilite questioned.

"Remember how God took care of the children of Israel on their journey?" Arvids spoke with his usual serenity.

"Ah, yes, He certainly did," Cilite murmured. She was reminded of the importance of keeping their focus on God's ever-present grace.

"God always takes care of His own and protects them," Arvids said.

The ship left the dock under cover of night, since in winter dark came between 2 p.m. and 3 p.m. The passengers had been instructed that there would be no lighting of cigarettes and no lights in cabins onboard.

Once inside, Arvids had not noticed the excitement building on deck. Russian planes were heard and spotted, and alarms started blasting. When he came out of the cabin, the crew was running for their gun stations to prepare to shoot back, and passengers were ordered to take cover.

161

Then, as if on cue, a low cloud rolled in, camouflaging the entire ship. Fog became so dense that no one could see Russian planes any longer – and neither could pilots see their intended target. People had to feel along the deck and walls to be able to walk through the thick precipitation.

When Arvids needed to escort Judite across the deck in the dense fog, she said, "Papa, please take me back to the ship."

The passengers could hear the roar of planes above and bombs splashing in the water, but they were safe under the cloud – in God's divine protection. For the remainder of the day as the ship slowly sailed out to sea, the fog hung close, providing a blanket of safety.

Although the wind was not severe, the passengers were affected by seasickness. Hallways and lavatories were full of people who had passed out and were oblivious to others stepping over them. The air reeked with vomit.

In the late evening of December 28, the shipped docked at Pilau, Germany, during a blizzard. Cilite and the two youngest children were placed on a truck; and the other women and children were ordered to walk more than a mile to an internment camp, which was a holding area for further assignment to prison camps. The site was encircled by tall barbed-wire fencing, and mean-looking guards jerked on the leashes of their vicious, trained dogs. This holding camp would be the refugees' home until they could be assigned to prison labor camps.

Initially the children were placed in separate barracks according to age groups. They were frightened since it was the first time they had been separated from each other, forced into crowded rooms among strangers – without their parents. The barracks were not heated, and there were no beds or cots. Everyone searched for a place to sleep on the scantily strewn straw on the floor. The men and boys were detained on the ship to help unload cargo.

At 12 p.m. Arvids and Janis arrived at the camp with the other men and found that the children had been assigned to separate rooms. Breaking the rules, Arvids and Janis searched each barrack – within sight of the guards. It took several hours, but no one stopped or questioned them as they gathered the families together and found a spot on the floor of one of the buildings to try to sleep. It was a relief to be together again and feel the safety of family.

In the morning they awoke to find smoke filling the room from the pot-bellied stove in the center. Although the barracks had no heat source, small cook stoves were located in some of the buildings for those who had brought food. The refugees stood in line to take turns boiling their one potato or soup on the stove. A deaf-mute family was being pushed and shoved, so Cilite ushered them to the front of the line. Soldiers walked in with a large can of milk and almost caused a riot. Each child had a metal cup to be filled; Judite nearly fainted while waiting for her portion. The meager ration of food did not satisfy the crowd's hunger, and Cilite was happy to have the farina she had traded for the cow. This helped the children – while it lasted. One day when Judite spotted red apples on top of a garbage pile, she became excited and climbed up to get them. She was disappointed to discover they were too rotten to eat.

The refugees had to wade through snow to get to the outhouses. Although they were not treated like prisoners, they were captives without rights.

At any given time at the internment camp, one or two of the girls in the group were ill. That was the case when they heard everyone was being shipped to a work camp. When time came to move out of the barracks, soldiers ordered all refugees to walk to the distant railroad station. Arvids refused, saying the children were too sick to walk the distance in the cold weather. He told the families to sit down and wait. After a period of shouting and cursing, the soldiers left them by the side of the road outside the camp. Finally another soldier yelled a command.

Arvids answered in Latvian.

"I will take care of you, but please do not acknowledge that I speak Latvian," the soldier said softly as he approached.

To avoid disclosing his identity, he ordered in German to follow him and then motioned for them to board a truck. They passed other refugees still walking to the train station. At the station the soldier escorted them to a warm car with soldiers in it, gave them food, and disappeared. How grateful they were for God's providence to provide a ride with a friendly Latvian – in a vehicle with heat!

* * * * * * * * * * * *

On January 2, 1945, the families arrived in the city of Konigsburg, Germany. Here they were to live under constant Nazi terror for a week.

At first glance they knew they were in trouble. Everything was altogether different. The internment camp they had left was surrounded by tall, barbed-wire fences with guards closely watching every move; now they were prisoners housed in large block buildings. At the previous camp they had slept on thin blankets or straw on the floor. Here Cilite spread her overcoat on the floor to provide a place for the children to snuggle together for warmth.

It was cold outside, and frozen bodies were stacked in a large pile. Nearby, in another big snow-covered pile was frozen, rotten cabbage. The new arrivals soon learned that the cabbage was to be cooked in water and served as soup. It smelled awful; yet the children eagerly gobbled their portions. Before long, everyone had the dreaded dysentery.

In the morning, all refugees – including children – were served coffee and a small piece of rye bread. The Nazis continuously shouted orders and propaganda, calling out individuals for interrogation. When the elderly or sick did not respond immediately, they were kicked and cursed.

Some of the refugees who had recently left their homes still had meager amounts of food with them. The Keikulises, Bartusevicses, and Mariana had run out long ago. A lady offered them a small sack of dried bread crusts.

The mornings started with loudspeakers blaring, "Achtung! Achtung! (Attention! Attention!)"

While the German national anthem played, the prisoners – including children – were forced to run out into the snow and line up in the courtyard for roll call and instructions for the day's work – orders interspersed with Nazi propaganda. Anna was sick with a high fever and confined to their room when the others went outside. The refugees were freezing as they stood in slush and snow. When Judite became cold and shaky, Cilite whispered, "Go inside."

Little Judite walked past the speaker and slipped back into the building unnoticed.

Years later, when Judite sat in a church service in the United States and heard a hymn sung to the tune of the German national anthem, she experienced sudden stomach cramps, and tears rolled down her cheeks. It brought her back to the harsh morning rituals in the prison camp.

On another morning when everyone was called into the courtyard, the Keikulis family happened to be on the front row. Fully armed guards walked up and down the rows picking out teenaged boys to ship to the front lines in an awaiting truck. Janis's name was among the first called, and he and the other boys were directed to stand in a separate line. Goodbyes were not allowed, and there was no information provided to families to indicate where they might contact their sons. The youths, as well as their loved ones, found it difficult to hold back tears. In his heart Arvids was calling upon the Lord, "Must I sacrifice my son to this senseless war?"

"No, his place is by your side," was the answer he heard in his heart.

Arvids stepped out of the line where he had been ordered to stay and went across the field lined with yellow shirts, party functionaries, and armed soldiers.

No one stopped him.

The Nazis continued yelling orders. Janis happened to be at the end of his line. All the boys' faces were pale and frightened, but none dared to glance back at their parents.

When Arvids came to Janis, he said, "Follow me, son. Your place is by my side."

Accustomed to obedience, Janis left the ranks despite the presence of an armed soldier next to him. Another youth turned to the soldier and complained about Janis's leaving. The soldier ordered him to shut up.

Before the eyes of the whole crowd, father and son returned to their places in the front row. The peace of God and His courage were upon Arvids, and it did not enter his mind to hide or be afraid.

"What are you doing?" one of the other parents questioned.

"You take care of your family," Arvids replied. "I am taking care of mine."

The prisoners spent a long time freezing on the field until the soldiers finished their procedure and left with the young men. No one noticed Janis anymore.

The next day Arvids was walking outside the camp during permitted curfew. He encountered a German stranger who asked, "Are you a Christian?"

Arvids was surprised by the man's friendly demeanor. Although he knew little German, Arvids soon recognized Bible verses being spoken. By exchanging scripture passages, Arvids managed to communicate to the gentleman that he was a pastor from Latvia and his family was imprisoned in the camp. The kind man followed Arvids back to camp and asked the commandant for permission to have the family as guests for dinner that evening.

To everyone's disbelief, permission was granted. It was an unexpected blessing to share a normal meal in a normal home at such a time. Again, using familiar scripture, they overcame the language barrier. The German brother stated that their church had been forewarned by the Spirit that trouble was coming. Some Christians had left the country, but he and his family had chosen to remain and minister.

While the Keikulis family was warming to the good-natured Christian fellowship, the German brother's wife noticed that Judite was lethargic and kept a blank stare on her face. As the families shook hands at the door, the hostess pointed to Judite and told her husband, "I'd like this one to return tomorrow to play with our daughter."

Once again, the German brother asked for – and received – permission from the camp commandant.

The next morning Arvids walked back to the pastor's home with Judite. The pastor's daughter sat on the floor, making motions that they were having a make-believe tea party. Neither child could speak the other's language but easily became absorbed in the activity. The little hostess "cut" her bread and put a slice on an imaginary plate for Judite and then for herself, smiling and nodding. Judite smiled and nodded back as she received it. Then the "tea" was poured into pretend cups, each girl stirring and resting the spoons. The girls held their cups properly as they sipped the tea, extending their pinkies. Between the "bites" of bread and "sips" of tea, they moved their mouths as if speaking, nodding their heads and raising their eyebrows with expression and smiles.

They were most surely having a proper tea party – two little girls from widely diverse cultures, in time of war, connecting in their hearts.

This experience was therapeutic for Judite, and Arvids and Cilite could see the light had returned to their daughter's sad eyes. Back in Latvia, Judite had loved the times when her mama had brought out Grandma's china teacups to serve tea or hot cocoa to family and guests. She had helped her mother serve and cherished the pleasant conversations.

Much later as an adult in the United States, Judy – as she was known – realized what a precious gift her Heavenly Father had provided. She enjoyed collecting china cups and tea sets, which she gave as hostess and wedding gifts. In the 1990s Latvia was free once more, and the Keikulis sisters began visiting their cousins. Over the years Judy brought or sent her older cousins beautiful china tea sets.

The following day a Latvian major visited the camp, and Arvids became acquainted with him. On that day the family was served a better portion of food – barley porridge.

Major Kripens told about the conditions at the front and said that this city would soon fall to the mounting Russian pressure. He expressed concern about the many Latvians here that would not have a chance to escape except for the few that possessed travel permits issued back in Latvia by the proper authorities. These were the same papers Arvids had been reluctant to pick up from the forestry office. Major Kripens assured him that the permits would allow the family to leave the prison camp. He advised Arvids to leave Konigsburg immediately and warned him not to surrender the documents to anyone. He said that trains would likely be filled to capacity by escaping German nationals who, as expected, would have first choice. The families were relieved at the news, and they all prayed for God's help and blessings.

Because of Major Kripens' influence, the camp officers came through the rooms asking who had special travel permits. Arvids was the only one to raise his hand. Madele Bartusevics quickly followed suit. She had written on their passports the same address that was on the Keikulises' documents. When the officer saw the same address, he granted permission for both families to leave the camp.

Mariana was told she would be sent to a different camp. She did not want to be separated from her loved ones and was clearly upset.

"Mariana, you fast and pray, and we will fast and pray," Arvids said. "God is able to make a way. We will be waiting for you at the station."

Although troubled, Mariana fasted and prayed fervently. She was uncomfortable being away from her family. That evening as she walked alone in the hallway of her building, tears streamed down her face.

A young Nazi soldier was approaching from the other end of the building, and he noticed her crying.

"Hey, Fraulein, why are you so sad?" he asked.

"I do not have any family," she said, daring to share her heart. "The family I came here with is more than my own family. Now they are leaving, and I am appointed to a different camp."

"Do you want to go with them?" he asked.

"Yes," she answered, "but I do not have a ticket."

"It does not matter," he said. "Give me some money, and I will get you a ticket."

By this time a young man from another refugee family had walked up and heard the conversation. Wishing to leave himself, he and Mariana both gave the Nazi soldier money for tickets. The soldier returned a short time later with tickets for two.

The next morning an order blared over the loudspeaker: "No refugees leaving today! The gates will be locked!"

Mariana and the young man wondered if that meant none of them could leave. In addition to train tickets, refugees needed permission slips to travel. The Keikulises and Bartusevicses had them, but Mariana did not.

Arvids went to Mariana at once.

"Mariana, if you want to meet us at the train station, you will have to use faith as your travel permit," he said. "Go to the gate and tell them you are going to town, and we will be praying for you. Then spend the rest of the day at the German Baptist brother's house. We will see you at the train station."

After praying with her family, Mariana walked alone – suitcase in hand – to the front gate, where she met two Nazi soldiers armed with machine guns.

"Guten morgen (good morning)," she smiled and said.

"Where are you going, young lady?" they asked.

"I'm going to town," she answered.

The soldiers waved her on. She wondered if they had forgotten the announcement over the loudspeakers. She did not hasten her steps or turn around but continued walking slowly to the German brother's house.

Due to God's intervention through Major Kripens and travel permits, the families found themselves leaving the well-guarded camp on January 9, 1945. Their appearance was ragged and sickly, and they knew their belongings were of no value to anyone except themselves. It was obvious that they had come from the war zone. Many of those remaining were from well-to-do families and had hung onto their most precious possessions.

The commandant released the Keikulises and Bartusevicses with courtesy, and provisions were provided for their journey to Sudetenland, Czechoslovakia. At the gate the guard addressed Arvids as "sir" and expressed his opinion that they should not have been in this kind of camp in the first place. Arvids was surprised at the special treatment.

The Nazi soldier who had gotten the tickets met Mariana at the train station to see that she made it onto the train safely. He took her to the front of the line, and soon Mariana was reunited with the rest of the family. She was keenly aware that when humans put their trust in God, He is able to drastically change outcomes – at times using one's enemies -- as Proverbs 16:7 states: "When a man's ways please the Lord, He makes even his enemies to be at peace with him."

The trains were jam-packed. People and luggage were pulled in through windows, and children were passed overhead like parcels. After a lot of pushing and shoving, everyone managed to find a seat. Arvids and Cilite, with Ilze in their laps, settled by a window.

Mariana and the young man who had also bought a ticket from the helpful soldier sat behind them. The conductor came down the aisle, checking tickets and travel permission slips. They all began to pray, since Mariana and the youth had not been able to obtain visas. The train was kept dark to avoid being spotted by enemy planes, so the conductor used a flashlight to check tickets. People were tired, and babies were crying. The family firmly believed if the Lord could bring Mariana this far, He could protect her further.

"Lord," Mariana prayed, "you are able to take me through. Please keep the conductor from questioning me."

Just then little Ilze told her mother that she needed to use the toilet. Cilite took the child to the door of the facility, finding it occupied. Ilze's expression and body language conveyed that she could not wait long, so someone handed Cilite a bucket. Setting it down near the toilet door, Ilze quickly used it, with Cilite trying to shield her for privacy. The conductor angrily turned from checking tickets and passed by just before he was to check Mariana.

"Schřeinerei für flugten ausländer (d---- foreigner!)" he shouted, leaving the car with a disgusted face.

In that moment Mariana's fate was decided by a toddler's physical need. It saved the day! Her companion's eyes were bulging, and beads of perspiration had formed on his forehead. Fortunately, darkness had provided the protection he needed to keep from giving himself away. When the conductor left, the young man breathed a sigh of relief, saying, "Thank God!"

The trip took about 30 hours. If a passenger had a pressing need to relieve himself, he was forced to do it through the window since all lavatories and hallways were full of people and baggage. When the train stopped in Dresden, the travelers were told they would have to wait there for the next train.

Connections were difficult due to the bombing and massive destruction of railways. The Keikulises and Bartusevicses stepped into the large station and glanced up to see a beautiful glass dome, an architectural masterpiece, with the sun shining through and smoke from the locomotives disappearing into the high structure. In normal times, the travelers might have thought this magnificent feature worth pausing to take a closer look, but on this day they had other priorities.

By this time, the children were extraordinarily hungry and weak. There was little energy left in anyone. The group found it difficult to stay together. Cilite was again loaded down with two coats, and Ilze lagged behind, physically exhausted and fatigued. Each child, with a small suitcase or knapsack, held another's hand, trying desperately to navigate through a mass of wall-to-wall bodies anxious to find an exit.

The war front was moving faster than any train could transport them to safety.

With the combination of a language barrier, loud announcements blaring on the loudspeakers, and constant shoving, Cilite became disoriented. Anna looked quickly from her papa to her mama. Responsible for Judite, whose hand she held, she also tried to check on Modra. As Arvids plowed through the crowd, he looked back over his shoulder and realized Cilite was overcome with it all.

With a twinkle in his eyes – something the children had not seen in months – he called out, "Hey, vecen (old lady)!"

In a split second Cilite regained her normal composure, and she was mad.

"Who are you calling an old lady?" she yelled back.

The playful comment had immediately accomplished what was needed. It was imperative that they move as one through the crowd. The children had expected their father's command of "peace," and they all giggled to see how their mama reacted to the teasing. Like little chickadees, they followed their leader through the congested station.

Since no train would leave until morning, the Keikulises and Bartusevicses spent the night in a large room on the second floor of the station, where they were brought some soup. Prisoners of war in the same room were not permitted to talk or sit but kept walking in a circle with hands behind their backs.

Compassionately moved, Anna joined in walking beside one of the men without saying a word, her hands behind her back. Cilite offered him some of her soup, but he declined, saying softly, "No, thank you. We're not permitted."

Then reaching into his pocket, he handed Anna a bar of soap, not missing a step in the forced rhythm of marching.

Chapter 6

Czech Labor Camps

Around midnight on January 10, 1945, the families arrived in a small town called Deutsch Kralup. This was in Sudetenland, which had been part of Czechoslovakia. It was still under German occupation. They stayed in a hotel provided especially for employees of the Latvian forestry department in the center of town.

On February 1 the families were relocated to the Hotel Ritter Von Kunevic in the town of Keller, a few miles out of Deutsch Kralup. The former rambling, old-fashioned hunting lodge had been converted into a voluntary work camp. The lodge mainly held refugees who were foresters needing shelter and provisions.

The Keikulises and Bartusevicses were pleasantly surprised that this camp had no armed guards or barbed-wire fences. Occupants were free to come and go at will and even walk into town.

Mariana was placed in a women's labor camp five-and-a-half miles away from Keller in a town called Komitau. There were 29 girls of nine different nationalities. Everyone was hungry, dirty, and depressed – which often led to loud arguing. Strewn on the bunk beds was straw teeming with bugs and lice. Mariana looked for a place to pray.

She was put to work in a metal factory where she would have to work on Sundays. During her curfew she walked the long way to see the Keikulises and told them about her dilemma.

"You know our stand that the scripture says the Sabbath day is holy," Arvids said. "If you want to serve the Lord, you must follow what He says."

After a time of prayer, the family said goodbye and embraced her with the words, "If we don't meet again here on earth, we'll see you in the presence of the Lord. Be faithful to Him."

On Sunday morning Mariana went to the office to inform the authorities of her decision not to work on the Lord's Day. Her commanding officer was a large woman with a reputation of being tougher than any man. Mariana asked if she could work extra hours on six days in order to have Sundays off.

"What is your reason?" the officer barked.

Mariana explained that she believed in the Lord and desired to obey His commands, one of which is to keep the Sabbath Day holy. Working on Sunday would be against her commitment.

The commandant was enraged, looking as if she could kill Mariana on the spot.

"I'm going to report you, and the Nazi soldiers will come and shoot you!" she screamed. "I want to see where your faith is when your brains are splattered across this wall."

The peace that passes all human understanding kept Mariana calm.

"I believe in the God that delivered Daniel from the lion's den and the three Hebrew children from the fire," she replied, without hesitation. "I believe in the same God that sent an angel to take Peter out of prison. If God calls me to die for His name, I'm ready."

The insolent woman called her commanding officer on the phone to report Mariana's outrageous request, expecting a verdict of death. In a minute she was heard saying, "Yes, sir. Yes, sir."

Obviously surprised, the officer hung up the phone and told Mariana she could work two extra hours on four days of the week to make up for her time off on Sunday. She seemed embarrassed to have to explain this to Mariana, since it was apparent nothing would have pleased her more than to have the girl shot.

Mariana walked out of the office victoriously, praising the Lord. On Sundays she would get permission to leave the camp and could meet the Keikulises in the woods, where they would pray and worship together, weather permitting.

One day she was heading down the road away from her building at the work camp to find a place to pray and read the Bible. Wherever she went, she had to remember to show an identification card with a number and photo on it.

Within a short time, a farmer riding an ox-drawn cart pulled up beside her and jumped down.

"What are you reading?" he asked.

"I'm reading the Bible, God's Word," Mariana replied.

"And what are you doing here?" he continued, staring at her photo ID.

"I'm at the work camp," she said. "Why? Do you read the Bible?"

As the man came closer, Mariana knew he had evil intentions. Raising her voice, she exclaimed, "Are you married? How dare you touch me? How dare you want to defile me!"

The farmer turned away and jumped back into the cart, leaving Mariana on the road.

Another time, when Mariana was stooping down to tie her shoe, she saw a guard ready to kick her. As she caught his eye, he yelled, "Are you Polack?" There was deep resentment for Poles from past occupations.

"Would you kick me less if I weren't?" Mariana responded.

Startled and ashamed, the guard turned and walked away.

"Lord, how long will I have to suffer not being treated like a human?" Mariana cried out to God.

"I will take you to the land where you will eat all you want, but when you are there, forget me not," she heard the Lord answer distinctly, as though audible.

How can that be? Mariana thought.

"Lord, my times are in your hand," she prayed. She soon forgot the incident and the promise.

Five years later, when Mariana was in the United States, she made 50 cents an hour working in a factory. Always grateful, she walked to work and back to save money. She was able to send packages to help displaced people still in camps hoping for immigration to America. She could buy all the white bread and bananas she wanted. Then she remembered God's promise to her in a desperate moment. "Yes, Lord," she murmured humbly. "Your word came true. I can eat all I want and whatever I want."

Mariana worked at large grinding machines in the sheet metal factory. Women were paid for their labor but had to buy coupons to eat meager fare in the camp's kitchen. One meal a day was served, and the menu was often rotten potatoes, occasionally served with a sauce. In the mornings they received only black coffee. On Sundays a bread roll was included. A loaf of bread was distributed at the beginning of the week that was to last seven days.

It seemed that in the bleakest of times God provided a special bright moment for the suffering. On a cold, wintry day Mariana was particularly hungry and whispered her need to the Lord as she walked outside. There, as if illuminated by a spotlight, she saw colorful apples lying in the snow in a ditch in front of her. As she picked them up, she noticed they were warm and fresh. With grateful anticipation, she bit into one, thinking she would hide the others for later.

She ate all three.

* * * * * * * * * * *

In the camp at Keller, the Keikulises were placed in a large room that held about 80 people, sleeping in double bunks next to each other. There were no mattresses in the bunks, just straw. Narrow walkways along the wall allowed crowded, limited access to the bunks. Although there were enough bunks for all family members, they usually chose to sleep two together for warmth in the unheated building. Cilite would stand at the foot of the bunks, tucking the children in with a brief prayer. In her prayer she was giving them into the Heavenly Father's care. Instead of ending with "amen," she said, "Sleep as though you were nestled in God's ear." More often, she ended with, "Even so, come Lord Jesus." Those words were like a security blanket to the children.

Food rations were meager and of little nutritional value. Here Arvids and Janis worked in the forest, since Arvids' identification card and travel permits from Latvia showed his experience. If they made or exceeded their quota for the month, they were given extra food rations – a larger piece of bread and a piece of smoked sausage.

The family's world had become dull and somber, and everyone was downcast from long months of malnutrition and sickness. Arvids noticed Anna specifically, that in conversation she no longer responded to the beauty of colors. There was a perceptible absence of any of the children's former antics and expressions. Arvids realized that his family needed a diversion, a glimpse of beauty to feed their souls.

So he began to plan and announced that they all would go with him and Janis to the woods the next day for a special event. His voice indicated they might discover something out of the ordinary.

Prayer and Bible reading were held daily in the room; but with so many people housed there, the Keikulises went to the woods for church services when weather permitted. On this particular Sunday Cilite dressed the children in their best, the one extra piece of clothing they had brought from Latvia. The girls started to perk up.

Their papa was waiting and explained that they were going to climb up the hill where he and Janis worked. It looked high and daunting to them.

"Do we have to go up there?" came the grumbles from the group, still frail from their recent experiences.

"Yes, indeed!" Arvids said excitedly.

Although the children were initially reluctant, their father knew how to tempt their tired minds with new discoveries awaiting them. Little footsteps became deliberate as spirits began to soar, and they hastened the pace. Stepping on crunchy snow, the group finally made it to the top of the hill.

When people's eyes are downcast, they give the impression that they are simply trying to exist. Arvids had recognized it was time to lift his family's eyes. How well he remembered what Jesus had said to His disciples in John 4:35-37:

Lift up your eyes and look to the fields...

It was a clear, sunny day. He began to point out how the sun reflected multiple colors on the snow.

"And look at that bird over there!" he exclaimed. "Do you see the bright color when he opens up his wings?"

Although they knew God had put the colors there, in their despondency the children had not recently taken the time to notice the splendors of nature.

Then with a grand gesture Arvids exclaimed, "Ahaha vota!" as he usually did when he had a surprise for the children. He asked them to stoop down to see the first wildflowers peeking through the snow's crust.

"Look closely at the colors, how they stand out," he said. He urged each child to examine the soft petals and focus on the delicate shades. The flowers and wild scallions represented new life.

Suddenly, as if slowly being awakened, the children began to make normal chatter among themselves.

"Ooh, aah, yes! That's so pretty!" they exclaimed.

They were seeing again that each new day, with all its twists and turns in the road, is a day God has given. Their papa had helped them see how God, their Creator, placed beauty all around, but they had to look for it and take time to fully appreciate it. Even though life had thrown them into hopelessness, their Heavenly Father was absolutely still at work. Satan, working through the Nazis and Communists, had taken away the dignity of man, but God never changed.

Hope was alive.

Arvids then unrolled a blanket for Cilite and the girls to sit on while he and Janis built a fire. Again he called out his familiar "Ahaha vota!" They knew a special surprise was coming, and everyone looked at him in anticipation.

Arvids brought out the loaf of bread and small smoked sausage for which he and Janis had worked harder to surpass their goal. Each child was given a pointed stick to harpoon a slice of sausage and place it above the hot coals. They had little patience for waiting and impulsively ate the sausages half-cold, asking for more. The bread was eaten with as much enthusiasm, and they relished each bite. Thus their monthly ration disappeared.

The group lingered a while longer talking about the sights they had seen, basking in dazzling sunshine beneath an endless blue sky. Making their way back down the hill, the Keikulis children no longer dragged their feet because they had "lifted up their eyes" and been renewed.

* * * * * * * * * * * *

At the camp the family was allowed about one pound of bread per day for seven people, plus a bit of margarine. Later they were able to secretly buy a few potatoes. Anna had begun showing signs of illness back in Germany, and Arvids and Cilite had assumed it was due largely to starvation and the challenging conditions. Also, the long train ride had been taxing and difficult. Now Anna was experiencing extreme abdominal pain and blackouts. Her body seemed to be deteriorating.

Years later, Anna was found to have had a ruptured appendix during that time in the prison and labor camps. It had developed into a tumor the size of a grapefruit and had to be surgically removed.

Because of Anna's weakening condition, a few locals tried to help. A sympathetic German lady brought in some broth, and the lady inn-keeper was compassionate with Anna in her suffering. She came and knelt by the bed, trying to offer encouragement by saying that every-thing would be fine. She had gone to her priest, who held a mass and lit candles for the sick girl. When the lady had described the pain and agony Anna was experiencing, the priest scrambled to find something to give her. Later the innkeeper and her little girl brought in a bright red apple the priest had sent. In those days, an apple in winter was a rarity, a precious gift.

Anna thought it was the most beautiful thing she had ever seen.

Cilite took Anna and Judite to a doctor in town in an effort to obtain increased food rations. Upon seeing the sick girls, the doctor stepped back and gasped, "Mein Gott, mein Gott (my God, my God!)"

He hesitated, not wanting to come too close. He handed Cilite a prescription for a pound of butter and some cod liver oil. They took the prescription to the store to buy food. However, if they did not salute, "Heil Hitler," they would be chased out, so they ducked behind others who were saluting.

Anna heard women talking when they thought she was asleep. They were saying that she was not going to make it. She pondered the pos-sibility. It seemed to her that a mere illness could not kill one after surviving all those bombs.

The Lord did spare her, though there were years of pain.

On Saturdays each refugee family was given a bucket of water to use for bathing and laundry. The well had been destroyed by bombs, making water a scarce commodity. The Keikulises strung up blankets around their bunk beds. One by one, Arvids made each child strip and wash. Then they would wrap themselves in a blanket. When everyone had bathed, Cilite washed their clothes in the same water and hung them outside to dry so they could dress again. If the children questioned whether the procedure was worthwhile, Arvids would insist that it was important, even necessary, to feel good about oneself in these crowded, unsanitary camps. Thus, as much as possible, they strove to preserve their dignity and self-respect.

Modra, now four years old, had developed a staph infection on the top of her head. It swelled up an inch-and-a-half, and her eyes were ringed in blue. The swollen area was larger than a fist, producing pressure and pain. Due to the crowded quarters, head lice were rampant, and there were no means of getting rid of them. Cilite tried to wash Modra's head and hair by melting snow in a bowl on the small woodstove, hoping to destroy the lice in her hair. Squeezing a rag in the boiled water, Cilite daubed the hot cloth on the cyst.

The little girl prayed weakly in the midst of her pain, "Dear Lord Jesus, I know you can heal me and make me well. Please take the pain away."

Modra's pleas touched a tender-hearted Latvian teacher in the room. She had some enamel jars of honey she had brought from home in suitcases of family valuables. As the need arose, she sold the items for food and other necessities. In a spirit of compassion she brought milk and honey to Modra.

The children continued to suffer the effects of malnutrition and substandard living conditions. Upon arriving in Czechoslovakia, Ilze developed severe dysentery and fever, causing hemorrhaging, and her large intestine had dropped out onto her mother's lap. Cilite could only push it back in – and pray. The child had stopped talking in sentences and had forgotten how to walk and talk.

The family had to teach her as if she had never learned before. Her baby talk the second time around was humorously different from the first time. She had a habit of repeating the last syllable of words and gave people names of her own invention. However, as she developed and grew, she became the family's healthiest child, with no sign of her former suffering.

Ilze, who was still a toddler, became increasingly weak. For the past year their diet had not included the vitamins and protein required for a young child to develop. They all had boils and sores on their bodies from severe deficiencies, and Ilze became so weak and feeble that she could no longer walk. She moaned "ma-ma-ma" endlessly. By now her stomach was badly swollen from malnutrition. There were boils on her head. For several months she could not talk or respond to anything. When someone lifted her up, her head rolled as if disconnected from her body, unable to support itself. Her body was thin and frail, while her head looked large in comparison to her body. Her abnormalities were frightening.

Anna was trying to recover from months of severe pain and high fever, and her teeth were loose. Arvids called the condition "zing" and told her to eat the small meals carefully. He assured Anna that her gums would become strong again once she had proper food. Judite was thin and frail, and her teeth had turned black. Modra was weak and suffered pain from the large cyst on her head. Janis walked gingerly with a limp and kept pulling up the sides of his boots. He had long ago outgrown them and cut holes in the leather, wrapping rags over the soles to make them wearable. He went to his daily work of cutting trees with his feet hurting. He also suffered from a painful boil on his neck, causing him to walk with a stoop.

Seeing his children's desperate condition and feeling helpless to provide for them, Arvids broke down and, like Job in the Bible, cried out, "Cursed is the day I was born! From this day we will never again celebrate my birthday" (Job 3:1). He left for work handing his piece of bread to Ilze, who could barely hold it, much less eat it. Ilze had been rocking back and forth. Taking the bread with trembling hands, she put it to her heart, still rocking. Cilite encouraged her, saying, "Eat it, Ilze. Eat it." And so she tried.

For so long Arvids had been the one to stimulate everyone's moods and outlook; now his face looked haunted, and his eyes were sunk in.

But Arvids hung onto the hope that God would answer their prayers. As days went by, his faith increased, and he decided to do that which had become a habit in his family and his parish, to anoint the dying person with oil, according to James, Chapter 5. Although the bottle was almost empty since oil had not been available during the final months of the war, he was able to shake one more drop out of it to anoint and commit Ilze into the Lord's hands.

When the family immigrated to the United States four years later, the children asked, "Papin, may we celebrate your birthday now?" Only then was the annual event resumed.

Cilite showed patience and quiet strength during the darkest times. When Ilze's dysentery was severe, the mother routinely pushing back the intestine as big tears streamed down her face unhindered.

However, she held her composure, and there was no sobbing or weeping – only plop-plop-plop as the tears fell onto her chest. When she daubed at Modra's cyst and picked out the lice, plop-plop-plop went the tears rolling down her cheeks onto her blouse. Then she put coals into the old iron to get it hot. Pushed back and forth over the seams of the dirty, smelly clothes, the iron sizzled as it hit lice. Again tears fell softly – plop-plop-plop. When the children had to put on the same unwashed clothes, they were warm, having been pressed and anointed with their mama's tears.

Behind each tear was a silent, heartfelt prayer.

Arvids and Cilite thought of trying to lance the swelling of Modra's cyst to relieve the pressure, but the infection was too far beneath the scalp. Cilite stood over Modra and shuddered. Blue lines had started down her temples. The child could no longer see or walk from weakness, but still she prayed – and her mother prayed, "There is nothing we can do for her, Lord. If your hand doesn't touch her, there is no hope."

A few hours later they saw 20 or 30 pin-sized holes in Modra's scalp begin squirting pus like little fountains. Arvids and Cilite wiped her head until all the liquid had drained and the swelling was gone. Modra fell into a deep sleep and rested well through the night. By morning all the blueness and swelling had disappeared, and her color had returned.

With that, Modra lost the hair on her head where the cyst had been. With typical feminine modesty, she was self-conscious of her baldness, and Cilite tried to comb the hair over on the sides as a cover. Before long, new hair began to grow in puffy little ringlets all over the top of her head, making her the object of attention with the pretty new hairdo. Until the new hair grew out as long as the rest of her hair, she had thick curls on top. Ladies and children often stopped to ask how her mother could achieve such an attractive style.

"I used to have a big sore on top of my head," Modra would proudly reply with a wide smile.

"Oh, I wish I could have a big sore like that – to give me such pretty curls," the other girls would say, with unabashed envy.

* * * * * * * * * * *

Around this time Anna asked her dad, "Papin, how come God is not answering some of our prayers?"

"Dear daughter," Arvids answered, "the rain falls on the righteous and the unrighteous alike, but always remember: We have Him. We may be uncertain of many things, but we are certain of God."

Anna was satisfied.

* * * * * * * * * * *

While living in Keller Arvids came upon a large trash pile during one of his walks. Soldiers had looted hundreds of former factories, businesses, and grand homes. Kicking around the pile he found a big bucket with a wide rim. The bottom was rusted out, but the sides and rim were solid. He took it back to the camp and cut an opening near the bottom, creating a small chimney on the side. It became a convenient portable stove for cooking outdoors. He could build a fire on the bottom from sticks and fit a pot or pan on the rim.

It was a small, simple device but one that provided a welcome diversion many times when the hours were long and discouraging. The entire family looked forward to gathering around the makeshift stove, to warm their hands and savor the aroma of whatever was cooking.

If Cilite found any suitable bones for cooking, she used them over and over to make soup, drying them afterward on the windowsill for the next meal. Everyone kept eyeing the bones, thinking of the flavor they added to the broth. These days they ate carefully to avoid spilling a drop or allowing a crumb to fall. Still the children searched the floor for possible stray morsels. They scooped up snow to make soup and dug wild onions to add nutrition and flavor in the broth. Slowly the meager diet started building up their bodies, and they began to recover.

When Arvids found a private time on his job in the woods, he voiced his prayers to God. It was good to release the burdens and cares in his heart for his family. His small salary was barely enough to buy a few potatoes. His boss often yelled at him, shaking his finger to show disdain and authority.

"You and I know that Hitler will lose," Arvids would firmly reply. The man was shaken and would mumble under his breath.

Cilite was happy for the few potatoes, preparing them in cod liver oil. Once she tried to fry a small fish in the oil. The taste was disgusting, but the hungry brood ate it anyway.

Arvids did not approve of begging because Psalm 37:24 says, "I have been young and now am old; yet I have not seen the righteous forsaken nor His descendants begging bread." Arvids' work ethic demanded earning and bartering for food they needed, so they used money or traded with the items brought from Latvia.

Whenever Janis could find time away from his job, he wandered around for hours bartering for food, covering many miles. He tried never to give up until he could return home with an item of food. Farmers grew tired of the begging refugees and chased them away. Occasionally Janis met one that was sympathetic, and he discovered a method that worked well. Cilite had sewed small sacks out of an old pillowcase, and he took a few with him on his journeys.

"Couldn't I have just a tablespoon of flour?" he would ask the farmers, holding up a small sack and looking pathetic. He was offering an exchange for the items brought from Latvia. Usually the farmers declined the items, seeing how ragged he was.

Yet such a small request was hard to turn down. With each trifling amount received, Janis would run and hide it in a secret place in the woods. At the end of the day, he gathered the sacks and carried a considerable little quantity back to the family. He would march into the room as if he had won a prize, bringing smiles all around.

He found another similar request that worked. Coming to a farmhouse, Janis would ask the farmer who opened the door, "Please, could we have just one potato?"

One day a farmer told him to come back in the evening, and he would find potatoes buried by a certain tree that was pointed out. When Janis returned to the tree, he was delighted to see a plant with potatoes attached to the roots. Hurrying back to the camp, he entered the room with a triumphant smile, unloading his treasure – a potato stalk with potatoes.

The family held a big event outdoors beside Arvids' handmade stove. Burning the stalks first, they carefully placed the potatoes in the coals, avoiding the red fire. Waiting for them to bake created hope in their hearts. To pass the time, Arvids began to tell a story about Latvia. When he finished, the others told anecdotes they remembered. Finally the potatoes were ready. They had turned black and were too hot to handle at once, but presently the entire family was enjoying a feast.

Happy faces told only a tale of charred potatoes, but it seemed more like a Thanksgiving dinner that God had provided.

After bedtime, sirens blared announcing another impending air raid, and everyone scrambled into a bunker. A lone American plane began bombing. Then there were more. The family had not considered the United States their enemy, but this time the blitz was coming from American planes overhead. It was the middle of the night, and sleeping families had been rocked from their beds. The refugees huddled together in the bunker, hoping for safety.

Families were already hard pressed, having come out of the Nazi prison camp. Now they were starving and diseased. To the children, the Americans in those planes were enemies. No one had been oppressed by them, but the reality was inescapable: People on the ground would be killed by the bombs. The sky lit up with searchlights, looking for planes. Before long, the Germans shot down one of them. As it whirled down in flames, the children broke into applause and cheering.

"You stop it! A man is dying in there," Cilite said sternly, her hand landing on Anna's face. The swift discipline brought Anna to the realization that no one is her enemy who still has life and breath, who was created in God's image, and who needs the opportunity to know Christ.

"Rather, pray that he has heard of the Gospel and it will come to light before he dies," Cilite concluded solemnly.

They were all reminded to value an eternal soul for whom Jesus had died – and that truth was no less commanding in these cruel, merciless times.

* * * * * * * * * * * *

Tired and embittered by years of German occupation and Nazi mistreatment, the Czechs looked to Russia for relief. Although the Keikulises were not officially prisoners, they were treated as unwelcome intruders by most. However, from time to time they were able to buy potatoes from local farmers. A few valuables that Arvids had placed in the knapsacks when leaving home still remained and could be traded for food. They occasionally exchanged one of their grandmother's embroidered silk linens or a silver money piece for food when money had no value. One particular linen towel was embroidered in bold, vibrant colors depicting Little Red Riding Hood and the Wolf. Arvids took it to a bakery and traded it for a loaf of bread, always bartering an item of value or offering money when he went to the stores.

People were afraid of being seen trading with camp residents lest they appeared to be aiding an enemy. The children's boots and shoes were tattered and worn; and usually when the older siblings went to ask farmers for food in exchange for the items, dogs were sent to chase them away. However, Janis continued to be tenacious; nothing seemed to discourage him. Finally, in pity, a farmer took the goods and told the youngsters where to find buried potatoes.

"Now don't take too much, but from time to time you may take what you need," he told them. "I don't want a mob of refugees coming at once."

Delighted, Anna and Janis filled their knapsacks and returned to the work camp.

* * * * * * * * * * * *

One day Arvids told Anna to wash up and put on her good dress – the one change of clothing that she had. There was no water, so Cilite filled a bucket with snow, melting it on the stove. It made only a small

186

amount of water, but Anna went through the motions of washing herself. She put on her clothes and brown coat and combed her hair. She felt dressed up.

This was to be a memorable day.

They would go to town and buy bread. On the way to the store a young Czech boy noticed Anna and, approaching with a friendly smile, asked, "Going to church?" She understood the word "kirke." Some Czechs had been kind since they had also been oppressed.

Arvids was making a special occasion of going to a store to spend the little money he had earned – about six dollars. They purchased two loaves of bread and a small bologna, delighted to bring something back to the family.

Arvids had the wisdom to take the children – as often as he could – out of the everyday doldrums full of lice, disease, loose teeth, and drab surroundings. To keep their children's souls from being ruined, he and his wife did their best to make ordinary things seem special.

They were still learning to seek and enjoy simple beauty in everyday existence.

In this camp Cilite tried to encourage a refined young woman who was bordering on despair. Mrs. Lange, a Latvian, was a dentist and her husband a forestry supervisor. They had two daughters who were ill, like most of the other children. It was obvious that this family had been accustomed to the finer things in life and now found it difficult to adjust to the desperate situation in which they found themselves, along with the other refugees. Disease, filth, and lice were everywhere. There was no room for privacy and little opportunity for cleanliness. Mrs. Lange got to the point of falling apart and cried out, "We are all going to rot and die here!"

Cilite began to speak about the Lord and His faithfulness, that He was a God of mercy and compassion who does not turn away from prayers offered in humility. On numerous occasions she was able to calm the distressed woman.

In their conversations, a group of Latvians sometimes discussed their petty philosophies. Their comments usually mirrored weakened faith, saying things like, "How could God have turned His back on our motherland? We were all good Christian people. How could we have deserved this?"

"Did our goodness really honor God?" Cilite felt compelled to reply. "Did our lives really glorify Him? God is just and holy, and He knows how to humble mankind so that we can begin to think of what is really important, to know Him, and to glorify Him and deny ourselves!"

When the complainers heard this, the room became quiet, and no one expressed any additional grievances – for a time, at least.

Mrs. Lange was one who respected Cilite's faith.

The Lange family was able to escape over the hazardous mountains before the repatriation process. Arvids and Cilite learned that they made it to West Germany after much difficulty and eventually went to Australia. Later that year while in the American zone, the Keikulises heard from one of the Langes' acquaintances. Mrs. Lange had begged her friend to please thank the Keikulis family if she ever found them. She had said, "They were like angels and helped us to keep the faith in the midst of trying circumstances."

* * * * * * * * * * *

Cilite had three large open sores on her leg, which had developed from vitamin deficiency. These took a year to heal. Some mocked, and people said she would rot and lose her legs with her faith still in God. When she prayed regularly, some would say, "Here goes the concert again." The comments did not deter Cilite from allowing her prayers to flow earnestly. Within seconds the whole room would become reverent, and her prayers affected the negative attitudes. The complaining diminished, and there was a perceptible return to kindness.

The city of Dresden, Germany, was approximately 12 miles across the northwestern border of Czechoslovakia. The Keikulis family had come through it a few months earlier while traveling by train. Camp residents could hear the noise of bombs dropping and the tremendous explosions that followed. During one heavy air raid, most of the children in the room began to scream. When Arvids shouted, "Peace!" they immediately stopped. The father of one of the families had been out begging for food for his family. Arvids did his best to console his children.

Later a family told of their terrifying experiences during the bombing in Dresden. Two couples and a single girl escaped the horror of the phosphorus bombs and told of tar in the streets, melting from the intense heat and making the roadway curvy and bubbly. People in bunkers were buried alive, including this family. Hysteria was rampant in the bunkers, and it was next to impossible to breathe. People began clawing ferociously with their hands. Finally, as daylight dawned, they emerged, squinting painfully in the brightness. Those that were able helped dig out other victims. Black, charred bodies quivered for days as their hearts continued beating. One girl told how she had dipped a blanket in water and darted through smoke and flames. She swam the river to get away. One of the families found her safe in a basement. Together, they fled to Czechoslovakia.

The bombing of Dresden meant the Allies were coming to stop the Nazis. Someone in the room had a radio, and the refugees gathered around it to hear news of the war, hoping the end was near. They heard Winston Churchill's famous speech, "I have nothing to offer but blood, toil, tears, and sweat ..."

The war was officially over on May 7, 1945; yet people were afraid to express their opinions. They were not sure whose side the next person was on and did not trust anyone – so no one slept restfully.

Russians had seized Mariana's camp and told the women they were free to go. Mariana took her little suitcase and prepared to leave. She noticed that many of the women just sat there. They had nowhere to go or did not know how to find their former homes. In countless cases, homes and loved ones had been lost.

She walked the five-and-a-half miles to Keller alone. She thought how heartbreaking it was that most of the women in the camp had showed no joy or relief; they had no destination. They did not know where to start to look for relatives or how to pick up the pieces of their lives and begin again.

The Keikulises had heard that Mariana's camp was bombed, so they feared for her life. Later they learned that during the fire bombs the resourceful girl had wet a blanket and spread it over herself for protection.

Soon after the end of the war was declared, the Keikulis family went outside to roast a few precious potatoes on the handmade stove. They were anxiously waiting for the vegetables to finish cooking when Ilze suddenly let out a shrill cry and took off down the road as fast as her little feet would carry her.

"Mara, Mara!" she cried, yelling the name she called Mariana.

The others sat in stunned silence.

Then in the distance they glimpsed Mariana with her suitcase – coming home. After months of separation, no one could move for sheer happiness and surprise. They saw the two figures embrace in the road. Then Ilze began pulling Mariana's hand to lead her to the rest of the family. In her excitement the little girl grinned from ear to ear, triumphant to have found her lost Mara. Ilze had been sickly for a long time, but like a burst of joy that lifts even the weariest spirit, this emotional reunion re-energized Ilze's heart with new strength.

The family was grateful for times like this that brightened miserable, depressing days.

But Anna stared intently at Mariana, wondering, if she is so happy, how come she looks so gray?

* * * * * * * * * * * *

Mariana had a delightful sense of humor, even in less-than-ideal circumstances – and a knack for picking up languages; in the prison camp she had learned to converse easily with women of nine different nationalities. From their window, the family had been watching soldiers march to a drill in the town square when Mariana called out in German, "Nas dar (hello)!" Instinctively the soldiers turned, and the family ducked down out of sight. A frustrated officer had to re-gather his disrupted troops.

Another time, Mariana's friendly, talkative manner had resulted in one of the guards at a nearby castle bringing the family over the fence for a grand tour of the ornate palatial structure.

* * * * * * * * * * *

The Allies were still miles away, and Russian tanks were approaching. The next morning everyone was standing in eager anticipation, expecting the Allied armies to arrive. They hoped it would be the British or Americans. Their hope was mingled with fear of the Russians and their brutality.

Then the dreaded news came.

"They have made a deal, giving Czechoslovakia to Russia," the radio announcer said. The people scattered in different directions in their efforts to escape.

"We can't run," said Arvids. "We might perish. We have to wait for the Lord to save us."

Cilite wondered why there had to be such severe judgment. They had heard people who escaped the horror speak without any concern for others.

"There are situations that we cannot understand, but we can know God is righteous," Arvids said. He quoted Psalm 145:17, "The Lord is righteous in all His ways."

The Czechs were not familiar with Communism and thought the Russians were their brothers – allies who had liberated them from the Nazi yoke. They soon learned different, but by then it was too late.

Czechoslovakia became the Russian zone. The Czechs were told they were being liberated from the Germans. The Russians took over because the Allies – i.e., Americans – stopped occupying. The Russians were thought to be allies in the war against the Nazis. The Red Army came in as "friends," so to speak. They promised the millions of refugees a return to their homeland. Everyone knew this was not good news, remembering former occupations and massive exiles to Siberia.

On May 9, 1945, the Red Army entered the area with characteristic brutal force. Czechoslovakia became the Russian zone. They were vindictive. Terror seemed to spread through the air. Children and women suffered the most. Furnishings from expensive homes were strewn across the fields for miles around, rotting away. Soldiers emptied all stores and sometimes wore as many as 10 watches on their wrists.

No one dared to resist.

Upon hearing the Red Army was approaching, most of the inhabitants of the camp had attempted to escape to the West the previous night, leaving everything behind. Sometime later it was found that the majority of them succeeded – with significant difficulty. The Keikulises

191

and Bartusevicses remained behind with the women who could not risk the dangerous journey.

When the Russian soldiers charged through the camps, they hunted for young women. As they approached the Keikulises' camp, a Latvian woman with long, blonde braids was looking for a place to hide. Outside the building were wooden doors stacked and leaning against the wall. The young woman ducked under the doors to hide. Seeing her squeeze under, Judite followed in curiosity. The woman signaled the girl to be still. The soldiers searched all around but passed over the hiding place.

On another occasion the women were cooking outside when soldiers approached. Everyone feared their intent. Sensing danger, Arvids immediately told the women to go inside, and he walked out to meet the soldiers.

"These are refugees, women and children who have suffered much in the war," he said, speaking in Russian. "Do not touch any of them."

The intruders may have thought this meant they were all Russian, since Arvids was speaking the language. Cursing, they asked for the German couple who ran the place. The couple had hidden in the woods.

"No, they took care of us," Arvids said sternly. "We're not handing over anyone!"

The soldiers lingered for a while, eating and drinking while the frightened refugees stayed inside. The couple had left their daughter, Annelise, at the camp, and Ausma Bartusevics was rocking her in her lap, trying to provide comfort during the tense episode. The child had started to cry when the soldiers asked about her parents. She kept asking if her parents were alive.

When Annelise's parents returned, news spread that the Russian army would arrive in full force by morning. Everyone scurried to grab a few necessities, dressing children, and ran en masse to the train station. A train was waiting for a locomotive that never came.

One evening a German girl had run in for safety, and the Keikulises hid her among their baggage. Several days later the Russian soldiers, angry that Arvids was protecting Germans, grabbed him and hauled him into the yard. The children watched at the window as their papa was brutally shoved and pushed up against a tree, presumably to be executed. At that moment the Lord gave Arvids courage to communicate with authority. Speaking fluent Russian, he appealed to their consciences, and they released him.

During their months in Czechoslovakia, the Keikulises usually spoke Russian to converse with Czechs. The children picked it up easily. One day Janis was again scouting for food when Russian soldiers approached him and called out in Russian, "Where are you going, malchik (boy)?"

"I'm looking for bread," Janis answered, also in Russian.

"Have you found any?" they asked.

"Not yet," replied Janis.

"Come with us," they said, with unmistakable friendliness. "We'll help you find some."

The soldiers took Janis into a bakery, where they commanded the baker to give him bread. The boy was uncomfortable taking something without paying for it but dared not resist.

"What part of Russia are you from?" the soldiers asked, walking back outside.

"Latviskaya rayon," Janis answered, adding Russian endings to his words to identify the Latvian region.

"Oh, we've never heard of it before," one of the soldiers said.

"Russia is a very big country," Janis quickly replied.

"Mala-gyets (clever boy)!" they said, smiling and slapping him on the shoulder.

Afterward it was a touch-and-go situation, depending on the level of drunkenness or state of the soldiers' minds as to whether suffering would be inflicted upon the refugees. Arvids used caution in dealing with the Russians and depended on the Lord for wisdom in each circumstance. There was no cunningness on his part. These were not reasonable men. Their intent was to loot, upheave, kill, and destroy. Everything they touched was left in devastation.

In the aftermath of the war, the families had no place to live, so on May 25, 1945, they were placed in the upstairs of the Hagensdorf Manor House, not far from Keller. This had once been a grand house, with its huge central courtyard, built and owned by an aristocratic German family. The Czechs had taken it over, turning the plantation into a collective farm. The Keikulises and Bartusevicses were each given a large room on the third floor, where they shared a toilet and sink. After months of living in cramped, filthy quarters, this place seemed luxurious.

Here the adults got jobs working the land. Seeing that the remaining refugees were not overjoyed about the Russian occupation and had no intention of returning to their home country, the Czechs knew the people were at their mercy, so they took merciless advantage of them.

To understand the conditions that existed in Sudetenland, one must remember that the area was inhabited by Czechs and Germans.

History records that the German occupation of Czechoslovakia (1938–1945) began with the Nazi annexation of Czechoslovakia's northern and western border regions, known collectively as Sudetenland, under terms outlined by the Munich Agreement (Wikipedia, 2015).

During Sudetenland's incorporation into Germany, the local Germans abused the Czechs, and now it was time for ruthless payback. According to custom, the Red Army killed, raped, and pillaged. Their deserters and newly-freed Russian war prisoners did the same. Armed robbery, rape, murder, and beatings were a daily occurrence. Hate had turned people into animals. The Czechs thought they would now join their "brothers," the Russians, in hate to repay the Germans. With unmitigated pride, they were convinced they would be the chosen race to conquer the world.

While at this plantation, Arvids and Mr. Bartusevics were sent by the landlord to the valley that had been a military post used by Communist forces. The Red Army had moved on, leaving unused supplies behind. The landlord hoped to seize some of these goods, so he sent the men out with a wagon to see what they could find. After having endured frequent periods of famine and hardships, the men were appalled at what they saw. The Red Army had left a revolting mess. They found loads of equipment and motorcycles, as well as butchered meat that had the stench of rot – piled higher and larger than an automobile. More mounds of goods and spoiled food lay scattered around. Stalls that had been built for horses were left with trampled oats instead of straw on the ground. Such a waste was sickening to behold.

Arvids was reminded of the fourth beast of the final world empire described in Daniel 7:19 in the Bible:

Then I wished to know the truth about the fourth beast, which was different from all the others, exceedingly dreadful, with its teeth of iron and its nails of bronze, which devoured, broke in pieces, and trampled the residue with its feet.

As they passed a small barracks that had obviously been hastily erected with fine wood intended for furniture, Arvids saw heaps of machinery, utensils, and broken glass. Knowing the area was noted for its fine china, Arvids thought that undoubtedly the soldiers had confiscated the most valuable items out of the homes, used them during their short stay, and then smashed everything before leaving. In some buildings the broken china was knee deep. Little could be salvaged that was worthwhile.

During this time Cilite continued to suffer with open sores on her legs that would not heal, a condition not uncommon among the refugees. Regardless, the landlord forced her to work and placed her in a position where she had to run behind a large harvester, with her legs swollen and bandages falling off.

Arvids had invited people in the area to come for worship on Sunday. Under the Nazis, Mariana had been given permission to make up her hours and join the services. Now that they were "liberated," the Czechs in charge demanded that everyone work seven days.

It seemed like things were worse than before.

One day Vali, the oldest Bartusevics girl, and Mariana had gone to search for food among the German farmers living in the area. On their way back they were spotted by two Russian soldiers in a fancy horse-drawn carriage. The soldiers stopped the carriage and told the girls to come aboard.

Mariana knew the intention was immoral.

"Vali, if you ever prayed, pray now because we are in real danger," she whispered as she nudged her 17-year-old friend. Obeying the soldiers' command, they prayed to themselves and managed not to show fear.

"This is how far we go; we live here," Mariana said as the carriage approached a small tunnel that opened to the courtyard of the manor.

The driver whipped his horse to keep going.

Mariana and Vali leaped off the moving carriage and ran into the building while the soldiers pulled the horses to a halt.

Mariana ran straight upstairs to the third floor. She knew if she stopped at the Keikulises' room with the soldiers in pursuit, the family could not lie to conceal her hiding. She spotted a chimney in the hall that had a small door in it. By crawling on her belly she made it inside and stood on a small platform built into the chimney. Vali had gone up to the next floor and had also found a hiding place. Standing in the dark nook, Mariana heard the heavy footsteps of the soldiers coming up the stairs, past the chimney, and down the hallway.

"Where are the two young ladies that just came in here?" she heard them ask as they went into the Keikulises' room.

"We haven't seen them all day," one of the family answered truthfully. "We don't know."

"We know they live here," the soldiers insisted. "We saw them run into the building."

They became angry and started swearing. After searching every floor, they finally left. The two families wondered where the girls were. At last Mariana came out, and her appearance left no doubt as to where she had been hiding. She was covered in black soot, with only the whites of her eyes showing – and a big smile. They had all been praying earnestly and thanked their Heavenly Father for protecting His children from being defiled.

On Sunday the landlord came to the Keikulises' room and ordered them to go to work.

When Arvids refused on religious grounds, the landlord summoned local militia. With great commotion a truck pulled into the courtyard; and the militia, carrying rifles and bayonets, started to jump down. Two soldiers ran up the stairs and rushed into the room, demanding that the adults report to work. The soldiers pressed their bayonets against Arvids' chest and Cilite's stomach.

Anna jumped off her bunk screaming, thinking the bayonets were going to penetrate. Running over to Mariana and pulling on her skirt she pleaded, "Mariana, you must go!" in hopes of preventing her moth-

196

er's death.

Mariana swung around on her heel.

"Depart from me, Satan!" she said, facing Anna with piercing eyes. "You don't know what you're asking me to do."

Anna ran into the bathroom, closed the door, and cried. In a few moments she realized that she had asked Mariana to betray her faith. She was only 10 years old, but it suddenly dawned on her that for the sake of keeping her mother she had asked Mariana to go in her place. There, kneeling by the toilet and bowing her head, she repented with bitter tears.

In those brief seconds of crisis the group recognized Satan as the opposition, and they stood firm, not giving in to fear. Cilite even stood up and stomped her foot in a show of courage and replied to the soldiers' harsh demand, "And what happened to Hitler and his work ethic?"

The soldiers gave them 20 minutes to decide whether they would work or not, making it abundantly clear that refusal would mean facing the firing squad.

The militia went outside and stood at attention, waiting for the execution of the refugees who had refused to go to work. They fired a few shots, with the intention of intimidating the people inside.

Anna came out of the bathroom and saw that everyone had dropped to their knees. Arvids did not expect the children to face the firing squad.

"Janis, you're a young man," he said, turning first to his son. "You need not die for your father's faith. You have much to live for, much to see, much to learn."

Janis's reply pierced the hearts of his loved ones, leaving a profound, lasting impression.

"Papa, to whom shall I go?" he said. "Only He has the words of eternal life."

These words from John 6:68 became the seal and testimony for the terrifying trial they were facing. The children's expressions changed to those of faith and determination to stand up for what they believed in. In solid agreement they realized there was no other way. They focused as one on the truths that were written on their hearts: Only Christ has eternal life. In Christ is fulfillment. If mortals gain the whole world, they are still the losers, so it is just as well to face death with Him because in Him is life. Death is only physical.

Without discussion, they were all thinking of the words of Paul the Apostle in Philippians 1:21: "For me to live is Christ, and to die is gain."

Anna understood the full implication of that moment. She needed to hear her brother's words, and in their simplicity and clarity they removed all fear of the possibility of dying. The family was prepared to be martyred if necessary. The peace and confidence of Christ came into their hearts. As they worshipped, time lost its importance. They were aware only of the presence of their mighty God.

Suddenly they heard a loud commotion outside, and they knew the soldiers were coming to get them. They were prepared, feeling no panic or fear. When they heard the motor of the truck, they ran to the window and, to their surprise, saw the soldiers taking off in a hurry. In that moment they understood that they had won the victory. It had nothing to do with changing their minds. They had won a spiritual victory when the decision was made that for them to live was Christ and to die was gain.

While the families had been on their knees, a miracle had occurred.

A Red Army truck loaded with Russian soldiers had pulled up in the courtyard, and someone told them the Czechs were preparing to shoot some Russian citizens. Because Arvids and Cilite spoke Russian fluently, most people had generally assumed they were Russians.

"Even on Sundays they are not allowed to rest," was the report given to the Russian soldiers.

Suddenly the group waiting on the third floor heard heavy footsteps coming up the stairs, and Russian officers burst into their room.

"Is it true that the Czech capitalist makes you work on Sundays and threatens to shoot you?" the officers demanded.

Having no difficulty understanding Russian, the Keikulises answered affirmatively.

"Come on down," the officers ordered, still in Russian.

The families followed the officers down the steps. In the courtyard the landlord and his staff were lined up with a Russian officer maliciously interrogating them. As the group approached, the officer pointed toward them and addressed the landlord.

"Do you know who these people are?" he demanded. "They are Russian citizens. How dare you abuse them?"

Pointing a rifle at the landlord and turning to Arvids, he said, "Say one word, and I will wipe out this nest of capitalists!"

Arvids was petrified because he knew the Red Army soldiers and their thirst for destruction. With great difficulty he was able to calm them down.

"You work these people seven days a week?" the Russian officer continued scolding the landlord. "From now on they work four days and get off three days!"

Observing their ragged clothing and appearance, the Russians demanded that the families be taken to the kitchen. There they saw a well-stocked pantry and were given food, the likes of which they had not seen for many months: butter, eggs, meat, and even strawberries. The Russian officer also ordered that his truck be loaded with plenty of food.

The landlord could not meet the quantities demanded, and he was forced to borrow from local farmers. Finally, the Czechs were given more orders on how to work and feed their Russian "comrades." The surprised believers were careful not to take advantage of the situation. God had used Communists, their greatest enemy at the time, to save them from the oppressors.

Before departing, one of the officers told the Keikulises to leave the camp and move to a place that did not have a commandant.

The date was June 23, 1945, when they walked to Klösterle, which the Czechs later renamed Klášterec nad Ohří.

They walked what seemed like 12 or 15 miles to the village and found a small, abandoned cottage across the road from a porcelain factory, where Arvids worked for a month. The first night they were plagued by bedbugs coming out of the walls. The following day Arvids and Cilite boiled water on an outdoor fire and put it in the cracks in the walls. Then they pulled the beds off the walls – and still were bitten.

The children were told to wear the flag of their country on their arms for identification. They were playing outside one day when they saw some Czechs trying to murder Germans in a fit of revenge. A terrified woman who was hiding and weeping in the bushes called out to the children discreetly, giving them two tennis balls in a hand-crocheted bag. Even in her desperate hour, she made an effort to be kind.

Ilze had begun to have asthma attacks while back in Latvia. Now, the asthma was causing her to lose her breath and her body to turn blue. Cilite would quickly shake the little body upside-down, and the child would breathe again.

Janis found an excuse to get away from the room when this happened. It was simply unbearable to see his little sister suffer so much – with her desperate gasps for breath, each one seeming like her last, and her eyes rolled back in their sockets.

For weeks Cilite sat by the stiff little body and prayed. People who saw the child's condition felt free to voice their bleak opinions, saying things like, "It would be God's mercy if she died rather than to live on as a vegetable."

Ilze looked so deformed that most thought she would have brain damage and be crippled. Cilite prayed for hours at night. When she was too tired to pray, she opened her Bible to Isaiah 53:5 and repeatedly ran her fingers over the verse:

> For He was wounded for our transgressions, He was bruised for our iniquities; the chastisement of our peace was upon Him, and by His stripes we are healed.

She continued this practice for hours, throughout many sleepless nights.

The two parents dealt with their child's illness in their own way. When Arvids was heavily burdened, he spent time walking through the forest, where he could open his heart and pray. He walked and prayed until he could return to his family with some encouragement. Cilite pondered the fact that one of her children was near death and wondered why Ilze had to endure prolonged agony. The devoted mother had pleaded to be off from work to care for her child, but was refused.

* * * * * * * * * * *

With the ending of the war in early July, the allied leaders – Winston Churchill, Franklin D. Roosevelt, and Joseph Stalin – met at the Yalta

Conference. The world rejoiced that Nazi terror had been stopped. Under the treaty Stalin had asked Churchill and Roosevelt to return his prisoners of war, in a process known as repatriation. With Russian tanks arriving all over Eastern Europe, refugees were told that the war had ended and they were to return to their motherland. This meant that the war-weary refugees were being turned over to the hands of the Red Army by the allied armies, bringing further stress upon the refugees, since most of them had already lived under the atrocities of this mob.

In a camp where the Keikulises had once lived, suicide was the choice of a thousand people who preferred death to being herded into trains that would take them back into the hands of the Red Army.

Fear and panic spread once more.

The Keikulises received notice that they were being deported and sent back to Latvia. Arvids went to a Czech doctor and described Ilze's condition. She had severe asthma, experiencing labored, uneven breathing and lapsed in and out of a coma for three months. The doctor said he could not come to see her and that she would die soon. He changed the status of the repatriation papers, and the family's stay was extended two weeks, giving them time to "bury the child."

Each time there was a threat of sending the two families with refugees on trains to Latvia, Ilze lapsed back into a coma, and the doctor gave two more postponements.

Years later, the family learned that their fears had not been unfounded. The millions of refugees that were put on trains never came near their motherland. When the trains crossed the borders, they were stopped and the refugees told to get out for a break. Then machine guns came out, and the people were shot to death. Eleven million Slavs and Baltics were murdered this way before the Americans realized what was going on and stopped the so-called repatriation. Sixty years later, in 2005, George W. Bush, the 43rd president of the United States, publicly apologized for this appalling process and for the annexing of the Baltic States to the Soviet Union after the war. (For additional information, see "Operation Keelhaul," Stanford Press.)

It was through faith and patience the family eventually saw God's promise fulfilled as they placed their trust in Him, according to

Hebrews 6:11-12:

Show the same diligence to the full assurance of hope until the end, that you do not become sluggish, but imitate those who through faith and patience inherit the promises.

Because of Ilze's severe sickness the Keikulis and Bartusevics families, along with Mariana, escaped the cruel fate; and they gave glory to their faithful, omniscient Heavenly Father.

* * * * * * * * * * *

Things had become relatively quiet by then, and Arvids was praying for a way of escape to the American zone, which was nearby.

One day a Czech man came up to Arvids and spoke to him.

"You are refugees with young children who are suffering," he said. "You must find a way to get food for your family."

He then told Arvids where to go to find the American military Office of Intelligence, where one could request to enter the American zone.

Following the man's directions, Arvids boldly approached a border checkpoint in broad daylight and gave the Russian his work pass that was written in the Czech language.

"Where are you going?" the guard asked in Russian.

Arvids did not answer.

The guard looked him over, studied the work pass on both sides, and waved him to go on, handing back his booklet. Once inside the American zone, Arvids found the United States Central Intelligence Agency (CIA) office. The kind officer on duty there initially said he had no authority to bring the family into the American zone. However, after Arvids pleaded, the man scribbled on a piece of paper: "This man is staying in Klösterle, interrogation satisfactory." It was signed "Special Agent Mark, CIC," with an accompanying signature that was illegible.

The willing agent was a blessing. The Czechs had no objection to their resettlement.

To get back into the Russian zone was also no problem, since the Russians accepted anybody.

Getting out was another story.

202

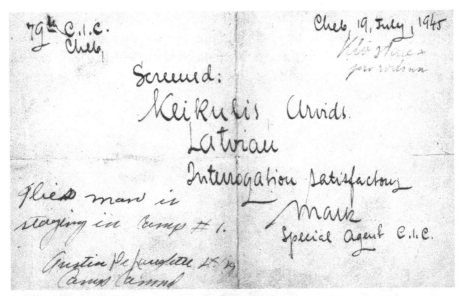

Scratch piece of paper given by U.S. Army Lieutenant & Special Agent in kindness.

After Arvids' success in acquiring papers of resettlement in the American zone, others were encouraged to try but were forbidden to board the bus to the border. Mr. Bartusevics also tried and apparently got lost, and no one had heard from him since.

The next step for Arvids was to go to the local city hall and get a permit to move. He knew the first incriminating questions would be "What is the country of your origin, and where do you intend to move?"

Luckily – or perhaps providentially – the young lady assigned to him was lackadaisical and rather absentminded. She skipped the first part of the question and asked only where he intended to move. He gave her the name of the city in the American zone.

No objections were raised.

On July 21, 1945, the families were preparing to move.

The Bartusevics family was also packing to come along, although they had no documents of any kind. Mr. Bartusevics still had not returned, and his fate was unknown. At the railroad station there was no problem getting extra tickets for the Bartusevicses and Mariana because the permit did not specify a number but simply stated "Keikulis and family." Two men in the group would have made things appear like there were two families, and the group was boarding the train without Mr. Bartusevics.

Castle at Elbogen (today Locket) where U.S. Command was at the end of the war. Papa received stamp that allowed to travel.

Across the Russian and neutral zones the trip went without incident.

As the train approached the American zone, it was stopped. The passengers sat stunned and frozen. The ominous stillness was broken by an incessant hiss of steam billowing from the locomotive. Then shouts, bellowed orders, and screams pierced the air. Several Czechs in civilian clothes, with guns drawn, boarded the train and began throwing people off furiously and pitilessly. People hurriedly gathered their belongings and assembled into family groups, expecting to find solace with the American sentries who were nonchalantly standing by, seemingly uncaring, only several yards away.

Outwardly Arvids remained calm as he gathered the others about him, but in his heart he was desperately calling upon the Lord.

Confusion and despair erupted – amid feelings of helplessness among the refugees, to have endured and come this far. It was but a few short steps to the American zone and freedom; yet now it seemed hopeless. The disheartened people stepped down from the train into an open field. As Arvids looked around in the midst of the milling mass, he saw that some women had broken through and were rushing toward the American guards with outrage. Their coats and dresses, which had once defined them as ladies of dignity and position, now looked incongruous as they beseeched the startled, embarrassed soldiers.

The women dropped to their knees and tried to kiss the soldiers' boots.

Then Arvids' attention was drawn to a well-dressed lady who had emerged from an American military tent on the other side of the border. She crossed the sentry line, walked straight toward him, and began to speak in German.

"You have a good chance to make it across, but you have to have a round stamp applied to your passport," she said. "You can get it in the city of Elbogen, about nine kilometers [5.5 miles] from here. When you get there, seek out the American commandant and ask him to apply the stamp I have described."

After providing a few additional details, she returned to the tent. Many of the passengers had the same need, but she had not approached anyone else. Arvids told the family to stay in the field, and he immediately went on his way to find Elbogen.

Left in the open, the people were defenseless. There was no shelter, and the train had taken off. Now they were without a destination and forced to wait for someone to make a decision about what to do with a group of destitute refugees. They felt numb, almost deprived of emotion. There they sat, dazed and dejected, speaking few words – their future more uncertain than ever. The whole situation of not knowing what to do, subject to the will of ruthless men, added to their insecurity. The family had no assurance that Arvids would get through the checkpoints and make it back. They wondered what had happened to Mr. Bartusevics.

They stayed in the field a whole day, with no one offering food or comfort. They were not entirely hopeless, but it was like being resolved to nothing. It was a strange, empty feeling. There was the possibility of never seeing their papa again, and the prospect of a military police-man's commanding them to go back to a work camp was uppermost in their thoughts.

They waited for the impossible to transpire, a small, ragtag bunch of people with all their worldly goods in the middle of a field. It was a deplorable situation. Cilite and Mariana rationed among the children the bits of food that was left. There was little to drink, and it was a hot, muggy day. The children could not understand the interruption and waiting; yet they were still grateful for God's protection. They had learned that when uncertainties arise, it is a good thing to be thankful to God for His faithfulness in the past and for who He is. To pass the time they prayed silently and began telling favorite Bible stories.

All the while, their eyes kept looking in the direction Arvids had gone, hoping for his return.

About halfway to Elbogen, his destination, Arvids felt someone com-ing up behind him. Looking over his shoulder, he glimpsed the outline of a soldier. His immediate reaction was a furtive "Oh, no!"

But then a friendly voice called out, "Howdy, howdy!" and Arvids turned around.

A smiling American lieutenant approached and asked where he was going. Having been accustomed to the sharp orders of the Nazi and Communist soldiers, Arvids was surprised to encounter what appeared to be a normal, kind person. He tried to explain his problem, using all the languages he knew. The lieutenant inquired about his nationality.

When the soldier heard "Latvian," he said to wait while he went to get an American-Lithuanian colleague at the American base. The second soldier was fluent in several languages, and he understood the predic-ament. Eager to help, they gave Arvids the American commandant's address in Elbogen.

Then they took him to the camp's mess hall and asked the chef to bring in some food. Arvids looked at the pile of food before him but could not eat for thinking about the hungry, bewildered family mem-bers waiting for him. Realizing the reason for Arvids' hesitation, the lieutenant asked the cook to make sandwiches for a "very large family" to take along.

The lieutenant escorted Arvids back to the road to Elbogen. Parting with a bear hug, he said, "Don't worry, Mister; you will make it to America!"

The thought had never entered Arvids' mind. As he continued his walk, he realized that God had sent this man to serve and encourage him – and to reveal the future that lay ahead.

Elbogen meant "elbow," referring to a river bend. Nearing the town, Arvids walked downhill and saw a bend in the river that bordered a knoll upon which stood a large, medieval castle. It looked like a huge fort, protecting the view of the municipality behind it. Across the bridge, the road led to a scenic German town that seemed to have escaped the destruction of war.

When Arvids reached the address that was given to him, a German maid answered the door and said that the commandant was not at home. Arvids persisted in asking where he was. The maid became nervous and frightened. She finally divulged that the man had left for a conference at the local castle, where no unauthorized personnel could reach him.

Having been encouraged by the Lord, Arvids headed for the road leading to the castle. At the entrance was an armed soldier chewing gum, with a serious look on his face. As Arvids approached, the soldier lowered his weapon and denied him entrance. Seeing no aggressiveness in the youth's face, Arvids moved aside and used his finger to lift his rifle, cautiously opening the door and entering the courtyard of the castle. The vast courtyard surrounded by the fort-like structure was empty, and Arvids wondered, where now?

Then he heard muted voices coming from the second floor. Following the sounds, he went up an outdoor stairway to the conference room. At the door was an armed Czech guard in civilian clothes who categorically refused to admit Arvids. Speaking in broken Czech, Arvids insisted that he must see the commandant to obtain the proper stamp on his document. The Czech looked him over with contempt, clearly repulsed that the visitor was dirty and ragged. He yelled, "Impossible!" and tried to throw him out.

But Arvids kept demanding, "I must!"

Finally tiring of the annoyance, the guard asked for his documents

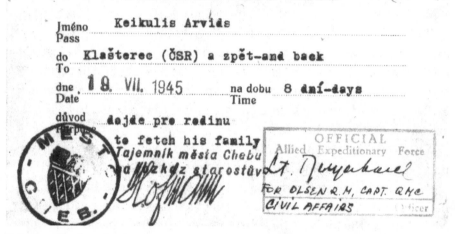

Document that had appropriate stamp to allow Family to travel, received at the Elbogen castle.

and went inside, leaving Arvids alone on the landing at the top of the stairs. A few minutes later he returned the papers – with the commandant's stamp and signature.

Arvids was relieved at clearing yet another hurdle. He left at once to go back to his family.

On the long trip back Arvids wondered how God had helped him surmount the difficulties. He thought of the young woman who volunteered crucial advice and the American lieutenant whom God had sent to encourage him. Suddenly he remembered the sandwiches, and he hastened his steps. What a pleasant surprise these would be to the children. During the long months of the war they had forgotten that tasty foods still existed.

Stars were out by the time he returned to the field. The family jumped to their feet at the sight of their papa returning with a large sack under his arm.

As they divided the sandwiches and began to eat, Arvids walked to the American zone and handed the newly stamped document to the border guard, who looked it over and asked Arvids to take him to his family. Arvids led him to the grassy patch where the 16-member group was sitting.

The guard scratched his head and inquired, "Aren't there two families?"

Arvids told him that the number included his sister's (in Christ) family whose husband had disappeared and that he could not leave her alone. Inwardly he thought, thank God, Americans are not servant of the letter. The man understood the problem.

A short time later the guard returned and for the second time asked for the papers. Then he read aloud, "Permission granted, Arvids Keikulis and family to reside in American zone."

Again he scratched his head and after a pause handed the papers back and said, "Well, OK!"

Then suddenly the unexpected happened.

From beyond the American zone they caught sight of Mr. Bartusevics approaching. The little group knew this could complicate the process, creating two families and more questions. Something had to be done quickly.

"See your papa?" Arvids whispered, turning to the Bartusevicses' three-year-old son, Janis. "Run to him and tell him to go to the railroad station, and we will meet him there."

When the train arrived, the two families boarded it and heaved a collective sigh of relief. Eventually everything worked out, but it could have turned into a catastrophe. The lost father returned to his family, and they were all able to get away from the horrible Communist control.

Left behind were 133 days of Nazi regime and 73 days of Communist terror and chaos. Although the future remained uncertain, they felt safe under the great American democracy's protection.

On July 22, 1945, the families traveled through Frankenbad and arrived in Eger, which was later renamed Heb. This was the camp where Americans were taking refugees to West Germany. There was widespread confusion – typical in the aftermath of war. The camp had closed the day before, and all former refugees had been shipped out. The new commandant did not know what to do with the influx of new refugees, and he turned them back over to Czech authorities for repatriation.

This was the low point of the day for the two families, who had already endured exasperating disappointment and delay.

The Russians began their propaganda indoctrination, saying that refugees had no legal rights. It was rumored that all of them would be taken to the Russian zone. Horror and fear spread like wildfire, as refugees continued to pour in from other places. The Keikulises heard that the Americans would be re-opening their camp. Thankfully, a bridge in this town had been bombed, slowing the forced evacuation. The Russians suggested that everyone walk down the steep slopes back to the railroad station.

Arvids replied that there was no way he could get his family with small children down the steep slopes and therefore would remain in the camp.

The families spent four days, July 22 through July 25, in the repatriation camp. Arvids insisted they had papers that granted permission to live in the American zone, not to return to Latvia. They were not treated badly, since it was the American zone, with freedom to come and go as they pleased -- and the days of rest were desperately needed.

Fasting had been routine for the parents and Mariana, but it was a rare occasion for the children. Now all of them fasted as they faced the potential threat of repatriation. Even little Ilze never asked for food.

They had heard of changes in the city. The American commandant had been instructed to receive refugees and set up offices under the Red Cross. Arvids went to show the American authorities his documentation and then returned to the Russian office. The families watched at the barracks window, where they could see him enter the second building. The officer banged on his desk while Arvids stood solemnly before him – with his loved ones watching and praying. Then Arvids came into the barracks, moving quickly.

"Pack up; we're leaving!" he exclaimed.

They grabbed their belongings and marched by the guards, looking straight ahead, and left the camp. Arvids pushed open the gate, guards stepping aside in disbelief while the two families and Mariana marched out triumphantly. They had taken advantage of the change in circumstances and moved out – to the displeasure and anger of the Communists.

Relieved, they walked up to the American zone. A soldier at the gate looked them over slowly, his eyes filling with tears. Then, with rare gentleness and kindness, he ushered them inside and served them a meal of warm soup. The camp was filling up with refugees. In fact, they later learned the camp had been full when they arrived, but the kind-hearted soldier at the gate could not refuse them.

The weary travelers thought they were in heaven. It was a time of warm sunshine for the children, the sky bursting with brilliant light. The soldiers served with big smiles. It was the first time the family had seen black soldiers, but they did not notice a distinction. A few handed out candy to the children, who remarked to their mother, "The soldiers are so kind!" It was their initial introduction to military personnel who were courteous and considerate.

After two days in the American camp, the refugees loaded onto the awaiting army trucks. Numerous Latvians and Ukrainians filled this column. There was no answer to their inquiries about the trucks' destination. Finally they pulled into Pilsen. After several turns through unfamiliar streets, they arrived at a large gate and saw a sign, printed in Russian, that read: "Russian Repatriation Camp."

Everyone was stunned. They all stood up in the trucks. They had been free under the Americans, and now freedom was again threatened and vulnerable.

The gates swung open, and the column of 20 trucks pulled in. To the right was a great field with dozens of barracks, and they could see uniformed Russian soldiers walking among them. The area was surrounded by a high fence.

The refugees in the trucks gasped in disbelief.

The Americans who brought them to the camp went into one of the buildings and stayed for some time. After an agonizing wait, the families saw the Russian officers come out, headed toward the lead truck of the column.

"Who wants to return to their motherland?" one officer called out loudly in Russian.

There was deathly silence.

He repeated the question, but again there was no response. He went from truck to truck and was visibly annoyed at the total lack of a reply. He became enraged and cursed.

Then the Americans went through the same procedure, stopping at each truck and repeating three times in German, "Who wants to go to West Germany?" Once again they were treated as humans having been given the right to choose.

The entire group raised their hands, shouting in a chorus as one, "To West Germany!"

The Russians followed the Americans around, cursing loudly. As soon as the rounds of all the trucks were finished, an American officer gave the command to start moving. Driving off the field and out the gate, they were still followed by swearing, threatening Russians.

The truckloads of refugees had been stunned by the drama that just transpired, but soon the reason for the outrageous theatrical procedure became obvious. Russian propaganda had claimed that the Americans were preventing refugees from returning to their homeland, and the unexpected stop at the "Repatriation Camp" had allowed the masses to communicate their wishes – and the truth – loud and clear.

The Allies had been on Russia's side to defeat the Nazi regime. Eventually the United States military recognized that something was seriously wrong. Refugees they picked up to take to repatriation camps were petrified. The soldiers became uncomfortable, since some had been close to the more-than-one-thousand who had committed suicide rather than fall into Communist hands. Everyone was talking about it in astonishment and dismay. Soldiers who came in the trucks were particularly troubled, as evidenced by their faces. They were intense as they instructed the refugees to respond exactly as directed.

After this, the families were taken to a railroad station to wait for the next train to West Germany. Before unloading, the soldiers warned that there would be Russian agents in civilian clothing asking questions and pressuring them to return to their homeland. Their advice was not to answer and to pretend that they did not understand Russian.

The soldiers were accurate in their assessment.

As soon as they disembarked, the refugees were surrounded by agents. Most of the people did not answer questions or told the agents, in German, that they did not understand.

"We know very well that you are Latvian and Ukrainian and understand every word we said!" the questioners said, as they grew angry and began to swear.

The refugees turned their backs and ignored them. It was a good feeling to know that Russia had no power over them here, but it was difficult to keep Russian children from speaking their own language. An old Russian woman and her daughter were carrying on a conversation in fluent French when the Russian soldiers walked by.

"Don't I know they're our people, pretending they don't know Russian and speaking French like that!" one of the agents snorted. "Huh!"

With tremendous relief, the travelers at last boarded the train destined for West Germany, first passing through a small remaining section of Russian zone. The German conductor could not hide his sense of humor. He walked among the refugees announcing with a twinkle in his eye, "Whoever has boots or watches, hold on tightly while we pass through the Russian zone!"

The long journey took them through many cities and stations, stopping frequently. Frightened and exhausted, the passengers tried to stay close to the train. There was nothing to eat, and by the second day they summoned one of their own who could speak broken English to ask the American soldiers in the front car how long it would be before they could get something to eat.

"Why, at every station there has been food set up for you!" the puzzled soldiers said.

No one had bothered to inform them.

At the next station they were led to a hall with food ready and waiting. Thankfully they took the sausage, canned milk, and bread, wasting no time in devouring the provisions placed before them.

Their journey to freedom was finally looking shorter.

Chapter 7

Displaced Persons' Camps

Despite encountering additional obstacles and delays, the Keikulis and Bartusevics families arrived in the old city of Eichstadt in Bavaria on July 31, 1945. Their first living quarters in the displaced persons' (DP) camp were located in barracks formerly occupied by the American military. They lived there in the Jäger Kaserne, which housed mainly Poles and Lithuanians, for one year, three months, and five days.

After the horrors of prison and labor camps and the repatriation holocaust, they had to become accustomed to their newfound freedom. Ironically, the barbed wire on the wall of the camp was there not to confine them but for protection. The Americans served the refugees with care and courtesy. Following nearly nine months of starvation, the refugees gratefully ate whatever remained of the soldiers' rations.

In the early part of their stay in Eichstadt, some of the men in the camp were arrested by the American military without being told the reason. Not all the men were taken, and the apprehensive refugees did not understand why some were chosen and some were not. There was no particular political background that distinguished one from another; yet approximately 300 men were arbitrarily taken from the camp. Their families did not know where they were taken.

Arvids Keikulis was among the ones arrested.

Through rumor, the families learned that the men were imprisoned downtown. Efforts to deliver supplies to them had been denied.

Arvids was jailed for several days. Again, he trusted the Lord for the outcome and his family's future. He was constantly interrogated with the same questions over and over again. His Russian interrogators asked where he was heading, where he had come from, and why he had not returned to his homeland. The Russians were still attempting to get all refugees back into their now-occupied countries. The Americans had to oblige and go to great lengths to prove that, in fact, these people did not want to return to those countries but preferred to go to West Germany.

After several days the men were released and returned to the refugee camp.

It was then they learned about some repatriation processes from which God had spared them. Had they made it into the American zone in their first attempt in Czechoslovakia – when they were taken off the train near the border – they would have been placed in an American camp that was immediately turned over to the Russians. Only after the U.S. military found out about suicides and parents cutting their children's wrists and then killing themselves rather than return to Communism did the Americans recognize the tragedy. Truckloads of people taking their own lives showed that Russians were to be dreaded just as the Nazis had been.

The Keikulis and Bartusevics families saw again how God had led their every step. It had been demoralizing to be ejected from the train in a field in Czechoslovakia, and they had been frustrated when their papers were not found to be in order. Yet these were transitory problems as far as God was concerned – part of a bigger plan to accomplish His purposes. How often His children may be disappointed when they are not aware of His perfect plan and timing! Looking back with a godly point of view, they could see that these had been minor delays. God always has His children's best interests – and eternal plan – in mind. It was a blessing to realize that through a temporary inconvenience He had spared them from certain tragedy.

Initially the refugees were placed under street watch. The Americans still did not know the type of people they were guarding. In the beginning a large number of soldiers guarded and marched, but their number gradually diminished and they became more relaxed and lenient. The soldiers soon realized the refugees felt secure in the camp and had no intention of running.

The establishment of self-government became the norm, and in each DP camp the United States base gave responsibilities to those refugees who showed a talent for leadership. Arvids' management abilities were recognized, and he was placed in charge of Building 3 on the hill, where the family was assigned to living quarters. They had an apartment of two rooms, one with a small kitchen, and a toilet shared with two other apartments. Mariana was considered part of the family and lived with them. Arvids was also in charge of the distribution of food and goods, which were stored in a large garage.

Their food came from the main kitchen. Arvids made wire handles which he inserted into two large coffee cans to serve as buckets for carrying food. Families were given an allotment of powdered cream and sugar for the coffee brought in from the kitchen. As the DP camps became more crowded, supplies could not always meet the demand to feed so many at once. At times food was skimpy, and the refugees were left hungry. They thought it was almost easier to adjust to having none than to having a little. The children had grown accustomed to searching for food, but they did not get used to the thick pea soup made from powder. Served almost daily in the cafeteria where they lined up for their meager fare, the soup earned the nickname "green terror." Nevertheless, it was sustenance they sorely needed.

Shower rooms at the Eichstadt military base were similar to those found in sports clubs or gyms. The refugees were allowed to take turns using them – alternating days for women and children, then men and boys. The stalls were clean and ample, with hot water and an open cold shower at the end of the row. The children loved running through the hot showers and ending in the cold one. It was invigorating, and Judite said the sudden change in temperatures reminded her of her mother's warm kiesel, a jellied fruit dessert with cold milk on it.

There was an interesting mixture of backgrounds, talents, and cultures among the refugees and countless ways they responded to conditions during the war and in the labor camps. Some continued to be stressed from their experiences, needing years to recover, and some were withdrawn; yet most were eager to take responsibility for getting on with life and making the best of it.

Although in the beginning there were no pencils, paper, or textbooks, educators among the camp's population began to organize grades for the children's schooling. Some students were not yet able to respond to the adjustment of order, but most were happy to have something to do. For months their minds had been dulled and intimidated by debilitating conditions; now it seemed like a fresh wind was returning their lives to a modicum of normalcy.

One particular teacher made a lasting impression on the students. War had inflicted its permanent wounds on him, inside and out. He was nervous, but the children knew he loved them and put his whole heart into teaching. He drummed facts and figures into their dormant minds in a way that stimulated a zeal for learning. It was only a short time until the children became occupied and interested. Although they were not required to attend school, they all showed up.

A science teacher named Mr. Kacis (Ka'-chis) – affectionately known as "Mr. Cat" – requested his students to bring samples of living things to class for identification and study. Little Ilze had heard about it, and for weeks she carried large insects into their building.

"This is for Mr. Cat," she would say seriously, only to open her fist to find a severely squashed specimen.

On their frequent walks, Ilze would spot a squirrel or bird and ask her papa to get it for her. Arvids explained there was no way he could catch the fast-moving creature. That did not stop his young daughter from insisting, "But get it for me, Papin!"

After several weeks the American soldiers realized the refugees were conducting school. It had been solely up to the teachers to capture the children's attention and keep them busy. Once the GIs found out about the classes, they brought in writing tablets and pencils, although the paper was of such poor quality that barely pressing a pencil on it would cause a tear. Still, it was better than none and proved to be a godsend for schoolwork.

To pass the time, the soldiers entertained with games and amateur magic tricks or brought in movies and sports balls, and they helped the boys organize soccer teams. Refugees showed their musical talents on piano and violin, wearing old tuxedos and performing like professionals in a music hall.

Arvids took on the responsibility of beautifying the grounds around their building. In the courtyard four flags flew: the American flag on the highest pole, then Lithuanian, Latvian, and Estonian. Residents planted flowers around the flagpoles, and Arvids formed flags out of multicolored pebbles on the ground nearby. The families were given garden plots to grow vegetables, and the refugees were elated to be able to work in the soil and watch their plants grow. They dutifully carried slop buckets to water the gardens. The gardens flourished, and trees were planted. Soon the place looked like a scenic park. In a matter of weeks the refugees could supplement their diet with the harvest from their labor. The women took turns in the camp's kitchen, making delicious soups that hungry diners appreciated. The vegetables brought back memories of food that had nourished them while growing up in their homelands.

Used clothing and shoes were brought into the camps – items much needed and appreciated. The refugees had worn out their clothing during the war period. Most people found something they could use from the deliveries. However, Judite could not find shoes to fit; supplies simply were not adequate to go around. If one found a pair that almost fit, he or she took them anyway and cut them into open-toed shoes to provide extra length. When the next shipment came, Anna's and Modra's shoes had worn out; and this time Judite got a shiny, black patent-leather pair. Her wide smile needed no words to express her pleasure.

The refugees were also given a small jar of petroleum jelly, called Brilliantine, and Keikulis family members found plenty of uses for it. Judite daubed some on her new shoes to keep them shiny.

In this camp Arvids and Cilite were allowed to hold religious services, and the majority of people who attended were Slavic. The couple was seeing their call to Russian ministry fulfilled.

Those who responded to the call of the gospel were grateful that God had drawn them to the Lord Jesus Christ when they had not known to seek Him. Arvids and Cilite remembered that they, as young adults, had prayed for God to give them a "good" family. His grace had brought them together and had recruited them to be part of His eternal family. They recalled how both had an interest in and burden for the

Russian people and had studied together so they would be able to share the gospel and pray in the Russian language. Now in the DP camps they were finding seekers of God's truth and believers who were likeminded and wanted to follow Christ.

One Sunday morning as the small congregation crowded into their room, Arvids noticed the entire front row filled with children. He had always loved the young ones, and their eager, innocent faces warmed his heart. He asked if any had a favorite hymn, memory verse, special request, or anything to share before they went to the Lord in prayer.

The first child looked down at his bare feet and said, "Let's pray for some shoes." The adults nodded in agreement.

The second child said, "Let's pray for some clothes." The adults again nodded in agreement, seeing many of the children in ragged clothes. The little girls wore dresses that Mariana had sewn from used flour sacks.

The next child's request was, "Let's pray for grandpa and grandma in the old country."

Again the adults nodded, murmuring, "Yes, let's remember our relatives."

And so it went down the line.

Near the end of the row was Modra, around four years old at the time, and her face had a funny expression. She was thinking about the candy jars in their store in Latvia. Throughout the war they remained in her memory, and she had dreamed about them.

"Let's pray for a whole pound of candy!" she said resolutely when it was her turn to speak.

The adults gasped at the frivolous request. "Oh, no!" they whispered. "We have too many other important things to pray about than to bother the Lord about candy."

Arvids thought for a moment. Then he spoke.

"No, I believe the children would be very pleased to have the candy, and we will pray about it this morning," he said.

They all had such a lack of energy from their diet through years without good food that Arvids knew little bodies needed a boost that sugar could provide. Ilze and the younger children did not know what candy was. So that morning, along with serious requests, they prayed that the

Lord would provide candy for the children.

Monday morning dawned – and along with it a delightful surprise. American soldiers arrived and got out of the trucks with bags in their arms. They saw the children running around in ragged clothes and called to them. As the scruffy little crowd responded, the soldiers reached into their bags and handed each child a Hershey chocolate bar. In spite of their appearance and circumstances, the children remembered the good manners they had been taught. In Europe, when speaking to an adult, little boys were expected to bow and little girls to curtsy.

Upon receiving the candy, Modra and Ilze curtsied several times and in broken English said, "Sank you, sank you!"

The excitement continued for some time. A while later the girls came running into their room squealing with delight and showing their parents armfuls of Hershey bars.

"Oh, where did you get all that candy?" Cilite asked, thinking they must have gotten them wrongfully. "Take it back, take it back!"

"Oh, no, Mama," Modra and Ilze insisted. "The Lord answered our prayer and sent the American soldiers with chocolate bars!"

That week the children had plenty of candy, and Modra went around the camp making sure they all understood who should receive the credit.

"Don't you forget it was all my idea," she reminded anyone who would listen.

In Eichstadt the men worked on a project building the Thompson Bridge in honor of their Austrian commandant. A celebration took place when the bridge was opened, and the commandant was invited. Cheaply constructed of wood, it washed away four or five years later; but for the men who were recovering physically and emotionally from the war, it provided worthwhile work and a needed sense of accomplishment.

Everyone looked for jobs. Mariana sought a job helping in the kitchen. She thought food might be left over to take back to the children, who were still weak from the previous two years. After praying about the matter, she found she was the first to be hired in the camp's kitchen. She was industrious, often working 16-hour days. The manager of the

First family photo for I.D. in D.P. Camp held in U.S. Army base.

Photo of sisters, 1st year in D.P. Camps.

storage house distrusted most of the camp residents, who were likely to steal; yet he requested Mariana to help after hours and gave her keys to the kitchen. She was assigned the responsibility of feeding the pigs, and a security guard watched over the kitchen while she prepared feed for the animals.

Mariana later worked in a bathhouse and supplied the families with passes to visit. After such a long time without the luxury of baths, the people relished a turn at this place. They made an entire evening of it, relaxing and perspiring in the steam room, followed by a shower. After the sauna, the participants splashed cold water from a wooden bucket as the final experience.

In her spare time Mariana made underwear for the women and children from clean flour bags. She had learned sewing from a Russian seamstress who altered and made repairs on donated clothing from America. Mariana had worked with her in her spare time when needed. As the children grew, she altered used clothes to make them fit. She became so adept that she could look at stylish garments and duplicate them.

Arvids was responsible for distributing the contents of the Care and Red Cross packages. He was so conscientious of being fair that he let others select first, and his family ended up with whatever was left. The DP camp required family photos to be taken for identification purposes. Naturally, all the residents wanted to look their best and scrounged for clothing presentable for the photos. In the most recent shipment were a few large dresses made of red-and-white polka dot fabric. Well aware of Arvids' consideration of others first, some of the women decided to trade so that the Keikulis family could alter the dresses to make matching outfits for their four daughters. Mariana sewed attractive dresses with white pinafores, which were fashionable for little girls in Germany at the time. The pinafores were made from flour sack material.

Church services were usually held in the Keikulis apartment. Mariana wished she could wear something attractive for the Sunday meetings. In one package she had found a large-sized dress in navy blue with light blue trim. She refashioned it into a tasteful jumper for herself and made an elegant blouse to wear with it from a used white parachute. Her talent blessed many people, and her creations made the women and girls feel feminine again.

Among the gifts and rations handed to the camp's refugees were cigarettes. Those who did not smoke could trade them for other needed items. Cigarettes could be sold in the black market for reasonable profit. Instead of trading his portion of cigarettes, Arvids burned them, saying, "If I consider it wrong, I cannot sell them to someone else."

Humiliated from losing the war, the Germans were becoming more openly kind to the refugees in the camps. Camp residents were free to leave, take walks, and enjoy recreation. Guards on duty at the entrances and exits were posted there solely for the residents' protection, observing who came and went. There were no restrictions. Local citizens were also kind to the refugees who ventured into town. The young people living in the camp frequented public swimming pools and gymnasiums and took advantage of programs offered in local high schools. The river was a favorite spot for swimming and fishing.

The countryside was picturesque with its flower-strewn hills and thick forests. Janis particularly enjoyed walks through the rugged terrain. While in Bavaria, the Keikulis family took a number of trips to Berchtesgaden and Garmisch-Partenkirchen to see the mountains.

On Sundays after church Arvids liked to take the young people on excursions through the fields and forests, often including other children in addition to his own. He taught them how he would call when they became scattered, using his familiar "haup, haup!" That was the signal for all the youths to scramble to get back together as he counted heads.

He tried to make the woods seem like God's vast cathedral. They gathered wildflowers, mushrooms, berries, rosehips, and whatever else they could find in the wild. On one occasion they found dark blueberries with pits inside and thorns on the branches. They picked and ate to their hearts' content. Judite felt her tongue getting numb and wondered what they were. At another place they found a tree with unusual nuts that were easy to peel. They were three-sided, smooth, and rich in oils but were never identified. Suddenly the children noticed the ground moving under their feet. They were standing on grey deer ticks and quickly brushed them off, searching each other's scalps. Bringing berries or mushrooms back to camp felt like an important mission

225

accomplished, since they knew everyone would later eat jam or cooked mushrooms with delight. The mushrooms satisfied their palates like meat.

These times provided a pleasant respite from pressures. Although the refugees struggled and worked hard to bring their lives into a more normal existence, there were still conflicts with unbelievers mocking and accusing the church group. Getting out into God's creation was much-needed therapy for their overall health. Arvids looked forward to teachable moments of building faith. He often scouted out ahead to find a special place for the children to "discover." When his eyes twinkled and his eyebrows lifted in anticipation of what was in store, the children responded with equal enthusiasm and excitement.

On one occasion, with a sweep of his hand and usual announcement, "Ahaha vota!" the children turned to see a picturesque clearing in the woods and a sparkling brook bubbling around a large rock in the middle. It looked like "big water" to the children. One by one, in dramatic strides, Arvids carried each child over and plopped him on the rock. Then he revealed a surprise hidden in his pocket – something to nibble on.

They would long remember the celebration: the day a gigantic rock was discovered in the middle of the dark woods.

And so it was that the refugees slowly and deliberately began to reclaim a more normal rhythm of life. They had to learn to relax and enjoy little things again. As they walked back, they wandered through an old cemetery, careful not to tread on delicate flowers. German cemeteries were kept trimmed and landscaped with an array of flowers that resembled a formal garden, making them fascinating places to visit.

Arvids obtained travel permits to go to other DP camps to witness and preach. Wherever he was invited, he went on a regular basis. When it was time to baptize new converts, they went into the woods and used bomb craters filled with rain water.

One night when the moon seemed biggest and brightest, Arvids and Anna climbed through the barbed wire and walked down to the river. There he baptized his oldest daughter and a few other new believers. No one was sure of the liberties pertaining to the ordinance of baptism, so they were discreet in their movements. It was a solemn, joyous occasion as they whispered prayers and softly sang hymns.

Walking back to the building in the moonlight, Anna felt as if she were walking on air. It was difficult to imagine not being a Christian, since her faith in Christ was real as far back as she could remember. She and her siblings believed as they were taught and shown. However, she was now aware of having made a lifelong commitment to Christ. She felt lighthearted, knowing she was following in the Master's footsteps.

Some of the rations of army food – and those later provided through the International Refugee Organization and Red Cross – were strange to the refugees. Envelopes of colored powder (probably Kool-Aid) tasted so good that the children ate it right out of the package. Once Judite opened a can of powdered cream and ate the entire contents, which was supposed to be a month's supply. When the family bowed their heads in prayer before meals, Modra covered her bowl with her hand as if to protect it. Another time they received an unlabeled can of vegetable soup. Not being told what it was or what to do with it, they simply tasted it and ate it out of the can. Later they learned it tasted much better to add water and heat the mixture. When it was Ilze's turn to say the blessing, she peeked with one eye and thanked God for every vegetable she could see floating in her soup, one by one.

They were also given vitamins and cod liver oil to boost their health. The children tried to run away before it was time to take their daily dose of the awful tasting oil. They lined up reluctantly, holding their noses, and ran away as soon as it was over, pleading, "Please! No more!"

Since many of the refugees traveled a long distance to attend church, the Keikulises planned to feed them after the services. Cilite and Mariana usually prepared a tub of farina whipped and sweetened, along with a pot of soup made with bacon drippings, onions, and oatmeal. Any soup bones they came across were used again and again, as had been practiced in the labor camps. The guests brought along bread or other items to supplement the Sunday dinners. It was not an elegant feast, but no one left hungry.

The families' encounters with Americans in Eichstadt demonstrated that the soldiers were humane and compassionate. The children soon discovered "tricks" to get the best from the guards, knowing exactly when the sentries would have their breakfast, lunch, and supper brought in. The soldiers had been ordered to eat at least some of their food, or it would be given to the frail refugees. The children often sat patiently near a sentry until a truck brought his meal.

One morning Anna and Judite were watching when a soldier received a breakfast of pancakes, syrup, and eggs. The pancakes were stacked with a large chunk of butter on top, and the contents of the plate seemed to literally float in syrup. The girls had never seen syrup in such abundance. The sentry looked at the girls and then started to eat. He took a big bite and pretended he was going to throw away the rest.

Then he glanced over at the girls, knowing why they were there, and asked, "Oh, would you care for this?"

Delighted, the two accepted. It was undoubtedly the most delicious thing they had ever eaten. They had never tasted anything like it before. They even drank his coffee and thought it was delectable. The soldier giggled as he watched them devour the food, relishing every mouthful.

On another occasion Janis had received pancakes via the same method. He was so excited he brought it inside and shared a mouthful with each of the others.

Kindhearted soldiers made a habit of conspicuously "throwing away" whole loaves of unopened bread at the side of the trash heap. They watched while delighted children retrieved them. Accustomed to dark breads, the white bread seemed like cake to the youngsters.

The family's introduction to peanut butter was an interesting experience. After opening the can and examining it, they realized it was made from some kind of nut. They did not know to put it on bread, so they began to eat it by dipping their fingers in the container. It tasted so good that they soon finished the whole can. Unfortunately they became violently ill since their stomachs were not ready for the unfamiliar food. They learned it was best to eat new, rich foods in small quantities to allow time for their digestive systems to adapt.

In Eichstadt the children were shown American movies, and they were captivated as they watched "The Last of the Mohicans." This was their first glimpse of the American Indian and cowboy. Judite screamed and ran home when she saw a cowboy hit by a tomahawk.

"Mama, mama, a man's been killed!" she cried.

"No, child, that's just a movie," Cilite explained.

"No, mama, it's real," Judite said. "I saw the blood coming out!"

During another movie, a woman who understood some English occasionally leaned over and explained a part of the movie to the girls.

"Is this a romance?" Judite asked.

"Yes," the lady replied.

"Oh, Anna," Judite exclaimed, "romance is bad. We have to leave. Papa wouldn't want us to watch it."

* * * * * * * * * * *

Eichstadt was a picturesque valley with a stream flowing through the middle of two meadows. It was green and lush, and the children loved roaming the poppy-covered hills. Acres of wheat fields were bordered with blue bachelor buttons and daisies. When Judite heard planes overhead, she instinctively ran behind a rock to hide. Arvids and Cilite told her the war was over, but Judite shook her head. For several months the children continued to run for cover at the sound of airplanes, their young minds conditioned to the perceived danger. When American tanks came through the base on an exercise, Ilze ran for cover trying to fit her body between a rainspout and the building.

On a crisp autumn day during the last week of October 1945, Arvids went to Anna and told her he wanted to take her on a special secret mission. She was to dress up in her Sunday best and comb her hair just right. They would be walking to town. Anna was excited as she dressed and prepared to go. October 28 was Arvids' and Cilite's wedding anniversary, and Arvids wanted to make it special. He had saved up several bars of soap from Red Cross boxes. After the war, soap was cherished more than money and made a good trade for other needed items.

"You and I are going to look for flowers for Mamin," Arvids whispered to Anna. "She hasn't had any flowers in a long time."

Arvids and Cilite had an extraordinary love relationship; they always functioned as a team. Even through trials and spiritual battles, they had a sweet, romantic fellowship underneath. Their love for each other provided comfort and joy. They had always been united and felt one another's strength and support. Arvids wanted his daughter to understand this kind of tenderness.

He had learned to speak German, and so they went into the first flower shop they saw. The shopkeeper was willing to trade for the soap. However, Arvids was not satisfied with the bouquet offered, so the lady told them about another place where they might find the favored flowers.

Arvids and Anna walked a long distance to two more florist shops. It was a misty, cloudy day, and Anna was feeling cold and wet. She felt like her toes would fall off.

At each shop Arvids asked if he could trade the soap for flowers for his wife's anniversary, but he still was not quite satisfied with the selections. They finally walked all the way back to the original shop and traded for the first bunch they had seen. Then they retraced their long walk to the second shop and added more flowers for the last bar of soap.

Now Arvids was satisfied with the gift.

When they returned home with the flowers, Cilite wept while the children squealed with delight.

"Can you imagine what we could have done with that kind of money?" she said. She was thinking of all kinds of needs.

Arvids did not try to argue or explain. He left her with the bouquet and took a walk to allow things to cool down. Cilite began to feel bad because her husband had made an admirable effort to get a few posies to celebrate their special day. When he returned, he consoled Cilite by calling her some favorite pet names, "Nu Dudin, dudin, balodin (Well, dovey, my dove)."

* * * * * * * * * * *

The DP camps were being reorganized to keep nationalities together. On November 5, 1946, the Keikulis family, along with Mariana and the Bartusevicses, were transferred to Ansbach, Germany. Here they lived and worked for two years and eight months. At first they were placed in a room in another former army barracks, where they celebrated Christmas that year. Arvids found evergreen branches which he nailed to a piece of wood to make a Christmas tree. The family made decorations out of scraps of paper and hung them on the makeshift tree.

Because of their Christian stance, camp authorities thought it would be humorous to assign the Keikulis family to live with a woman who was thought to be a prostitute.

"Put the 'holy ones' with the crazy woman," the refugee organizer said.

So the family was moved to the third floor of a large building to share an oversized room with a woman called "Onion Julie" and her current male friend. Julie was suspected of having a venereal disease, and the couple was known for violent fights.

Evidently a degree of persecution followed the Keikulises to the DP camps.

As they settled in, Arvids and Cilite attempted to section off their living area by hanging up army blankets. Later Arvids built tall wardrobes that helped to function as a partition. The children had heard rumors and were curious to see their new neighbors.

"A sinner is only a sinner, but we will be kind to her," Cilite said.

At first Julie played the part. She read the Bible aloud, selecting only those passages where stories of sinful deeds of murder, incest, and unfaithfulness occurred. Then she would exclaim loudly, "Huh, what kind of God is that?" When Julie and her friend got into intense arguments, pots and utensils came flying over the partitions.

Julie had lived in the same labor camp as Mariana at one time, and she called Mariana the "crazy Bible reader." She had told others, "Whenever there was an air raid, we all fell to the floor and hid. Mariana would grab her Bible and start to read."

Cilite reached out to Julie in love. The woman had taken in laundry to wash and iron to earn money, and Cilite often helped her with it. Julie saw that Cilite not only talked Christianity but lived it every day.

The children also sought her friendship and engaged her in conversation. Little Ilze liked to run around the wall of wardrobes and with a quick smile shout "sveiki (svay-kih, meaning hi)!" Judite helped Julie take care of her chickens. With the money saved, Judite bought two pairs of shoes, which she and Modra wore later on their trip to the United States.

Before long, Julie's attitude softened, and she became friendly, even offering delicacies her partner had brought. As the family treated her like a friend, their kindness was reciprocated. They lived together as good neighbors, to the surprise of many who anticipated severe problems.

Julie proved to be a good neighbor, but her mouth was in the habit of yelling profanity. Out of curiosity the children tried to listen to some of her expressions. Janis would reprimand them, saying, "I'm going to tell Mamin, and you're going to get killed!"

In Ansbach, Arvids and Janis obtained work in a warehouse, loading and unloading trucks for the International Refugee Organization. Since the two would not accept cigarettes as payment nor did they drink alcoholic beverages, the authorities trusted them and placed them in charge of delivering large columns of supply trucks to refugee camps. Arvids and Janis welcomed the opportunity to see the countryside and meet people of different nationalities. By then they could speak English and German well enough to handle the job.

Janis felt important, riding up front in the American army truck and being responsible for the safe delivery of supplies. Most of the drivers were recruited from the camps, many of them Ukrainian. Not having much money, if any, unscrupulous men tried to find means of getting something for themselves. The Americans knew how much gas was required to drive a mile. The sharp drivers knew how to take advantage of the engines and the terrain, sometimes coasting downhill to save on their allotment of gas.

Janis kept a constant watch in his rearview mirror to ensure all the trucks in his convoy were following, and occasionally he would notice that he had lost one. Drivers tried to pull off the road for one excuse or another to attempt black marketeering. The shrewd drivers would take a jerry can – a metal gasoline container used in the military, originally made by the Germans – of gas to sell to the locals. This was just one method of black marketeering for profit. It was Janis's responsibility to see that this did not happen. Once the drivers tried to leave him on the road, pretending they thought he was on the truck. Another time a lady in one of the camps approached the convoy and asked if she might get a ride to another camp. With good-hearted intentions, Janis agreed and promised to return as soon as his invoice was signed. Upon returning to his truck, he found the lady and the entire convoy gone. He walked 25 miles home that evening.

Another way the black marketeers made money was to alter a 50-pound sugar sack by sticking a pole into the bag, pouring in a bucket of water, and stirring the mixture. This increased the volume of the sugar by 10 to 20 pounds. Then when the sack arrived at the camp, the crooks gave the original correct weight and kept the difference to sell. Sometimes the thieves were so intent on making a buck that Janis's life was actually in danger.

* * * * * * * * * * * *

During the early months in Ansbach, Anna also had begun to experience chest pains, shortness of breath, and temporary fainting spells. Physical activity in school became increasingly difficult. She decided that she must have tuberculosis.

She knew her papa had suffered with it, so she was familiar with the symptoms. She began perspiring heavily at night, and her parents spent much time praying for her and trusting God. Finally Anna stopped mentioning the severity of the discomfort and pain in her chest. It was too much for her young mind to figure out, so she stopped talking about it. She did not want to worry her parents and had heard of others being sent to hospitals far away. There was no medical care nearby.

Americans encouraged self-government in the camps, so teachers taught classes from memory and medical personnel used their skills to diagnose illnesses and conditions. Most often they did not have equipment or medicine to cure the ailments. As a norm, patients were not sent to German hospitals.

Eventually, medical personnel were sent to the camps to examine the refugees. One of their first assignments was to administer tuberculosis tests. Anna was terrified to see her results.

"How will you know if I have TB?" she inquired of the medic.

"If this one little scratch grows into a boil, you can be pretty sure that you have it," he answered.

It was the wrong thing to say. The skin reaction was only a sign that one had been in contact with the disease. Anna's scratch grew into

233

a boil. She hid it from her family. In three days, when she went in to report it, the medics said she needed to have chest x-rays immediately. With that, she gave up fighting the pain and came down with a high fever. She became quite sick, and upon arriving at home Arvids and Cilite put her to bed. She was too ill to return for the chest x-rays.

Under camp authority they had to call a doctor. He was grave about her condition and saw little hope for her recovery. Between the delirium of heavy fevers, Anna heard the physician tell her mother that she had water in her lungs. Because of high fever, she was bleeding at the mouth and had a serious case of pneumonia. Upon hearing this, Anna was relieved that she did not have tuberculosis. It did not occur to her that pneumonia could be fatal. The doctor suggested that she be placed in a hospital, although there was no cure available.

"We are Christians, and we believe in the Lord," Cilite quietly told the doctor. "May we keep her here and pray for her?"

"Who am I to fight such faith?" the doctor replied. "God help you. There is nothing we can do for her in the hospital anyway."

Anna continued to be extremely ill and weak from the loss of blood and weight. Arvids had been away on a trip. When he returned home to find his daughter so sick, he called the Christians to come and gather around her bed to pray. Anna could not comprehend what they said or how long they were there, but she knew they were praying. She awakened in the middle of the night and realized the fever was gone. She lay there trying to figure out how many days she had been sick but had no recollection. Cilite had pulled a cot up next to Anna's bed so that she could feel her every movement or if she needed help. Anna did not want to awaken her mother, but she could not wait until morning to find out what day it was.

The camp authorities did not permit Anna to return to school for six months, but she began to recover rapidly. The story of her complete recovery reached the doctor who had visited.

Four years later, when all family members were required to have a series of physical examinations to be permitted to immigrate to the United States, they were concerned that the scars on Anna's lungs might prohibit their clearance. The physical exams and tests took two weeks. When medical professionals evaluated Anna's x-rays, they called them "healed scars from wet pleurisy." Doctors in America said they were from pneumonia, and eventually all the scars healed. God used these experiences as a steppingstone in Anna's life of faith.

The surgeon who operated on Anna when she was 25 said that a large cyst had grown on her ovary as a result of the ruptured appendix. Anna's Bible college had called a special chapel service to pray for her. A few days after the initial operation, the doctor scheduled an emergency surgery for an infected gallbladder. However, when time came for the second surgery, her infection had healed, and gallbladder removal was no longer needed. God had protected her through the years when she had been in a near-gangrene condition and had intervened once again.

During this time, the children took turns coming down with common childhood diseases, so the Keikulis room often resembled an infirmary, and school was prohibited to keep diseases from spreading.

As in Eichstadt, Arvids and Cilite were allowed to hold Sunday church services while in Ansbach. Slavic refugees from other camps came from as far away as 25 miles to join the believers for the weekly meetings. After morning worship the congregation sometimes took a train to a Ukrainian camp to hold an afternoon service, where there were mostly Catholics.

The group had heard of a lady who had given birth to a baby without a digestive tract. The hospital tried to keep the infant alive with blood transfusions and intravenous feeding, but she remained seriously ill. The same doctor who had visited Anna spoke to the mother of the abnormal baby in Ashaffenburg.

"Look, there is a man and his family who really have faith in God and pray," the doctor said. "In your case, we cannot help your baby. It wouldn't hurt if you visited this man."

During the Sunday service the believers were surprised to see a woman walk in carrying a frail, discolored baby and drop to her knees in front of Arvids. They immediately knew who it had to be. In her traditional manner she attempted to kiss Arvids' feet, which is the Orthodox custom when meeting a priest. Arvids restrained her. She begged him to pray that her child would live. She handed him the frail baby, which she had taken from the hospital without permission. The baby's skin

Russian congregation in D.P. Camp.

2nd photo of Russian converts in D.P. Camp.

First Sunday school class for children.

was discolored – a bluish yellow – and her eyes were not clear.

Arvids felt the awesome responsibility placed upon him. He prayed a short, simple prayer. When he returned the baby to the mother, she opened her purse and lifted out a prepared bottle and began feeding the infant. The small group of people stood quietly and were astonished when the baby began sucking. The mother carried out her duty routinely, and – just as routinely – when the child finished the bottle, the woman began to change the diaper. Everyone watched and saw that the baby had soiled the diaper normally.

When the woman went back home, her husband and the police were searching for the baby. Instead of happiness resulting in the aftermath of this act of God's grace, harassment began. Some of the men in that camp behaved as if they wanted to kill Arvids. They threatened to call the police.

"Go ahead and call them," Arvids said. "They will arrest you. We have freedom of religion here. If you go to the United States, they will jail you for interference."

* * * * * * * * * * *

Converts and seekers came to the Keikulis camp for church services, and new believers were baptized. One man had beautiful children's books, which he loaned to the Keikulis family. Arvids read and translated them from Ukrainian, and the bright-colored illustrations fascinated the children.

Baptizing new convert in crater made by bomb.

The older men who worked with Janis decided to play a trick on him, taking advantage of his youth and innocence. There were no grapes in Latvia; therefore, the Keikulises were not familiar with grape juice. Arvids had shown Janis pictures of grapes, bananas, and other fruits that grew in some parts of the world. When the men offered Janis grape juice, he trusted them, having worked with them for several years. First smelling it and then tasting it, Janis did not become suspicious and drank it down. He was somewhat disappointed, expecting it to be much tastier.

"Here, you need the vitamins," the men said. "Have some more."

"No," Janis stammered. "Save some for yourselves."

"Drink!" they said, handing him another cup.

They stood around to watch. Janis felt warm and unbuttoned the top of his shirt. The next morning he learned they had actually given him vermouth wine and expected him to become drunk. It would have been fun for them if they had managed to get the minister's son in trouble.

Germany was filled with an abundance of spectacular ancient castles that provided interesting destinations for sightseeing. In his spare time Janis loved to travel, and he and his friends sought out places to explore. Gone were the ruthless Nazis and soldiers, and the youths had plenty of energy stored up. On one occasion the boys discovered a secret underground passageway in a castle. With lit matches in hand, they gingerly made their way through a long, dark tunnel. With extended arms, they ran their hands along the walls for direction. Suddenly the walls ended, and they realized they had arrived atop a deep, forbidding precipice. That ended their spirit of adventure for the day, and the explorers were relieved to crawl back above ground to daylight.

The family once again enjoyed walks through the woods. Arvids remembered that during his childhood the forests were his refuge to escape the unhappiness at home. In his early Christian walk, the woodlands had become his prayer rooms where he spent many hours meditating and communing with God. He gained strength and spiritual refreshment from those experiences.

The children shared their father's love for the outdoors, and they often accompanied him on the excursions. In Bavaria the beauty of the woodlands was tainted by the unavoidable tick population; the family literally had to peel them off their covered bodies. In Germany they explored scenic forests, and the cities were clean and beautiful, even with the destructive evidence of war. There were numerous parks and public places to enjoy. The forests were kept healthy and unblemished, and fallen or unsightly dead trees were seldom encountered.

There was a spiritual hunger among Russians in the camps, and the Lord blessed Arvids' and Cilite's ministry there. Another baptismal service was held for new believers, and this time Judite was among them. The sun's rays that beamed radiantly through the trees seemed to match the significance of new believers' obedience and confession; the humble, spiritual atmosphere was enhanced by the wonder of God's creation. A baptism was always a special occasion, and this was no exception.

Camp residents were again able to supplement their diets as their garden plots provided fresh vegetables. It was a special treat to have new onions or other home-produced items for meals. Wanting to help pull weeds one day, Ilze had inadvertently gathered a handful of flowers from someone's garden. She looked dismayed when she was corrected.

The American soldiers continued to be a pleasant change to the refugees' former dealings with the military. Prior to learning to be at ease around them, the children had tried to hide from men in uniform. Now they saw friendly American GIs, and the little ones returned the smiles. At Christmas the GIs picked up all the children in the camp and took them to a party. There the Keikulis children saw their first Santa Claus, who passed out gifts and treats with the help of the soldiers. The Red Cross and Care organizations had provided games such as checkers, dominoes, and Chinese checkers. European children were not used to a Santa Claus who invited them to sit on his lap. Most of them stared in awe, but all had a pleasurable time and came home with gifts of crayons, toothbrushes, hard chocolate, and foodstuffs such as sweetened canned milk and canned pressed ham.

One day the American camp authorities and the Association of Refugee Leaders announced that they would provide a tour bus to go into Switzerland to see the Alps. Cilite immediately said, "No way!" but Janis was thrilled, having inherited an appetite for adventure from his papa. He often traded his allotment of soap and other amenities, accumulating items others deemed as prizes. The Germans needed soap and canned fish that the refugees had received in Care packages and were eager to barter and help arrange the bus tour. Soon Arvids, Mariana, Janis, and Anna had exchanged their cherished possessions and boarded the bus headed for the Alps.

The vehicle was filled, taking excited passengers to Salzburg, Austria, and down into the famous salt mines. Most nights were spent on the bus. Passengers ate whatever rations they had brought with them, mostly stale bread or sardines. The weather was chilly, but everyone was having an enchanting time. One night the tour coordinator secured rooms for the entire group. Small beds were shared, and the down comforters were luxurious. Even the frozen water in the bowls on the washstands the next morning did not dampen the spirits of the travelers. In the dining room they were served hot coffee and tempting soft rolls. They savored each sip of coffee and lingered on each bite of the fluffy rolls, even coddling the bread.

Anna enjoyed counting the tall bridges they traveled over. The trip was an exceptional, much appreciated opportunity, a feast for the eyes and soul. The refugees were inspired and renewed as they beheld the grandeur of stately mountains and forests, bright colors in the land-scapes, architecture in large buildings and homes, and even the serenity of cows grazing in green pastures. On Lake Geneva the group went for a boat ride that took them between the majestic peaks. It really did seem like heaven.

Lacking proper warm clothing, Anna cuddled close to her father, never complaining. As she sat close to him, she suddenly realized how skinny he had become

Chapter 8

The Land of Freedom

Immigration was initiated by the United Nations Relief Rehabilitation Administration, and the Keikulis family began to consider their possibilities. Because of their large family, they did not expect to receive permission to go the United States, so they initially signed up for Brazil and Venezuela.

After a time they succeeded in establishing contact with American Christians. A tall, chubby American chaplain of Russian descent went with Arvids to the various camps, where they met with small church groups in each. When discussing the immigration issue, Arvids told the chaplain that he had applied for sponsorship to South America, Australia, and Canada but had not heard back from them. He thought the problem was that the family was too big.

"I've been given the responsibility to find a pastor to help with the incoming Russian immigrants in Philadelphia," the chaplain said.

He put Arvids in contact with an American woman named Clara Eagle. She pastored a small Ukrainian church in Newark, N.J. This church had sponsored the Bartusevics family, who had left a few months earlier. Clara worked diligently to assist Arvids in his efforts to emigrate.

When word came that the Assemblies of God had agreed to sponsor the Keikulises, through a Russian church, to assist Pastor Paul Demetrus in Philadelphia, Pa., Arvids and Cilite bowed their heads, vividly remembering when the call to minister to Russians was revealed early in their marriage. They had made a commitment at that time to follow Christ and reach out to Russians with the gospel.

Prior to the departure of groups of refugees for their new homelands, emotional goodbyes and small ceremonies took place in the camps. There were brief speeches focusing on gratitude and hope for a new future. Before departing, women and teenaged girls received a bag of cosmetics to prepare for their new destinations. Inside they found a compact, lipstick, and creams for beauty aids, which they were eager to try. However, some of the children thought the lipsticks were crayons to be used for creative artistry.

After corresponding with their secured sponsors in America, the Keikulis family went to work to obtain the necessary papers for immigration. Some of the congregation left for Brazil and Venezuela, but Arvids and Cilite could not help but notice their own travels always continued westward – just as God had intended.

The camp population decreased rapidly as families awaited their turn in the quota system into the new world. The free countries had established annual quotas based on the numbers of immigrants they could accept and accommodate. Mariana, with a different last name, could not be listed with the Keikulis family. She read an announcement on a bulletin board that single men and women could sign up to be sponsored by those needing maids and servants. Seeking a way to get to the United States, she registered.

When the family obtained the required sponsorship from the church in Philadelphia, Mariana's papers were still not processed. No one understood the delay but continued to pray about the matter. When it was time to leave for the processing and medical exams, the family was heartbroken to leave Mariana behind. Tearfully, they promised to keep praying and to do all they could to find her a sponsor if she did not leave soon.

After the Keikulises had begun the process for immigration, Arvids received a letter from a Christian youth who was concerned about the Lord's work. He explained that he had met a Russian doctor on a train after World War II. He had witnessed to the doctor and upon parting obtained his address.

"I know you will be going through the city where this doctor lives when you receive your physical exams," the young man wrote. "I think it would be worthwhile to look him up because he is really thirsty for God, and I think you can speak to him better than I can."

With all the documents finally ready, the Keikulis family left Ansbach in military trucks bound for Schweinfurt, Germany. Since they had to wait in this city for their turn for physical exams, Arvids looked up the address of the doctor, and he and Cilite went to find him.

After knocking several times, a woman finally came to the door and said, "The doctor is not seeing anyone today" and shut the door. Arvids continued to knock, and again the woman came out and repeated, "The doctor is not seeing anyone. You are wasting your time."

Arvids and Cilite realized that the doctor must have thought they needed special favors for their exams, so they told the woman they had received the address from a young man the physician had encountered on a train.

Then the couple was allowed to step inside to meet the doctor, his wife, and a grown daughter. The wife and daughter were both nurses. The doctor explained why he had not come to the door. He was the main physician assigned to examine refugees who had tuberculosis, and many refugees begged him to lie on their papers so they could gain entrance to the United States. He had remembered seeing the documentation for their family with five children, and no one had tuberculosis. It was common in a large family to find at least one member with tuberculosis.

The conversation then took a more personal tone. The doctor told his guests that he had studied for the Orthodox priesthood before going into medicine.

"I know the Bible, but I couldn't argue with the young man I met on the train," he said. "What is it that's different with him? I could see it on his face, and I see it on yours. How could this young man know the Bible as he did? I know he wasn't educated, but he could speak of the Bible in a way that I couldn't."

They talked for a long time about Jesus Christ and His free gift of salvation. Arvids had never felt quite this way as he witnessed to the family; he was aware they were taking in every word with faith and a thirst for truth. They all knelt and prayed together, and the hearts of the three responded to Christ's invitation. They confessed Him aloud and praised Him with their hands raised heavenward.

For a long time the little group did not want to end their newfound fellowship. The doctor told Arvids and Cilite that they would be going to Australia but did not have a forwarding address. They parted as old friends, now with the common bond of their Savior's love.

Most of the refugees were nervous about passing their physicals to receive permission to immigrate to the United States, Brazil, or Australia. People with communicable diseases were automatically prohibited from going to the country for which they were being processed. However, if they had an abnormal disorder, they were not rejected from entrance but bypassed and delayed for future examination – often waiting months before being called again.

Among themselves, the refugees were known to classify doctors and examiners as "kind and considerate" or "strict and severe." The Keikulises had been warned of a stern examiner, and it was their fate to get him. The children wore their best clothes, with faces scrubbed and hair neatly combed. They lined up against the wall in the examination room. The examiner walked over and, without changing his expression, patted a few of them on the head.

He must not be so bad, the children thought and began to smile shyly.

"Don't forget!" the doctor snapped just when they started to relax. "I have the authority to decide your destiny."

He started to question their intentions and asked Janis what kind of work he would do in the new homeland.

"I will do any kind of work given me," Janis answered politely.

As the examiner continued with each child, they noticed that he became more at ease, and he even pulled at one of the girls' braids.

"This family has permission to immigrate to the United States," he dictated to his secretary. She flashed a wide smile, to which he quickly retorted, tongue-in-cheek, "This is serious business. Don't get carried away!"

Thus he completed his formal duty.

After a few weeks in Schweinfurt, the Keikulis family was sent to another camp north of that location. The next and final camp was Grohn, outside Bremerhafen. In each camp they went through different screenings, which added pressure to their already fragile nerves. At times it almost seemed worse than the cruelties they had endured during the war.

When Anna was examined, scar tissue was found in her lungs, and the doctor wanted to know what had taken place. He spoke of calcium spots on her lungs. The parents spent anxious moments wondering if these abnormalities were associated with tuberculosis. Upon returning to the barracks, worry and concern filled their minds. It was stressful to wait several days before knowing the outcome for their future. Then the news came that they had passed and were approved for entry into the United States of America.

What a magnificent, perfect relief!

On July 9, 1949, the Keikulis family embarked on their journey to America aboard a troop ship named General Leroy Eltinge. Cilite was sick during the entire trip. The crew was kind to the children, providing treats such as apples and candy bars. They showed the children how to avoid seasickness.

"In your mind, smell the earth," they said. "Every time you feel like you're going to get sick, just close your eyes and in your imagination pick up dirt in your hand and smell and feel it."

Amazingly, the technique worked. One stormy night most of the passengers were thrown out of their bunks. The children scrambled, eyes closed, picking up clumps of imaginary dirt and smelling it. Then they went back to bed.

The children were free to roam the large deck. Here they saw more American movies, which they found captivating. One was a Bob Hope movie, and another featured Charlie Chaplin. There was a playroom full of toys, but through an oversight it was not shown to the children until the last few days of the trip.

The young ones were fascinated to look through a large metal grate that was part of the bathroom floor. Below they could see the lower floor, on which many adults were experiencing the consequences of seasickness. "Smelling the earth" evidently had not worked for them.

As Ilze and a little boy her age were walking around the ship, her friend showed her a box of strange powder in the bathroom. He told her that mixing the powder with plenty of water would make lots of bubbles. To satisfy her curiosity, she scooped a couple of handfuls of the powder into the sink and turned on the faucet full blast. Soon there were suds overflowing onto the bathroom floor.

Ilze had discovered American detergent. Her excitement was somewhat abated when she got into trouble over the incident.

One day the passengers were called on deck to see whales swimming close to the ship. Another time the crew pointed out tall cliffs, identifying them as part of England. The food served on the ship was scrumptious, and there was plenty of it. During the final days of the trip, the refugees were shocked to see numerous crates of apples and oranges thrown overboard. After years of near starvation, such waste was deplorable, and Cilite could not keep from crying.

The soon-to-be immigrants had heard much about America, the land of promise. Their expectations ran high. It had been eight days since their departure from Germany.

As the ship approached the Boston harbor, the atmosphere overflowed with excitement and anticipation. Everyone pressed at the rails to see. However, the filth of the harbor and the surrounding city was a disappointment, though soon forgotten.

Upon disembarking, each child was greeted by an immigration official offering a large ball or another toy. Clara Eagle met the Keikulises; and they rode two taxicabs to a station, where they boarded a bus for Newark. They were intrigued with the black women and children, having seen only a few black soldiers in Germany. When the girls saw an empty seat next to a black woman on the bus, they argued over who would sit in it.

As the family rode through the streets of the cities, they stared in awe at the sights. After the buildup of stories about America, they could not believe the litter in the streets of New York. Modra stared with wide eyes at the city lights at night – soaring skyscrapers with windows lit up and bright-colored neon signs everywhere.

"How can the Americans pay their electric bill?" the girl exclaimed.

When the family arrived at Clara Eagle's home that night, each girl received a large stuffed animal. Judite had a "Bambi," Modra a dog, and Ilze a panda bear. The next morning they were treated to an American breakfast – a choice of cereals out of a box, with milk and sliced ba-

Russian church in Philadelphia.

nanas. One of the cereals made a crackling noise while soaking up the milk. It was an unfamiliar meal to the newly arrived immigrants – but nevertheless delicious.

After two weeks they were taken to Philadelphia by car, where they met Paul and Ruth Demetrus and their two little girls, Karen and Judy. The Keikulises were given an upstairs apartment over the Demetruses' living quarters.

Next door was the church Paul and Ruth had started for Russian immigrants. Here Arvids felt at home and was jubilant in helping Brother Demetrus pastor the Russian congregation. He knew he had arrived at God's destination for him and his family.

For the next six years the church sponsored many Russian families and helped them start a living the way the Demetrus family had helped the Keikulises. Ruth was gifted in teaching Sunday School. Church services were conducted in Russian, but Sunday School for the children was taught in English. The elementary school was located across the street, so the children were learning English in school, on the street, and in Sunday School. Anna and Judite were placed in a special school that taught English and acquainted students with American culture – Anna in high school and Judite in junior high.

Several months after the Keikulises arrived in the United States,

Mariana was working as a cleaning woman in a refugee hospital approximately two miles from their former camp in Germany. One day a Jeep vehicle came, and she was taken to people who asked questions concerning her desire to immigrate to the United States as a maid.

Two weeks later she was told to prepare to leave for Schweinfurt, the screening camp. She had no idea of her destination or the identity of her sponsor. Still, she hoped she would be going to United States, where she could work and support herself and perhaps meet her spiritual family again. She had prayed that she would pass the physical examinations and questioning. There were rumors of blackmail and jealousy, and this was the last big hurdle to complete.

When Mariana asked who her sponsor was and where she would be going, she was told, "O. Brooks in Virginia."

I am not going to write Mama and Papa Keikulis, she thought at first. I'll just surprise them after I get to America.

However, she felt a restlessness and a strong urge to go ahead and write. Finally, she sent a note saying she would soon leave for the United States and included the name and address of her sponsor. Upon receiving the letter, Arvids took it to Clara Eagle, who could find out the best way to contact Mariana upon her arrival.

Clara sent a special delivery letter to the sponsor's address asking if Mariana might be able to visit her family for a few weeks before starting work in Virginia. The letter came back stamped "Address Unknown." Not to be discouraged, Clara next sent a telegram. Western Union told her they could not deliver the telegram. Checking with immigration authorities, Clara was told that it looked suspicious, that "O. Brooks" had likely changed addresses too frequently. Then Clara contacted Church World Service, who in turn contacted the Keikulises to see if they would be responsible for taking care of Mariana when she arrived.

As it turned out, Vali, the oldest Bartusevics daughter, whose family was already in the United States, was married to a man named Janis Jansons. He was working in a factory where he mentioned to his boss the unusual circumstances of Mariana's mysterious sponsor and that she would be coming on the General Blackburn ship. Janis's boss asked for a photo of Mariana.

"Don't worry," he said. "I will arrange for plainclothes police to meet her at the ship."

Before docking, Mariana heard her name called on the loudspeaker. Startled, she wondered if she would be sent back to the refugee camp. She went to the captain.

"Here, you have a telegram," he said." Can you read and speak English?"

"Not very much," she answered.

"Well, what languages can you speak?" asked the captain.

"Russian, Lithuanian, Latvian, Ukrainian," Mariana replied.

"Well, then, let's speak Russian," the captain continued, reading and interpreting the telegram: "Mariana, do not leave the port until you see Clara Eagle. Signed Janis Jansons."

Mariana was confused and tried to figure out the message. What if my sponsor comes; what will I do? she worried. She could not sleep that night.

In the morning the refugees were lined up alphabetically to get their papers stamped and fingerprints taken in preparation for disembarking. Suddenly, two plainclothes men walked up to Mariana.

"Is your name Mariana Greitans?" one of the men asked.

"Yes," she replied. She thought they might be from her sponsor.

"Is this you?" asked the man as he pulled out her photo.

"Yes," she said.

Then the men led her to the head of the line, explaining in English to the authorities at the desk. Mariana did not understand. The immigration officials found her papers, stamped them, and took her fingerprints. Then she was led off the ship. Mariana was in a daze, momentarily thinking of the angel taking Peter out of prison. The men guided her to another desk and explained again in English. Next she was placed in a sectioned-off room and told to sit down and wait until she saw a woman named Clara Eagle.

Suddenly Clara Eagle and Papa Keikulis burst into the room.

"Praise the Lord, Mariana, that we got here!" Clara exclaimed, hugging Mariana.

"Where is my sponsor?" Mariana asked feebly.

"You're not going to see him, ever!" was the reply.

"What happened?" murmured the astonished young woman.

"It'll take me a while to explain it all," Clara said reassuringly.

After investigation it was concluded that "O. Brooks" was an alias name, and the intentions were not legitimate. Mariana was relieved that friends and family had been led by the Lord to protect her from a bad situation.

She went to Philadelphia and lived in a third-floor room above the Keikulises' apartment.

The Philadelphia neighborhood where the Keikulis family and Mariana lived was comprised of many ethnicities. Within a two-block walk were grocery stores and several small shops. Carts on the curbsides were always full of fresh produce. Most of the shopkeepers and street merchants were Jewish immigrants who were fluent in Russian, and Arvids and Cilite were rarely forced to practice English.

While in Germany they had heard rumors that in America people could get all the white bread they wanted – anytime they wanted it. Cilite had imagined this impossible, so it surprised her to see store shelves full of bread every time she went. At first she bought large quantities of staples such as Crisco shortening and stored them under the bed, in case the stores ran out. Gradually she learned that grocery shelves in this land of plenty were always stocked.

Once when the family had a loaf of Wonder Bread on the table, they all began to spread mayonnaise on the slices, adding fresh slices of tomatoes to make sandwiches. Janis reminded them of his prediction when they had been starving in the labor camp.

"Someday we will eat all the white bread we want," he had said.

It had finally become true.

Epilogue

Open Doors, Open Hearts

Fond memories of the Keikulis sisters...

After many attempts to communicate with friends and family in the old country, in 1955 a reply finally came from Mama's sisters in Liepaja. The letter had traveled for many months through the Russian mail system and arrived torn and tattered. Thus it was for the next 30 years that a steady stream of relief packages was sent to dear family members and Christian friends who were under the oppressive Communist occupation.

Mama and Papa were keenly aware of the suffering church behind the Iron Curtain and continued to not only send support to them in sacrificial giving but also lifted them up in prayer. Papa's letters never arrived, as he was black-listed. Mama learned to intersperse news of family with encouragement from God's Word. They learned that some of their minister friends were exiled to the severe gulags (prisons) in Siberia, leaving their wives and children to fend for themselves. Believers met in small groups in homes called underground churches.

Besides their ministry of generosity, Mama and Papa also had a fruitful Russian language radio ministry. They prepared Bible studies, and Mama recorded them for more than 10 years. Paul Demetrus produced the "Voice of Truth" Radio Ministry, and response letters came from all over the world, wherever Russian-speaking people resided.

Mama and Papa had openness of heart for always being available to all whom the Lord would bring to their simple but warm country home in Bucks County, Pa. The three-room cottage on five acres of mostly woods was nicknamed "The Farm" by visitors from the city. Some were friends from our old neighborhood in "Philly" and some from the Russian church. Everyone was welcomed with joy and made to feel as family.

Papa had turned the woods into a beautiful park with intersecting paths lined with rocks. These were kept clean throughout the warmer months. Each path had a road sign, one for each Keikulis sibling. As the children married, a circular clearing called a wedding ring connected to a new road named for the spouse.

There was a special picnic area among large rocks with a place for a campfire and a rail for resting the sticks used for harpooning hot dogs and marshmallows. A natural wild grapevine allowed children to swing "Tarzan-style" from one boulder to another. In the middle of the woods was a "Lover's Lane" that led to a bench positioned against a vertical side of a rock for comfortable seating. On Sunday afternoons Mama and Papa, holding hands, would walk through the paths. Ending on Lover's Lane, they stopped at the bench and spent time recounting many memories of God's blessings.

No one remembers asking, "May I bring or invite 'so and so'?" Friends, acquaintances, and strangers were welcomed. Some stayed days and some weeks or for the summer. We can't remember ever running out of food. Mama had a beautiful spread for every meal.

Each day, usually after supper, everyone gathered in the living room for devotions that included the singing of hymns and reading of Scripture in Latvian and English. One of the sisters would translate. Papa would give a brief lesson or sermon from the Bible. Then there was the closing in prayer. Often an individual or couple would find personal time to share their heart or ask questions

Sitting at the kitchen table, Papa would listen, exhort, or encourage but quickly open God's Word for the instruction or building of faith.

Once Anna asked Papa how it was that he always seemed to have the right word of encouragement for every situation.

"Each morning I review before the Lord opportunities to minister

Family after six years in U.S., John's wife Olga, 1956.

to someone, asking the Lord to lead someone to my very doorstep with whom I could share His goodness and love," he answered without hesitation.

After the daughters married and moved to various locations, Mama and Papa would come for a visit. Often they had the opportunity to minister in their churches. Mama would sing "His Eye is on the Sparrow," and Papa would exhort the congregation to follow God wholeheartedly in the walk of faith. When friends gathered in our homes, Mama and Papa would minister in an informal setting. While we went into the kitchen to prepare refreshments, people would gather closer to "draw" from their life's experiences of walking close to Jesus. The college students especially would be sitting at their feet asking questions and listening raptly.

Whenever reuniting with friends of bygone days, we daughters were so blessed to find many following the Lord's paths with their families, children, and grandchildren. A similar theme was heard from each, "No matter what difficulties I have been through, I felt Mama and Papa's prayers following me. I knew what they had was real and that I needed that relationship with Christ."

Homegoing

Mama and Papa prayed daily for Latvia and the Suffering Church worldwide. They subscribed to ministries that reported news of saints in closed countries. They prayed for God to strengthen believers in their difficulties and for the Lord to meet their needs.

When praying for their own children, Mama and Papa often prayed, "Lord, You know the trials they need so that their faith can grow and they would know You more."

In 1982 Papa was found to have leukemia. After several blood transfusions in the hospital, he was sent home. In the spring he began longing to see his Savior face to face. He was able to stand and pray a prayer of blessing on his children, giving strong handshakes to his sons-in-law and hugging the daughters and grandchildren.

On Sunday morning, May 9, 1982, he and Mama had their devotions. Papa was talking about going to heaven.

"I still need your teaching because I am not yet like Sarah, who called Abraham her Lord (I Peter3:6)," Mama said.

"There'll be no more teaching," Papa answered. "Everyone (family members) will have their own trials."

"Oh, Papa!" Mama sighed.

Papa took a few tissues from a box, forming them into a ball. With a twinkle in his eyes, he threw the ball, hitting Mama's nose. They both laughed.

"This is my last trial," he said, rising to his feet, "and I want to be alone." He walked to his room and climbed into his bed.

Respecting his wishes, Mama, Judy, and husband Jim waited outside the door. In a minute they heard a pleasant sigh. Looking in the room, they saw Papa in bed, his hands folded in prayer. There was a sweet look of contentment on his face. He was with the Lord.

Seeing Papa's countenance Mama began to worship. Such joy filled her heart! She asked Jim not to cover his face so the other family members would not need to grieve after seeing him.

On the day of his homegoing Mama insisted she go to Sunday evening service to give her testimony. News spread, so the church was filled with friends.

Mama got up with her face aglow and said, "Well, darlings (she called everyone that she prayed for 'darling'), your church has a new widow! But she is happy widow, because Papa won the victory and he is with Jesus Christ. Hallelujah!"

O death, where is your sting? O hell, where is your victory?
(I Corinthians 15:55)

Papa had won his last battle.

Mama had thought she would be a "scaredy-cat" without Papa, but God gave her overflowing joy and contentment. She lived three more years as a happy widow. She had the excitement of knowing the details of Ilze and John's first trip to Latvia. Upon their return, she cherished the photos and stories of their meetings with relatives and the remnant of the church members and pastors.

Mama went to be with the Lord on July 4, 1985 – a fitting date, considering her frequent rendering of "God Bless America!"

With great excitement and anticipation the sisters, along with their husbands, began visiting Latvia in 1984 and 1986 while it was still Latvian Soviet Socialistic Republic. We longed to meet our relatives and dear friends that Mama and Papa had prayed for and ministered to for 30 years through letters, prayers, and packages. Back then the number of luggage pieces was not restricted but could be searched and confiscated. Traveling with 14 trunks of gifts for the suffering church, we were backed with much prayer. When waiting in the customs line in Tallin, Estonia, we purposely went to the end of the long line. We observed many items being confiscated from passengers' luggage in front of us. However, when our turn came, we were motioned through quickly.

On our first journey our bus from Tallin arrived at the hotel in Riga at midnight. Our relatives were standing in the rain waiting to greet us. Each one was holding a beautiful bouquet of flowers. What a happy reunion to finally meet face-to-face Aunt Irma, son Andris with wife Diana, and daughters Sandra and Evita! We were

Getting acquainted with sweet family in Latvia. 2nd visit back to Latvia.

Cilite's sister Irma with Diana, daughter-in-law & grandaughters Sandra and Evita.

permitted to visit their apartment in Riga, but other friends who traveled distances by car or train came to see us at our hotel. For the first time we could meet our parents' dear old friends whom we had come to know from letters, photos, and prayers.

Daily we took a different group to the hotel restaurant and then to the "Dollar Store" meant for tourists with American dollars. As we encouraged and urged our guests to express their needs, there was a pile on the table for the different families each day. The clerks became kinder as they saw the love and care between our new friends. These became beautiful deeper relationships. Before departure we shared the contents of the gifts we brought from the U.S. The believers had been meeting in underground house churches. Some of our parents' peers had been exiled to Siberia for eight or more years.

It was a great honor to meet with Arvids Kumins, who had led our parents to Christ. Although he was slightly bent with age, his eyes flashed and voice boomed like he was preaching. John West, Ilze's husband, and Harry Johnson, Anna's husband, were delighted to hear the man speak excellent English. When asked how he fared in prison, he exclaimed, "I preached the gospel; I baptized new converts and served communion!"

Surprised, Ilze asked, "How could you do that in prison?"

He began to knock on the door of the car to demonstrate the Morse code. As his voice became louder, one of his daughters said, "Papa, 'they' are listening!" The years of Soviet control made most people very cautious.

"What can they do to an 86-year-old man?" Brother Kumins exclaimed. He had served two terms in Siberia and had hitch-hiked throughout Russia and Latvia several times preaching the gospel.

On our second trip in 1986 we took a chauffeured van to a grassy park outside Saldus, desiring some privacy. There we found a private place with arranged logs on the ground for a meeting place. Brother Kumins needed something to lean his back on so Ilze, sitting behind him, placed her knees right up to his back for support and her hands on his shoulder blades. The small group sang three verses of "How Great Thou Art" in English and Latvian. Then

Meeting Arvids Kumins, 1984.

Last member of House Church in Pampali. Marija Gaislar, 1994.

Brother Kumins closed in prayer. What a sweet, memorable service! Returning to the van the chauffeur grabbed our hands, and with tears streaming down his cheeks he said, "Thank you for not forgetting us. It means so much to us!"

When the Soviet Union fell in the early 1990s, the sisters asked the Latvian Christian leaders how they could help the church that had been so restricted under Communist domination. We were then invited to bring mission teams to encourage ministries and to help equip pastors and church workers. On the first mission trip Ilze had requested to hear testimonies of how the believers persevered under heavy persecution; so there were three moving testimonies of valiant courage to risk worship and witnessing in order to live out their faith.

One dear lady was sent to a severe prison in Moscow, and the Lord enabled her to live through it and return.

Each year in the schools students were questioned, "Where did humans and the world come from?"

To answer "God made man and the world" meant that student would receive a flunking grade in science and history, which would keep them from attending college or music conservatory and usually kept them from getting the best jobs. Three young girls had lived silently in the parsonage attic making copies of the Scriptures. The pastor's five children never knew they were up there. The girls never saw the light of day. The pastor's wife would bring them food after her children were asleep. The girls usually stayed at one place around six months and then moved on.

At the conclusion of the testimonies Janis Eisans, the pastor and bishop of the Baptist Union, stood up and said, "Communism said that religion would completely die, but God had the last word!"

When it came time for the U.S. team to minister, a chime choir (bell choir) prepared to play. As the first chords sounded Latvia's national anthem, which had been forbidden for 50 years, the congregation stood quickly and began singing "God Bless Latvia." The song rang out with strong, heartfelt thanksgiving for bringing freedom to publicly acknowledge God's leadership and provision to meet to worship without incident or dread of repercussion.

Anna and Ilze experienced overwhelming emotion and felt the congregation's victory of God's triumph. Never in their wildest dreams could they have imagined this blessing. After years of sharing the burdens for Latvia's Church and friends and relatives, only the Lord could have allowed them to come full circle and be able to worship openly with these dear people and give God the glory.

Truly, God had the last word.